Responsibility to protect

This volume explores in a novel and challenging way the emerging norm of the responsibility to protect (R2P), adopted by the United Nations World Summit in 2005 following significant debate throughout the preceding decade.

This work seeks to uncover whether this norm and its founding values have resonance and grounding within diverse cultures and within the experiences of societies that have directly been torn apart by mass atrocity crimes. The contributors to this collection analyze the responsibility to protect through multiple disciplines—philosophy, religion and spirituality, anthropology, and aesthetics in addition to international relations and law—to explore what light alternative perspectives outside of political science and international relations shed upon this emerging norm.

In each case, the disciplinary analysis emanates from the global South and from scholars located within countries that have suffered from violent political upheaval. Hence, they draw upon not only theory but also first-hand experience with conscience-shocking crimes. Their retrospective and prospective analyses could and should help shape the future implementation of R2P in accordance with insights from vastly different contexts.

Offering a cutting-edge contribution to thinking in the area, this is essential reading for all those with an interest in humanitarian intervention, peace and conflict studies, critical security studies and peacebuilding.

Rama Mani directs the project on "Ending Mass Atrocities: Echoes in Southern Cultures." She is a Senior Research Associate of the Centre for International Studies at the University of Oxford and a councillor of the World Future Council, Hamburg.

Thomas G. Weiss is Presidential Professor of Political Science at The CUNY Graduate Center and Director of the Ralph Bunche Institute for International Studies.

Routledge Global Institutions

Edited by Thomas G. Weiss
The CUNY Graduate Center, New York, USA
and Rorden Wilkinson
University of Manchester, UK

About the series

The Global Institutions Series is designed to provide readers with comprehensive, accessible, and informative guides to the history, structure, and activities of key international organizations as well as books that deal with topics of key importance in contemporary global governance. Every volume stands on its own as a thorough and insightful treatment of a particular topic, but the series as a whole contributes to a coherent and complementary portrait of the phenomenon of global institutions at the dawn of the millennium.

Books are written by recognized experts, conform to a similar structure, and cover a range of themes and debates common to the series. These areas of shared concern include the general purpose and rationale for organizations, developments over time, membership, structure, decision-making procedures, and key functions. Moreover, current debates are placed in historical perspective alongside informed analysis and critique. Each book also contains an annotated bibliography and guide to electronic information as well as any annexes appropriate to the subject matter at hand.

The volumes currently published are:

54 The Responsibility to Protect (2011)
Cultural perspectives in the global South
edited by Rama Mani (University of Oxford) and Thomas G. Weiss (The CUNY Graduate Center)

53 The International Trade Centre (2011)
Promoting exports for development
by Stephen Browne (FUNDS Project) and Sam Laird (University of Nottingham)

52 The Idea of World Government (2011)
From ancient times to the twenty-first century
by James A. Yunker (Western Illinois University)

51 **Humanitarianism Contested (2011)**
Where angels fear to tread
by Michael Barnett (George Washington University) and Thomas G. Weiss (The CUNY Graduate Center)

50 **The Organization of American States (2011)**
Global governance away from the media
by Monica Herz (Institute of International Relations, Catholic University, Rio de Janeiro)

49 **Non-Governmental Organizations in World Politics (2011)**
The construction of global governance
by Peter Willetts (City University, London)

48 **The Forum on China-Africa Cooperation (FOCAC) (2011)**
by Ian Taylor (University of St. Andrews)

47 **Global Think Tanks (2011)**
Policy Networks, and Governance
by James G. McGann (University of Pennsylvania) with Richard Sabatini

46 **United Nations Educational, Scientific and Cultural Organization (UNESCO) (2011)**
Creating norms for a complex world
by J.P. Singh (Georgetown University)

45 **The International Labour Organization (2011)**
Coming in from the cold
by Steve Hughes (Newcastle University) and Nigel Haworth (University of Auckland)

44 **Global Poverty (2010)**
How global governance is failing the poor
by David Hulme (University of Manchester)

43 **Global Governance, Poverty, and Inequality (2010)**
edited by Jennifer Clapp (University of Waterloo) and Rorden Wilkinson (University of Manchester)

42 **Multilateral Counter-Terrorism (2010)**
by Peter Romaniuk (John Jay College of Criminal Justice, CUNY)

41 **Governing Climate Change (2010)**
by Peter Newell (University of East Anglia) and Harriet A. Bulkeley (Durham University)

40 **The UN Secretary-General and Secretariat (2nd edition, 2010)**
by Leon Gordenker (Princeton University)

39 Preventive Human Rights Strategies in a World of Acute Threats and Challenges (2010)
by Bertrand G. Ramcharan (Geneva Graduate Institute of International and Development Studies)

38 African Economic Institutions (2010)
by Kwame Akonor (Seton Hall University)

37 Global Institutions and the HIV/AIDS Epidemic (2010)
Responding to an international crisis
by Franklyn Lisk (University of Warwick)

36 Regional Security: The Capacity of International Organizations (2010)
by Rodrigo Tavares (United Nations University)

35 The Organisation for Economic Co-operation and Development (2009)
by Richard Woodward (University of Hull)

34 Transnational Organized Crime (2009)
by Frank Madsen (University of Cambridge)

33 The United Nations and Human Rights (2nd edition, 2009)
A guide for a new era
by Julie A. Mertus (American University)

32 The International Organization for Standardization (2009)
Setting standards
by Craig N. Murphy (Wellesley College) and JoAnne Yates (Massachusetts Institute of Technology)

31 Shaping the Humanitarian World (2009)
by Peter Walker (Tufts University) and Daniel G. Maxwell (Tufts University)

30 Global Food and Agricultural Institutions (2009)
by John Shaw

29 Institutions of the Global South (2009)
by Jacqueline Anne Braveboy-Wagner (City College of New York, CUNY)

28 International Judicial Institutions (2009)
The architecture of international justice at home and abroad
by Richard J. Goldstone (Retired Justice of the Constitutional Court of South Africa) and Adam M. Smith (Harvard University)

27 **The International Olympic Committee (2009)**
The governance of the Olympic system
by Jean-Loup Chappelet (IDHEAP Swiss Graduate School of Public Administration) and Brenda Kübler-Mabbott

26 **The World Health Organization (2009)**
by Kelley Lee (London School of Hygiene and Tropical Medicine)

25 **Internet Governance: The New Frontier of Global Institutions (2009)**
by John Mathiason (Syracuse University)

24 **Institutions of the Asia-Pacific (2009)**
ASEAN, APEC, and beyond
by Mark Beeson (University of Birmingham)

23 **UNHCR (2008)**
The politics and practice of refugee protection into the twenty-first century
by Gil Loescher (University of Oxford), Alexander Betts (University of Oxford), and James Milner (University of Toronto)

22 **Contemporary Human Rights Ideas (2008)**
by Bertrand G. Ramcharan (Geneva Graduate Institute of International and Development Studies)

21 **The World Bank (2008)**
From reconstruction to development to equity
by Katherine Marshall (Georgetown University)

20 **The European Union (2008)**
by Clive Archer (Manchester Metropolitan University)

19 **The African Union (2008)**
Challenges of globalization, security and governance
by Samuel M. Makinda (Murdoch University) and Wafula Okumu (McMaster University)

18 **Commonwealth (2008)**
Inter- and non-state contributions to global governance
by Timothy M. Shaw (Royal Roads University)

17 **The World Trade Organization (2007)**
Law, economics, and politics
by Bernard M. Hoekman (World Bank) and Petros C. Mavroidis (Columbia University)

16 **A Crisis of Global Institutions? (2007)**
Multilateralism and international security
by Edward Newman (University of Birmingham)

15 **UN Conference on Trade and Development (2007)**
by Ian Taylor (University of St. Andrews) and Karen Smith (University of Stellenbosch)

14 **The Organization for Security and Co-operation in Europe (2007)**
by David J. Galbreath (University of Aberdeen)

13 **The International Committee of the Red Cross (2007)**
A neutral humanitarian actor
by David P. Forsythe (University of Nebraska) and Barbara Ann Rieffer-Flanagan (Central Washington University)

12 **The World Economic Forum (2007)**
A multi-stakeholder approach to global governance
by Geoffrey Allen Pigman (Bennington College)

11 **The Group of 7/8 (2007)**
by Hugo Dobson (University of Sheffield)

10 **The International Monetary Fund (2007)**
Politics of conditional lending
by James Raymond Vreeland (Georgetown University)

9 **The North Atlantic Treaty Organization (2007)**
The enduring alliance
by Julian Lindley-French (Center for Applied Policy, University of Munich)

8 **The World Intellectual Property Organization: Resurgence and the Development Agenda (2006)**
by Chris May (University of the West of England)

7 **The UN Security Council (2006)**
Practice and promise
by Edward C. Luck (Columbia University)

6 **Global Environmental Institutions (2006)**
by Elizabeth R. DeSombre (Wellesley College)

5 **Internal Displacement (2006)**
Conceptualization and its consequences
by Thomas G. Weiss (The CUNY Graduate Center) and David A. Korn

4 **The UN General Assembly (2005)**
by M.J. Peterson (University of Massachusetts, Amherst)

3 **United Nations Global Conferences (2005)**
by Michael G. Schechter (Michigan State University)

2 **The UN Secretary-General and Secretariat (2005)**
by Leon Gordenker (Princeton University)

1 **The United Nations and Human Rights (2005)**
A guide for a new era
by Julie A. Mertus (American University)

Books currently under contract include:

The Regional Development Banks
Lending with a regional flavor
by Jonathan R. Strand (University of Nevada)

Millennium Development Goals (MDGs)
For a people-centered development agenda?
by Sakiko Fukada-Parr (The New School)

Peacebuilding
From concept to commission
by Robert Jenkins (The CUNY Graduate Center)

Human Security
by Don Hubert (University of Ottawa)

UNICEF
by Richard Jolly (University of Sussex)

FIFA
by Alan Tomlinson (University of Brighton)

International Law, International Relations, and Global Governance
by Charlotte Ku (University of Illinois)

The Bank for International Settlements
The politics of global financial supervision in the age of high finance
by Kevin Ozgercin (SUNY College at Old Westbury)

International Migration
by Khalid Koser (Geneva Centre for Security Policy)

Global Health Governance
by Sophie Harman (City University, London)

The Council of Europe
by Martyn Bond (University of London)

Human Development
by Richard Ponzio

The United Nations Development Programme (UNDP)
by Stephen Browne (The International Trade Centre, Geneva)

Religious Institutions and Global Politics
by Katherine Marshall (Georgetown University)

South Asian Association for Regional Cooperation (SAARC)
by Lawrence Saez (University of London)

The Group of Twenty (G20)
by Andrew F. Cooper (Centre for International Governance Innovation, Ontario) and Ramesh Thakur (Balsillie School of International Affairs, Ontario)

The UN Human Rights Council
by Bertrand G. Ramcharan (Geneva Graduate Institute of International and Development Studies)

The International Monetary Fund (2nd edition)
Politics of conditional lending
by James Raymond Vreeland (Georgetown University)

The UN Global Compact
by Catia Gregoratti (Lund University)

Security Governance in Regional Organizations
edited by Emil Kirchner (University of Essex) and Roberto Dominguez (Suffolk University)

UN Institutions for Women's Rights
by Charlotte Patton (York College, CUNY) and Carolyn Stephenson (University of Hawaii)

International Aid
by Paul Mosley (University of Sheffield)

Maritime Piracy
by Bob Haywood and Roberta Spivak

For further information regarding the series, please contact:

Craig Fowlie, Senior Publisher, Politics & International Studies
Taylor & Francis
2 Park Square, Milton Park, Abingdon
Oxford OX14 4RN, UK

+44 (0)207 842 2057 Tel
+44 (0)207 842 2302 Fax

Craig.Fowlie@tandf.co.uk
www.routledge.com

Responsibility to protect

Cultural perspectives in the global South

Edited by
Rama Mani and Thomas G. Weiss

Routledge
Taylor & Francis Group
LONDON AND NEW YORK

First published 2011
by Routledge
4 Park Square, Milton Park, Abingdon, Oxon OX14 4RN
605 Third Avenue, New York, NY 10017

Routledge is an imprint of the Taylor & Francis Group, an informa business

British Library Cataloguing in Publication Data
A catalogue record for this book is available from the British Library

Library of Congress Cataloging in Publication Data
Responsibility to protect : cultural perspectives in the global South / edited by Rama Mani and Thomas G. Weiss.
p. cm. – (Routledge global institutions ; 54)
Includes bibliographical references and index.
1. Humanitarian intervention. 2. Genocide intervention. 3. Human rights. 4. Political violence–Developing countries–Prevention. 5. Human rights–Developing countries. I. Mani, Rama. II. Weiss, Thomas George.
JZ6369.R46 2011
327.1'17091724–dc22
2011004004

ISBN13: 978-0-415-78184-8 (hbk)
ISBN13: 978-0-415-78185-5 (pbk)
ISBN13: 978-0-203-80728-6 (ebk)

Typeset in Times New Roman
by Taylor & Francis Books

Contents

Contributors

Arjun Karki is President of Rural Reconstruction Nepal and International Coordinator of LDC Watch, a global alliance of civil society organizations that works in 49 UN-defined least developed countries (LDCs). In addition to work on democracy and human rights in Nepal, he also coordinates the South Asia Alliance for Poverty Eradication. He holds a doctorate in Development Studies from the University of East Anglia and post-graduate degrees in Management and Implementation of Development Projects from the University of Manchester and in Research Methods from the University of Bradford. His latest books reflect first-hand experience in conflict analysis and peace building in Nepal and other LDCs and include *The People's War in Nepal: Left Perspectives* (2003); *Whose War? Economic and Socio-Cultural Impacts of Nepal's Maoist-Government* (2004); and *Democratic Failure, National Insurgency and the Rise of Bellicist Culture* (2005).

Jean-Marie Kayishema is Associate Professor in the Faculty of Arts and Humanities at the National University of Rwanda where he is also Director of the University Centre for Arts. He has also taught at the University of Burundi and in Canada. He obtained his PhD in Literature from the Université de Laval. A playwright and theater director, he has produced numerous plays focusing on Rwanda's myths and legends, and he directed the Spectafrique Theatrical Company in Montréal. His latest co-authored book is *Anthologie de la littérature rwandaise moderne* (2009).

Nita Luci is a lecturer at the University of Pristina, Departments of Ethnology and Sociology, and ABD in the Department of Anthropology at the University of Michigan-Ann Arbor. Her research focuses on topics of gender and manhood, body, memory, and violence. In addition to her academic pursuits and career, she has also worked in the area of contemporary art (such as editing the publication of four supplements in the daily *Koha Ditore*, titled "Women n/or Witches, Focusing on Issues of Representation, Feminism and Art"). She is a member of the network Forum 2015 and an adviser for the UNDP project Women's Safety and Security Initiative. Her recent publications include one co-authored chapter and volume: "Events and Sites of Difference: Marking Self and Other in Kosovo" (2009); and *The Politics of Remembrance and Belonging: Life Histories of Albanian Women in Kosova* (2006).

Rama Mani directs the project Ending Mass Atrocities: Echoes in Southern Cultures. She is a Senior Research Associate of the Centre for International Studies at the University of Oxford and a councilor of the World Future Council, Hamburg. She was previously Executive Director of the International Centre for Ethnic Studies in Colombo, Director of the New Issues in Security Course at the Geneva Centre for Security Policy, and a policy adviser and strategy manager on conflict in Africa to Oxfam (GB), with postings in Ethiopia and Uganda. She has a PhD in Political Science from the University of Cambridge, and an MA in International Affairs from Johns Hopkins University. She is the author of *Beyond Retribution: Seeking Justice in the Shadows of War* (2002 and 2007), and several journal articles and book chapters.

Mutombo Nkulu-N'Sengha is Director of the Global Village Forum and Associate Professor at California State University where he teaches "World Religions," "Religion, Violence and World Peace," and "Indigenous Religions of Africa and the Americas." Born in the Democratic Republic of Congo, he studied at the Institut Saint Pierre Canisius, Kinshasa, Pontifical Gregorian University and Biblicum, Rome, and Temple University. Fluent in seven languages, he previously taught philosophy, religion, politics, and history at Haverford College, Temple University, and Montclair State University. He is associate editor of the *Journal of Ecumenical Studies* and a member of the American Academy of Religion, the Global Dialogue Institute, the Global Ethic Center, the African Association for the Study of Religions, the Institute of Signifying Scripture, and the Religious Consultation on Population, Reproductive Health, and Ethics. His publications in French, Italian, and English include four recent book chapters and thirteen articles in the *Encyclopedia of African Religion* (2009).

Yolanda Angulo Parra has a Philosophy PhD from the National Autonomous University of Mexico. She is Chair, Founding Member, Director, and Senior Researcher of the Center for Genealogical Studies for the Research of Culture in Mexico and Latin America; a founding and active member of the Ethics National Seminar; member of the Association for Philosophy and Liberation, the Center for Global Justice, and the Philosophical Association of Mexico. She was previously Professor of the National Autonomous University of Mexico (1989–2004), Research Professor of the Autonomous University of Puebla (1998–2001), and visiting professor at many universities. In the University of Tepeyac she designed and coordinated the Master in Humanities (1998–2001). Her most recent books are: *Ethics and Values* (2009); *Manual on How to Teach Social Sciences* (2009); and *Philosophy* (2007).

Jyoti Upadhyay is an anthropologist and development practitioner with roots in Nepal, India, and Wales. Having completed a BSc in Social Anthropology, she later completed an MA in International Development and Management at the Development Studies Institute of the London School of Economics and Political Science. She has worked on a variety of research projects, including anthropological research on female circumcision among the Marakwet of Western Kenya, and issues around "country ownership" of multidonor trust funds in post-conflict states, specifically in Nepal, where she is currently based.

Thomas G. Weiss is Presidential Professor of Political Science at The CUNY Graduate Center and Director of the Ralph Bunche Institute for International Studies, where he directs the United Nations Intellectual History Project. Past President of the International Studies Association (2009–10) and Chair of the Academic Council on the UN System (2006–9), he was previously editor of *Global Governance*, Research Director of the International Commission on Intervention and State Sovereignty, Research Professor at Brown University's Watson Institute, Executive Director of the Academic Council on the UN System and of the International Peace Academy, a member of the UN secretariat, and a consultant to several public and private agencies. He has authored or edited some 40 books and 175 articles and book chapters about multilateral cooperation. His latest authored volumes are: *Humanitarian Intervention: Ideas in Action* (2007); *What's Wrong with the United Nations and How to Fix It* (2009); *UN Ideas That Changed the World* (2009); and *Global Governance and the UN: An Unfinished Journey* (2010).

Foreword by the series editor

The current volume, dealing with an idea that has captured the global public policy *Zeitgeist*, edited by Rama Mani and Thomas G. Weiss, is the second in what we anticipate will be a growing number of research volumes in our "global institutions" series that examines crucial global problems and possible global policies and solutions. *The Responsibility to Protect: Cultural perspectives in the Global South* consists of specialized and critical chapters by first-rate analysts and offers a cutting-edge contribution to thinking in this area.

In addition to these research volumes, the series strives to provide readers with user-friendly and short (usually 50,000 words), but definitive guides to the most visible aspects of what we know as "global governance," as well as authoritative accounts of the issues and debates in which they are embroiled. We now have over 50 books that act as key reference points to the most significant global institutions and the evolution of the issues that they face. Our intention has always been to provide one-stop guides for all readers—students (both undergraduate and postgraduate), interested negotiators, diplomats, practitioners from nongovernmental and intergovernmental organizations, and interested parties alike—seeking information about most prominent institutional aspects of global governance.

The new research stream incorporates lengthier works by key authors as well as edited compilations, the collective wisdom from which helps push the envelope on important topics linked to global institutions. In this case, a glaring absence in mainstream thinking about peace building and security has been the unavailability of analyses conducted by scholars living and working within societies affected by violent conflict and mass atrocities, and by analysts outside of the fields of international relations and law. Here, Mani and Weiss have assembled a group of "unusual suspects"—including theologians, artists, anthropologists, sociologists, and community organizers—who have themselves endured and observed war-torn societies.

Ideally, these volumes will be used as complementary readings in courses in which other specific titles in this series are pertinent—in this case, we point readers to a host of books on humanitarian and human rights issues as well as key security, regional, and Third World organizations.[1] Our aim is to enable topics of importance to be dealt with exhaustively by specialists as well as enabling collected works to address issues in ways that bring more than the sum of the individual parts, while at the same time maintaining the quality of the series.

As always, we look forward to comments from our readers.

Rorden Wilkinson, University of Manchester, UK
February 2011

Notes

1 Jacqueline Braveboy-Wagner, *Institutions of the Global South* (London: Routledge, 2009); David Forsythe and Barbara Rieffer-Flanagan, *The International Committee of the Red Cross* (2007); Leon Gordenker, *The UN Secretary-General and Secretariat* (2nd edition, 2010); Julian Lindley-French, *The North Atlantic Treaty Organization* (2007); Gil Loescher, Alexander Betts, and James Milner, *UNHCR* (2008); Ed Luck, *The UN Security Council* (2nd edition, 2011); Julie Mertus, *The United Nations and Human Rights* (2nd edition, 2009); Edward Newman, *A Crisis of Global Institutions?* (2007); Bertrand Ramcharan, *Contemporary Human Rights Ideas* (2008), *Preventive Human Rights Strategies in a World of Acute Threats and Challenges* (2010), and *The UN Human Rights Council* (2011); Rodrigo Tavares, *Regional Security: The Capacity of International Organizations* (2010); Peter Walker and Daniel Maxwell, *Shaping the Humanitarian World* (2009); and Thomas G. Weiss and David A. Korn, *Internal Displacement* (2006).

Foreword

Mohamed Sahnoun

Co-chair, International Commission on Intervention and State Sovereignty

Co-chair, International Advisory Board, Global Centre for the Responsibility to Protect

> I have come into this world to see this:
> the sword drop from men's hands even at the height of their arc of anger
> because we have finally realized there is just one flesh to wound.
>
> Hafiz[1]

Since the birth of the responsibility to protect (R2P) norm a decade ago, the view that I defended vociferously among others in the International Commission on Intervention and State Sovereignty has become a firmer conviction: namely, the most important dimension of R2P and the primordial responsibility of the international community of states is the *prevention* of mass atrocity crimes. By this I do not mean superficial prevention. Today more than ever, we need to work very hard to make prevention much more comprehensive, strategic, and persuasive in order to affect changes in policy and in action. Furthermore, if we fail despite our best preventive efforts and are obliged to take forceful protective action, then at least such action will be more credible to skeptical governments and individuals. Forceful protection will not be viewed as being parachuted in from nowhere but will have followed clearly and consequently a long-term, committed effort to save lives and to resolve the root causes of hatred and bloodshed. If R2P is to be credible, morally and politically, action based upon its tenets must reflect solidarity and must serve the interests of the vulnerable and not the powerful.

This is not new! In all societies, however diverse their cultures and spiritual traditions, we find traces within ancient legends as well as within historical experience that fortify the principles of protection and prevention. These historical experiences and cultural contexts generate an elaborate system of ethics that are the foundation for legal responsibilities. The injunctions of contemporary international human rights law and international humanitarian law mirror those of cultural values and philosophical ethics; and the two mutually reinforce each other. The value of helping one's neighbor is inherent in all cultures. So too are offering hospitality to strangers and solidarity with the weak and suffering. In fact, not helping a person in distress is considered a crime in many societies.

Rama Mani and Thomas G. Weiss are to be saluted for having worked together with a distinguished team to produce this set of essays focusing on the cultural perspectives in the global South around the R2P norm. This breakthrough volume makes an essential contribution to the elaboration and application of the responsibility to protect. The three thematic chapters on spirituality, philosophy, and aesthetics provide us with a wealth of universal human values, ethical obligations, and aesthetic expressions that underpin the R2P norm and particularly the prevention of mass suffering. The three case studies detail the cultural ethnocide that led to genocide in Rwanda, the decade of nonviolent organized civic resistance that preceded ethnic cleansing in Kosovo, and the cultural practices and institutions that provided protection to rural communities despite the paralyzing dynamics of fear during the Maoist war in Nepal. They highlight the importance of prevention and demonstrate the tragic cost when early opportunities to prevent mass atrocities are missed. In short, this volume examines the wealth of our heritage of cultural wisdom that can help us ground more deeply the R2P norm, drawing on universal values of care, hospitality, and solidarity.

In order to strengthen the responsibility to protect, we need to draw lessons from previous actions and interventions. Very importantly, we need to demonstrate consistently in all our future conduct that we have genuinely learned lessons from past failures and will not repeat them. This goes for the United Nations and other intergovernmental organizations as well as for major powers. Only then will people around the world, and especially in war-torn countries, overcome their distrust and become more open to R2P. The case studies underline several culturally specific lessons from the experience of countries that have undergone atrocities. The lessons are all the more powerful because they reflect the first-hand perspective of local populations.

One of the lessons from these essays is that R2P's peace building pillar is not as prominent as it should be on the international agenda. We simply cannot allow this vital preventive dimension of R2P to be gradually minimized among international priorities. Mass atrocities inflict wounded memories; if they are not healed, they will re-emerge more painfully and violently later. If we make serious efforts to heal memories in war-torn societies, we find a vast positive human capital that had been eviscerated by the wounds of the past. This capital can become the bedrock of society to prevent future violence. That is what peace building is all about! Moreover, genuine and substantial support for peace building, healing traumatic memories, and resolving past problems adds credibility to the entire R2P enterprise.

Another lesson lies with peacemaking processes. We should surely have learned by now that if civic actors are more closely associated with peace negotiations—holding the genuine long-term interests of all sectors of society in mind—the resulting agreements are bound to be more constructive, beneficial, and durable. These essays demonstrate the remarkable commitment of ordinary people to build peace in their own societies. Far from media attention or international assistance, time after time we encounter civic activists, scholars, youth, and spiritual leaders who demonstrate the resilience, solidarity, creativity, and ingenuity to protect their communities amidst deathly violence.

It is indeed by working with civil society and grass roots populations and by understanding and respecting the complexities of each culture that the United Nations can build credibility and trust. In fact, they alone would enable the world organization to justify coercive R2P action when required. This insightful volume so ably edited by Rama Mani and Thomas G. Weiss rightly focuses on the countries of the global South and the former Yugoslavia, and it increases the decibel level of the voices of local actors in analyzing how to prevent, react, and rebuild. This book deserves to be widely distributed and read by both practitioners and scholars because violent armed conflicts are likely to continue to occur, especially in the global South, as societies take giant strides toward democratization and vie to meet the demands of the global market economy. All countries have to learn to weave their way through these cataclysms without resorting to repression and violence; they have to learn to promote human security and not only safeguard the state security of their regimes.

Building such capacities for peace and eschewing the resort to grisly violence has its roots in traditional culture. UN member states, particularly in the global South, must rely more than in the past on their own citizens; they must tap the vast but forgotten wealth of their own local wisdom; they must revitalize their own time-tested cultural values and traditions. Industrialized countries should encourage the developing world to do so by showing more understanding, support, and compassion.

Notes

1 Daniel Landinsky, trans., *Love Poems from God: Twelve Sacred Voices from the East and West* (New York: Penguin, 2002), 159.

Acknowledgments

We are immensely grateful for the support and input that we were able to draw upon trans-nationally for this unusual and engrossing multicultural undertaking.

First, we thank those who took a leap of faith in investing in the idea of this exploration of largely unexplored terrain. The Arsenault Family Foundation was the first to come forward with seed money in December 2008, which made it possible to kick-start the undertaking, and they renewed support for additional field consultations. The Carnegie Corporation of New York, longtime supporters of research in conflict prevention and peace building, provided the most substantial part of the funding. We thus are particularly grateful to Steve Del Rosso and Bob Hayward for their personal involvement. We encourage others to join them in funding research by local scholars directly involved in conflict prevention and peace building so that their otherwise inaccessible findings can be more readily available.

As in many such undertakings, the list of persons to whom the editors owe an intellectual debt is lengthy. We cannot mention the scores of individuals who attended seminars, conferences, and other gatherings during the two-year duration of this project, but we would nonetheless like to indicate those to whom we owe the most.

Our association with the Centre for International Studies (CIS) at the University of Oxford was particularly beneficial. We thank first and foremost our friend the CIS director, Richard Caplan, for his unfailing support and for hosting Rama Mani as a senior research associate. We are also grateful to Sarah Travis for her organizational help and input throughout, particularly in setting up the project website and in organizing the first conference of authors in Oxford in January 2010. We are grateful to numerous faculty members at the university and elsewhere who gave us vital feedback at this conference and earlier. We also appreciate research assistance in summer 2009 by Patricja Skys and Miriam Bradley, graduate students of the Oxford Department for Politics and International Relations. In Geneva, the Heim Foundation hosted Rama Mani and provided a welcoming home for her research.

Closer to home at the Ralphe Bunche Institute for International Studies at The Graduate Center of The City University of New York where the project was based, Nomvuyo Nolutshungu faithfully provided thoughtful support throughout while Nancy Okada ensured that we both spent and conserved our funds judiciously, with the able assistance of Zaida Ramirez. This support was especially in evidence during a conference in October 2010 to solicit comments from outsiders on the penultimate drafts of the chapters now in this book. Before that meeting and after, Danielle Zach performed the remarkable task of patiently helping to edit and shape the texts from our contributors and to pull this volume together; quite simply, it would not have appeared in its current shape or in such a timely fashion without her assistance. Our close association with the Global Centre for the Responsibility to Protect was a great asset, and we thank its executive director, Mónica Serrano, for her encouragement and cooperation throughout.

We express our appreciation to our contributors not only for their insights and evident commitment but also for the collective journey of learning through their respective disciplines and courageous life stories. Despite geographic, disciplinary, and personal diversities and logistic challenges, the project was truly a team effort. Rama Mani is particularly indebted for her first-hand exposure to the cultural wealth and wisdom of the case-study countries during two sets of field visits. She is deeply grateful to the many artists whom she met to discuss the contribution of art and artists to the responsibility to protect in general and peace in particular. She appreciates the input of Koulsy Lamko, Nadera Shelhoub-Kevorkian, and Ang Choulean earlier in the project.

A major contribution to our research was collaboration with local universities and institutes for two sets of local consultations in the summers of 2009 and 2010. The initial round was held with a diverse cross-section of local scholars to solicit preliminary input for the case studies. In addition to our contributors, we are grateful to: Shyaka Anastase and the Rwanda Governance Advisory Council and Paul Rutyasire and the Centre for Conflict Management of the National University of Rwanda for convening the Rwanda workshop; Qerkin Berisha and the Human Rights Centre of the University of Pristina for the Kosovo consultation; and to the Rural Rehabilitation Network for convening the Nepal workshop.

A year later a second round of consultations was especially useful in the case-study countries to get concrete feedback from knowledgeable local experts on the penultimate drafts of the three country studies. Additionally, conferences were organized with university students to seek their insights about the R2P norm and the project, with relevance to their country's conflicts. In addition to Arjun Karki and Jyoti Upadhyay, we would like to single-out Om Gurung, head of the Department of Anthropology at Nepal's Tribhuvan University, for invaluable assistance in pulling together eminent scholars and civil society experts as well as some 150 enthusiastic graduate students. In Kosovo, Nita Luci convened the animated scholars' workshop with the Faculty of Philosophy at the University of Pristina. In Rwanda, Jean-Marie Kayishema convened an academic seminar with faculty members at the National University of Rwanda and organized meetings with the members of the University Club for Reconciliation and Unity and with a University Cultural Club's dance troupe, all leading to lively discussions and inputs. The eye-opening student comments suggest a useful avenue for further collaborative research.

Additionally in April 2010, the project organized a consultation in Mexico City to discuss early findings from the thematic papers and to ensure maximum cohesion among them. Yolanda Parra Angulo kindly hosted the gathering at the Centre for Genealogical Research in Mexico City. Additionally, she organized a seminar with students at the Autonomous University of Mexico for lively and critical feedback. Cambodia was a possible case study at the outset of this project and while that case did not prove to be feasible, we are grateful to Vice Rector Neth Barom for convening a consultation at the Royal University of Phnom Penh and to Vice Dean Kim Sovan Kiry for organizational assistance.

Finally, we are indebted to the parents of the R2P norm, the members of the International Commission on International Intervention and State Sovereignty (ICISS) and especially to the co-chairs. We are singularly grateful to Mohamed Sahnoun, the Southern voice of wisdom within ICISS and our spiritual guide in this project; we are especially honored that he has graced these pages with a moving and personal foreword. We also thank Gareth Evans for his unflagging championship of the norm, without which it would have died a silent death many times over.

Despite the demands of this project, fortunately life continued with many wonderful developments in our personal lives: Thomas G. Weiss joyfully married his daughters Hannah (to Marcus Muller) and Rebeccah (to Ahmad Filsoof) and became the proud grandfather of Amara. Rama Mani married her soul-mate Alexander Schieffer and saw her son Arjuna leave home to start high school in Paris. We express our profound appreciation and loving devotion to our spouses, Alexander and Priscilla Read, and to our children for their unflagging forbearance and engagement in this and all our undertakings.

Rama Mani and Thomas G. Weiss
Geneva and New York
January 2011

Abbreviations

AIDS	acquired immunodeficiency syndrome
BCE	Before the Common Era
CE	Common Era
CPA	Comprehensive Peace Agreement [Nepal]
CSO	civil society organization
DRC	Democratic Republic of the Congo
EU	European Union
HIV	human immunodeficiency virus
ICISS	International Commission on Intervention and State Sovereignty
ICRC	International Committee of the Red Cross
KLA	Kosovo/a Liberation Army
LDC	least developed country
NATO	North Atlantic Treaty Organization
NGO	nongovernmental organization
OHCHR	Office of the High Commissioner for Human Rights
R2P	responsibility to protect
UK	United Kingdom
UNDP	United Nations Development Programme
UNMIN	UN Mission in Nepal
US	United States
WMDs	weapons of mass destruction

Introduction

Grounding responsibility and protection in culture and politics

Rama Mani and Thomas G. Weiss

This volume explores in novel and challenging ways the emerging norm of the responsibility to protect (R2P), adopted by the United Nations World Summit in 2005 after a decade of significant debate among governments as well as scholars from the global South and North.[1] The essays here seek to uncover whether this norm, as well as its founding values and practical applications, have resonance and grounding within diverse cultures and within societies that have been torn apart by mass atrocity crimes. Despite the growing global consensus around R2P, the norm still encounters difficulties—both political and operational.

The contributors to this collection analyze the responsibility to protect through multiple disciplines—philosophy, religion and spirituality, anthropology, sociology, and aesthetics—to explore what light alternative perspectives outside of political science and international relations shed upon this emerging norm. In each case, the disciplinary analysis emanates from the global South and from scholars located within countries that experienced violent political upheaval. Hence, they draw upon not only theory but also first-hand experience with conscience-shocking crimes. Their analyses could and should help shape the future implementation of R2P in accordance with insights from vastly different contexts.

It is with some pride that we indicate the extent to which this volume is unusual in its aspirations and ambitions, in the breadth of disciplines used to examine this emerging international norm, in the diversity of contributing authors, in its geographical and cultural spread. It is unusual also as an edited book in English with many contributors who normally teach and write in other languages. It is ambitious in its combination of rigor, engagement, and authenticity, emerging from the personal commitment of the authors to overcoming the legacy of violence in their own societies, which many of them have endured and witnessed in addition to analyzed.

The humanitarian enterprise itself and many of the concepts and practices in this endeavor are hardly uncontroversial.[2] What are the boundaries of "culture"? Does the "global South" make sense as a construct with the apparent end of geography? What exactly is "local" and what is "international" in the fluid contemporary global context? Which so-called values and practices have served over time to protect and liberate and which have oppressed or confined populations under threat? All of these questions, and many more, swirl about in the pages that follow.

This introductory chapter begins by explaining the origin and objectives of this publication and situating it within the genesis and evolution of the norm of the responsibility to protect. It then outlines its potential contribution, notwithstanding the challenges of the methodology and approach. We provide a brief overview of the chapters and the key questions emerging from them, suggesting how this publication could contribute both to academic investigations and to the development of international policy to prevent mass atrocities. In the concluding chapter we draw in greater depth on the lessons that emerge from each of the chapters to make policy recommendations and suggestions for further social science research.

The genesis and evolution of R2P: an accelerating yet unfinished journey

Since its emergence as the subject and title of the 2001 report by the International Commission on Intervention and State Sovereignty (ICISS),[3] the responsibility to protect has shaped international responses to egregious violations of human rights. Given R2P's declared goal to change the terms of humanitarian discourse, questions arise as to how far it presently is from the status of an international norm. How long can a norm be described as "emerging" before it truly has emerged? R2P surfaced in an attempt to move beyond the counterproductive and toxic backlash to the purported "right to humanitarian intervention" asserted in the early post–Cold War years as the response to complex emergencies. Since the international response in northern Iraq in 1991, this term had often led to largely circular tirades about the agency, timing, legitimacy, means, circumstances, and advisability of using military force to protect human beings.

The central normative tenet of the responsibility to protect, as envisaged first in the 2001 ICISS report and embraced later by the UN's 2005 World Summit, is that state sovereignty is contingent and not absolute. Each state has a responsibility to protect its own citizens from mass killings and other gross violations of their rights. If that state, however, is unable or unwilling to exercise that responsibility, or actually is the perpetrator of mass atrocities, its sovereignty is abrogated while the responsibility to protect devolves to the international community of states, ideally acting through the UN Security Council. The twofold responsibility in this framework—internal and external—draws upon earlier work by Francis Deng and Roberta Cohen on "sovereignty as responsibility."[4] The ICISS report and the World Summit Outcome document moved away from humanitarian intervention as a right (that is, one that could be deployed and perhaps manipulated without consistent adherence to rigorous standards and accepted principles). Both emphasized the need—and indeed the responsibility—for the international community of states, embodied by the UN and mandated since its creation to deliver "freedom from fear," to do everything possible to prevent mass atrocities. According to the R2P doctrine, military force should be deployed after all alternatives have been considered, attempted, and have patently failed to end mass atrocities, and in circumstances when it has reasonable prospects for success. Military intervention to protect the vulnerable is further constrained, in the summit's language, only to cases of "genocide, war crimes, ethnic cleansing and crimes against humanity." The shorthand for these crimes is "mass atrocity crimes."

The R2P agenda, however, comprises more complex and subtle responses to mass atrocities than the use of military force, ranging from prevention to post-conflict rebuilding in order to protect civilians at risk.[5] While the World Summit ignored post-conflict peace building and emphasized prevention and reaction, this book examines the full spectrum of prevention, reaction, and rebuilding as part of the original ICISS conceptualization of the responsibility to protect. It is important to ensure that R2P does not become synonymous with everything that the UN does. In addition to and halting mass atrocity crimes, the value added of R2P consists of proximate prevention and proximate peace building—that is, efforts to move back from the brink of atrocities that have yet to become widespread or efforts after mass atrocity crimes to ensure that they do not recur.

The responsibility to protect should not be viewed narrowly. It is not, and this cannot be said too frequently, *only* about the use of military force. R2P is not a synonym for humanitarian intervention although proponents sometimes lapse into this language. This task is especially pertinent after rhetoric issued by the administrations in Washington and London disingenuously morphed into a "humanitarian" justification for the war in Iraq when weapons of mass destruction (WMDs) and links to Al Qaeda proved non-existent. The Iraq war was almost a conversation stopper for R2P, as critics and even supporters tended to look askance upon humanitarian justifications for military force.

R2P is above all about taking timely preventive action, identifying situations that are capable of deteriorating into mass atrocities, and bringing to bear diplomatic, legal, economic, and military pressure in timely fashion to prevent or end suffering. There must be action long before the only option remaining is the US Army's 82nd Airborne Division, and additional commitments are necessary after deploying outside military forces.

At the same time, the responsibility to protect is not about the protection of everyone from everything. Broadening perspectives away from reaction has opened the floodgates to an overflow of appeals to address too many problems. For example, part of the political support at the World Summit reflected an understandable but erroneous desire to use R2P to mobilize more support for root-cause prevention, including investments in economic and social development. It may be emotionally tempting and even morally compelling to say that the international community of states has a responsibility to protect people from HIV/AIDS and small arms, or the Inuit from global warming. However, if R2P means everything, it amounts to nothing. The international community of states will once again stand by in impotent silence when machine guns or machetes result in mass murder because there is no universal norm to call upon, no deployable mechanism of protection to implement rapidly.

With these caveats, nonetheless, the R2P norm breaks new ground in several ways. In addition to the usual attributes of a sovereign state that students encounter in international relations and law courses and in the 1933 Montevideo Convention—people, authority, territory, and independence—there is another: a modicum of respect for basic human rights. The traditional emphasis on privileges has made room for modest responsibilities as well. Moreover, when a state is unable or manifestly unwilling to protect the rights of its population—and especially when it is the perpetrator of abuse—that state temporarily loses its sovereignty along with the accompanying right of nonintervention. In short, the traditional rule of noninterference in the internal affairs of other countries no longer applies in the face of mass atrocities. Moreover, ICISS turned the language of humanitarian intervention on its head and moved away from the label detested in large portions of the global South. The merits of particular situations should be evaluated rather than blindly blessed as "humanitarian." For anyone familiar with the number of sins justified by the use of that adjective during the colonial period, this change marked a dramatic shift away from the rights of outsiders to intervene and toward the rights of populations at risk to assistance and protection and the responsibility of outsiders to come to the rescue.

In what Gareth Evans calculates as "a blink of an eye in the history of ideas,"[6] the developments since the release of the ICISS report in December 2001 suggest that R2P has moved from the prose and passion of an international commission toward being a mainstay of international public policy. It also has substantial potential to evolve further in customary international law and to contribute to ongoing conversations about the responsibilities of states as legitimate sovereigns. In 2004 the UN's High-level Panel on Threats, Challenges and Change issued their report titled *A More Secure World: Our Shared Responsibility*, which endorsed "the emerging norm that there is a collective international responsibility to protect."[7] Former UN secretary-general Kofi Annan endorsed it in his 2005 report, *In Larger Freedom*.[8] The most significant normative advance came in September 2005, when heads of state and government unanimously supported the responsibility to protect in paragraphs 138 and 139 of the World Summit Outcome document, which gave R2P its own subsection title. In addition to the official blessing by the UN General Assembly in October 2005, the Security Council made specific references to R2P on two occasions: the April 2006 resolution 1674 on the protection of civilians in armed conflict expressly "reaffirms the provisions of paragraphs 138 and 139," and the August 2006 resolution 1706 on Darfur, which was the first to link R2P to a particular conflict.

In addition, UN secretary-general Ban Ki-moon appointed a special adviser for the prevention of genocide (Francis M. Deng) and a special adviser tasked with promoting R2P (Edward C. Luck). He has referred to the implementation of R2P as one of his priorities and released *Implementing the Responsibility to Protect* in January 2009.[9] In this report, Ban details a "three pillar" approach for implementing R2P, which includes the protection responsibilities of individual states, international assistance and capacity building, and timely and decisive response from the international community.[10]

The point of departure for the interactive dialogue of the UN General Assembly in July 2009 was the secretary-general's report, which resulted in resolution 63/208, a significant marker in R2P's normative trajectory.[11] The positive movement continued in August 2010 with another interactive dialogue[12] around a report on early warning from the secretary-general,[13] and resolution 64/245 in December 2010 that approved the new joint office focusing on the four mass-atrocity crimes. The cumulative impact in a generally more supportive atmosphere is described by Ramesh Thakur and Thomas G. Weiss as "the most dramatic normative development of our time."[14]

It is worth reviewing briefly the norm's path over the last two years. In 2009 state members of the Group of Friends of the responsibility to protect in New York, the UN special adviser, and civil society picked up the mantle from previous "norm entrepreneurs"—that is drawing upon successful recent campaigns to forge wider constituencies for such issues as banning landmines and establishing the International Criminal Court. Initially, many feared a deliberate dilution of the September 2005 commitment. On the eve of the debate, *The Economist* noted that R2P opponents had been "busily sharpening their knives."[15] The Nicaraguan president of the General Assembly, Father Miguel d'Escoto Brockmann, was a confirmed critic who called R2P "redecorated colonialism."[16]

However, R2P-naysayers were deeply disappointed and surprised by the discernible shift away from antipathy toward enthusiasm. It was to be expected that countries that had suffered terrible atrocities made rousing pleas to strengthen and implement R2P—e.g., Rwanda, Bosnia, Guatemala, Sierra Leone, and East Timor—and that a wide variety of countries such as Chile, Republic of Korea, and all of the countries in the West expressed their firm support. Less expected was the widening consensus evident from remarks by 92 countries and two observers who addressed the General Assembly. Only Venezuela directly questioned the 2005 World Summit agreement, and in all only four countries expressed opposition and sought to roll back the earlier consensus: Cuba, Nicaragua, Sudan, and Venezuela. Of special relevance were affirmative remarks from major regional powers that had previously been reticent or even hostile, including Brazil, India, Japan, Nigeria, and South Africa.

The tone of the August 2010 interactive dialogue echoed the positive tenor of July 2009 and went further, revealing again the backing of governments, North and South, for the objective of preventing and halting genocide, ethnic cleansing, war crimes, and crimes against humanity. Among the 42 countries that took the floor, constructive comments came from some that had previously been skeptical—including Cuba, Egypt, and India—suggesting that consensus on R2P within the UN's membership was deepening. The establishment of the joint office, a proposal from the secretary-general to combine Deng's and Luck's efforts with support from the regular budget, was contested (once again with Cuba, Venezuela, and Nicaragua leading the opposition, this time joined by Algeria) but approved at the 11th hour.

Then the Security Council made precedent-setting operational references against Libya early in 2011: resolution 1970 had unanimous support for a substantial package of measures (arms embargo, asset freeze, travel bans, and reference of the situation to the International Criminal Court); and resolution 1973 imposed a no-fly zone. In addition, the Human Rights Council referred to R2P for the first time in resolution S-15/1, which led to the General Assembly's resolution 65/60 that suspended Libyan membership in the council.

Mustering the cross-cultural political will to give real and consistent protection to civilians is never going to be easy, but Libya may be a pivotal moment for what Shannon Beebe and Mary Kaldor call "human security intervention."[17] As the situations in Tripoli and elsewhere across the wider Middle East unfold, acute dilemmas for humanitarians[18] and policymakers will remain. If the Libyan intervention goes well, it will put teeth in the fledgling R2P doctrine; if the Libyan intervention goes badly, it will redouble international opposition and make future decisions more difficult. However, for the moment the usual spoilers are on the defensive, and support in the global South—for instance, in the calls from the Arab League and the African Union—suggest that cultural and political reinforcements are not exclusively found in the global North.

Thus, the General Assembly showed in 2009 and 2010 considerably more enthusiasm for implementing the 2005 consensus than for moving backward. R2P is in fact at the beginning of a long normative journey. As with all humanitarian initiatives—beginning with the Geneva Conventions 150 years ago—time elapses before new norms stimulate routine change and compliance. As David Rieff reminds us, "there is considerable evidence of changing norms, though not, of course, changing facts on the ground."[19] At the same time, the pace of the journey has accelerated. Today, the R2P norm meets widespread consensus in the General Assembly, albeit more with a focus on prevention and capacity building than on protection and post-crisis peace building. The resistance to taking protective action and to viewing sovereignty as responsibility has faded but not completely disappeared. These seismic attitudinal shifts in international relations, so long fettered by non-interference in domestic affairs of states, herald a new dawn for those seeking to halt mass atrocities once and for all. Surely it is not quixotic to say no more Holocausts and Rwandas—and to mean it on some occasions.

From global principle to local cultural perspectives

Our research addresses exactly these two central concepts underpinning R2P: responsibility and protection. How are they viewed from the perspective of different disciplines, and how are they treated in societies that have actually experienced mass atrocities? Despite the progress made by the R2P norm in gaining wider acceptance and overcoming resistance since the time we conceived this project, there remains considerable ignorance or misgivings about R2P in some circles. We remain persuaded of the need to better understand the sources of support and sustenance for effective human protection and the responsibility to provide such protection among a variety of cultures and traditions. The motivation for commissioning these essays is obvious to Oscar Arias, "culture matters,"[20] but what is obvious to the Nobel laureate and two-time president of Costa Rica has been less obvious to R2P norm entrepreneurs. In scholarly terms, such knowledge is valuable; in more utilitarian terms, it also could provide a means to design and implement more effective, appropriate, and culturally acceptable means, both internal and external, to protect affected populations.

Thomas G. Weiss has been intimately associated with the crafting and evolution of the responsibility to protect, having served as research director for the International Commission on Intervention and State Sovereignty, and then as interim executive director of the incipient Global Centre for the Responsibility to Protect, established in February 2008 by supportive governments, foundations, and nongovernmental organizations. As part of his long-standing research about humanitarianism, he directly experienced reactions around the world to the preliminary discussion of the ICISS report and has had a front-row seat for diplomatic confrontations and compromise at the UN in New York over the evolution and application of the R2P norm.

Rama Mani's long-term work on peace building as a scholar and practitioner across different continents revealed to her the existence of a wealth of cultural, philosophical, spiritual, and aesthetic wisdom in every society pertaining to the dignity and protection of human life, which remained untapped but essential to rooting peace. During her time in Sri Lanka as executive director of the International Centre for Ethnic Studies, she also experienced first-hand how, during civil wars, governments misunderstand and fear the R2P norm, rather than seeing it as a potential ally.

Both editors were aware of an urgent need to go deeper into our understanding of the R2P norm and its application in diverse cultural contexts and disciplines. Not least this would allow us to differentiate the hostility of some governments toward the notion of sovereignty as responsibility and their reticence to protect their own populations from the expectation and demand for protection from mass atrocities expressed by ordinary people, and reverberated in their cultural and social values, beliefs, and traditions that reinforce such humane protection.

Often governments refer to cultural specificity to rationalize or justify their opposition to the protection afforded by human rights generally, and to R2P specifically.[21] Arguments about cultural relativism are indeed what had dogged the debate around human rights through the Cold War and the early 1990s.[22] Was this really so? Were there really cultures that could justify the massacre of a civilian population or resist and condemn attempts to intervene to save threatened lives? Were there really religious and spiritual values that would vindicate abandoning fellow human beings? Were there philosophical worldviews within certain societies that might consider massive loss of life and ethnic cleansing to be acceptable? Were there not spontaneous and embedded aesthetic expressions to condemn such violence and call for protective action when the lives of entire populations were threatened with annihilation?

Or rather, we asked ourselves, would we not uncover within the multiplicity of philosophical, religious, spiritual, cultural, and aesthetic traditions and practices also a multiplicity of explicit and implicit references to acceptable and appropriate ways to prevent mass violence and to protect lives? Would we not find innumerable expressions of sovereignty as responsibility and historic instances of humanity trumping tyrannical sovereignty? We decided to investigate within different traditions the values, principles, and practices of protection as well as effectively of the sources of responsibility for such protection, particularly in the acute circumstances of mass atrocity crimes and threats to survival.

For example, religious beliefs and values have long been considered as factors contributing to a humanitarian ethic. Charity and justice are longstanding religious values. Christianity's notion of love and compassion includes the idea of charity and obligations to strangers.[23] *Zakat*, which roughly translates to voluntarism, is one of the five pillars of Islam and reflects Islamic identity, commands various forms of charity, and is intended to foster solidarity within the community.[24] *Tzadakah* and the idea of repairing the world make charity and good works part of the Jewish identity.[25] Although there is tremendous historical and cross-cultural variation regarding whether faith demands a missionary impulse and whether charity extends to those outside the community of the faithful, many religions hold that charity is a cornerstone of religious identity.[26] While charity or justice are injunctions in the Judeo-Christian religions, in older spiritual traditions service to and solidarity with others go beyond injunction and are living values or principles emanating from the supreme wisdom of the inherent unity and interdependence of all life and creation. The millennial Hindu philosophy of the *Upanishads* declares that "Wisdom means a life of selfless service," because the wise "realize that all life is one" and "are at home everywhere and see themselves in all beings."[27] The southern African concept of *ubuntu* popularized by Archbishop Desmond Tutu underlines fundamental interdependence—I exist because you exist—which renders solidarity with and protection of the other instinctual and natural.[28]

We were drawn, in parallel, by the logic of investigating and exposing the analysis and perspectives of scholars affected by violence, to explore their views about the protection of threatened populations. Our intuition was that on-the-ground views were not adequately reflected at UN headquarters in the debates on R2P or even in academic and policy analyses about normative consolidation. We believe that this initial research could provide a building block on which social scientific analyses of public opinion in affected countries might be conducted. Such research has been modest to say the least. A 1999 survey of affected populations in several war zones reports that fully two-thirds of civilians under siege who were interviewed in 12 war-torn societies by the International Committee of the Red Cross (ICRC) wanted more intervention and only 10 percent wanted none.[29] A 2005 mapping exercise of operational contexts for humanitarian agencies finds that recipients rightly "are more concerned about *what* is provided than about *who* provides it."[30] While it was not our intention to conduct opinion polls, we believed that giving local scholars the wherewithal to conduct their own analyses in consultation with civil society could provide a different snapshot.

In the field of post-conflict peace building that emerged in the early 1990s, 10 years of practice signaled to senior UN officials that external assistance without local engagement was futile. By the mid-2000s UN secretary-general Kofi Annan noted that "country ownership of peace building is essential," and the UNDP administrator Mark Mallock Brown underlined the consequent need for "building indigenous support for reform."[31] As expressed unequivocally by the UN official who oversaw the deployment of the UN's most ambitious peacekeeping missions with extensive peace building mandates, Jean-Marie Guéhenno, then UN under-secretary-general for peacekeeping: "The primary responsibility … should ultimately rest with the men and women of the country concerned … It is they who will have to determine what system of law is best suited to their local culture, traditions, and norms. It is they who have most at stake."[32] In short, UN officials routinely included local ownership in their speeches. Studies of peace building also began to include this as a mandatory component of peace building's growing repertoire, albeit still writing from an external observer's perspective, with the continuing silence of local voices.[33]

Few Western scholars of peace building have attempted to ground their work within the fertile soil of culture through anthropological or aesthetic perspectives.[34] There is considerable literature treating different religious interpretations of or perspectives on human rights and humanitarian law, primarily focusing on Judeo-Christian and other monotheistic religions.[35] Likewise, since the early 1990s the literature has grown on cultural mechanisms of conflict prevention and resolution.[36] The fields of cultural anthropology and cross-cultural psychology address conflict and mass atrocities within different cultural contexts.[37] This research project seeks to go beyond these analyses, hopefully breaking new ground that could help shape and deepen the evolution of the R2P norm.

One glaring absence in mainstream thinking about peace building and security has been the unavailability of analyses conducted by scholars living and working within societies affected by violent conflict and mass atrocities. Such literature is often locally published, written in the local idiom, and frequently does not circulate beyond national borders. It has scant impact, therefore, on shaping international discourse and practice. This book begins to tap such scholarship and examine the issue of protection and the norm of the responsibility to protect emerging from these societies.

When they do address it, analyses of peace building tend to regard "culture" as an undifferentiated amalgam, a timeless unchanging monolith.[38] Furthermore, within peace building and security, most references to culture, whether anecdotal or academic, focus on its propaganda value to foment violence—for instance, by the Nazi regime or Radio Milles Collines in Rwanda. While acknowledging numerous previous instances of the manipulation of religion, philosophy, art, and other cultural practices for violence throughout history, our focus in this volume is substantively different. Our view of culture as a complex, endlessly adapting, and differentiated composite, and its importance for protection and peace building, is more akin to that expressed by Zimbabwean scholar David Kualemu:

> How people look at themselves and each other, their cultural beliefs and ideals all enter into how these people are going to build their social world and how they will behave in this world … I do not mean to accept cultural determinism that postulates that certain cultures are more democratic, more peaceful … Every cultural tradition has within it tools for peace and democracy just as it has tools for undermining these. It is up to members of each cultural tradition to identify aspects of their traditional practices which

> best help human centred development … by expanding people's choices and building peace.[39]

We decided to differentiate several of the principal elements that constitute culture, however contested the concept. Thus, we chose to distinguish and ask authors in Part One of this volume to explore:

Beliefs: the different ways in which human societies seek to construct and structure their beliefs about the place of the human being within the cosmos and the relationships between humans, the earth, and the divine. This led us to an examination of religious and spiritual traditions, both organized and theistic, as well as diffuse and regarding the entire cosmos and all creation as divine.

Values: the fundamental underpinnings of different worldviews of human society that shape interactions of rightful conduct. This led us to an examination of philosophy and ethics.

Manifestations: the expressions in various creative forms by individuals and societies that are shaped by such diverse cultural practices, especially those that emerge when these societies are under stress. This led us to an examination of aesthetic traditions and artistic expressions.

We asked contributors in the first three chapters to explore through the lenses of spirituality, philosophy, and aesthetics how individuals and societies in different parts of the global South approached and responded to human suffering and particularly threats to the lives and survival of vulnerable populations. Are there values, beliefs, practices, or manifestations that express how such threatened populations must be treated? How might they be afforded protection, by whom, when, and in what guise? Who might bear responsibility for responding to provide such protection? How might such threats be prevented, deterred, mitigated, or resolved in diverse spiritual, philosophical, and aesthetic traditions?

While exploring the extent to which R2P is embedded or at least reflected within diverse cultures and contexts, we also deemed it essential to analyze concrete experiences in order to explore whether different contexts made a difference to the prevention of mass atrocities or the protection of people when conscience-shocking violence erupted. The challenge was to situate this research within societies that had experienced mass atrocities and determine the resonance of the responsibility to protect as reflected across beliefs, values, and manifestations. Sadly, we had no shortage of possible cases from which to choose. We were tempted to opt for ongoing or recent cases of mass atrocities that remain a blight on the international public conscience and cry out for the application of the responsibility to protect—Darfur, the Democratic Republic of the Congo (DRC), Myanmar, Zimbabwe, and the list goes on.

However, we wanted some historical distance from the tragic events in order to permit more objective scrutiny as well as safety for our researchers. At the same time, we sought a rich diversity of cases that would enable us to compare R2P across a variety of cultural, spiritual, philosophical, and aesthetic contexts. Therefore, the second half of this book explores the traction of cultural perspectives for the following three key case studies:

Rwanda in East Africa, where genocide ran rampant in 1994, and where outside intervention was deeply criticized as being far too little too late. This tragedy sparked a cottage industry of analysis about the importance of prevention and recalled, once again, the pledge of "never again."

Kosovo in Southeast Europe, where the military intervention by the North Atlantic Treaty Organization (NATO) in 1999 faced a storm of controversy about whether the use of military force was too much too soon and legitimate if illegal, and whether "humanitarian war" was an oxymoron. Along with Rwanda, Kosovo was the second major crisis of the tumultuous 1990s that stimulated the establishment of the International Commission on Intervention and State Sovereignty.

Nepal in South Asia, where violent civil war ended as recently as 2006 with the country still in the early and uncertain stages of tenuous peace building. Here international attention has, by contrast, been rather limited; however, it would appear that widespread anticipation of mass atrocities in 2004–5 was perhaps prevented due to timely civic activism. Yet, some internal and external observers fear that deeper fissures have opened in society, which might yet result in unprecedented levels of violence.

These countries offer a wide array of religious, philosophical, cultural, and aesthetic diversity. Rwanda's three ethnic groups of Hutu, Tutsi, and Twa share the same language and mythically are siblings made by the same god; the population was converted almost entirely to Catholicism by Belgian missionaries and remains largely so, but vestiges of earlier cultural and spiritual traditions are re-emerging, and new evangelical churches are spreading, after the genocide. Kosovo has an almost exclusively Albanian population, with pockets of Orthodox Christian Serbs. Albanians are putatively Muslim, but strongly secular and Europeanized with the influence of Kosovo's 50 years in the former

Yugoslav Federation, and are more deeply attached to their ethnic Albanian identity than to Islam despite a resurgence of religiosity since the war. Nepal has a complex mosaic of ethnicities, castes, languages, and religions. Hinduism is the religion of the majority and of the historically dominant elite, while Buddhism is the predominant minority religion. Yet solidarity or a feeling of shared brotherhood remains strong among all Nepalese, despite this deep cultural diversity. Moreover, the three selected countries differ greatly in terms of nature, scale, and impact of violence as well as their experience with regional and international attention and intervention—or negligence and inaction. While not seeking to be exhaustive or definitive, the three heterogeneous case studies nonetheless permit generalizations to be teased out across cultures.

The objective of examining thematic areas, on the one hand, and country case studies, on the other hand, is to allow cross-fertilization and cross-analysis. In short, the thematic examinations in Part One provide windows for the deeper analysis of the cases in Part Two, while the cases provide substantiation and grounding for the more theoretical analysis in the thematic chapters.

Finally, cognizant that the norm and practice of R2P would continue to evolve even during the process of conducting this project, we asked our contributors to refer to the three stages formulated by ICISS—namely the prevention stage before mass atrocities, the protection stage in the midst of such crimes, and the post-crisis peace building stage. Authors also refer to the three pillars delineated in the secretary-general's 2009 report and, as we shall see in the conclusion, call particular attention to prevention and capacity building that emerged as crucial in each case.

Looking from the inside out

It was clear to us that if the study was to have a claim to credibility and authenticity, the choice of authors and the design of our book would be essential. No matter what approach was followed, we were aware of possible shortcomings or criticisms. In the interest of truth in packaging, we briefly spell out how and why we proceeded as we have.

We were aware that the thematic cultural issues would necessarily be broad rather than deep in a volume that seeks to pioneer using religion and spirituality, philosophy and ethics, and aesthetics in the study of an emerging international norm within a fraught global political context. For this reason, we knew that the authors would have to be persons of stature, depth, and breadth of knowledge. In addition to a deep personal understanding of the nature of mass atrocities, they also would have to be at ease with running the risk of being criticized for having attempted the impossible. Our task also was complicated in that we also wished to ensure that each chapter, while providing cross-cultural analysis, would be rooted within one geographical region. Consequently, we launched a search across faculties in Africa, Asia, Latin America, and the Middle East. We are delighted that Yolanda Angulo Parra from Mexico and Mutombo Nkulu-N'Sengha from the DRC decided to accept our offer to participate in the thematic section of this project. We are also grateful to Koulsy Lamko from Chad for his early advice and contribution to the chapter on aesthetics by Rama Mani from India. The thematic authors gathered in Mexico City in April 2010 and received feedback from local scholars, which helped in finalizing their chapters.

Our case studies also required careful selection. We first identified locally based scholars so that the analysis in each chapter was engaged, credible, and grounded. We also decided to hold a first round of interdisciplinary consultations in each of the country cases. The first round was held early in summer 2009 and involved partnering with local universities and research institutes and assembling a group of 10 to 20 scholars from diverse disciplines to provide input about their perceptions of the R2P norm within the context of their country's particular cultural context and experience of mass atrocities. This also created a larger cross-disciplinary peer group for the authors to draw upon in researching and writing their chapters.

In Rwanda, we benefited from a jointly convened effort by the Rwanda Governance Advisory Council (GAC) and the Center for Conflict Management of the National University of Rwanda, Butaré. In Kosovo, the Human Rights Centre, Faculty of Law, University of Pristina, organized the session. In Nepal, the Rural Reconstruction Network (RRN) organized the sessions. We are elated with our team of country authors: Jean-Marie Kayishema in Rwanda, Nita Luci in Kosovo, and Arjun Karki and Jyoti Upadhyay in Nepal.

Almost without exception, participants in the consultations in all three countries were directly or indirectly affected by armed conflict or atrocities. In Rwanda, several scholars had been refugees prior to the genocide; others were displaced or became refugees during the genocide; and the majority has devoted the last 15 years to rebuilding Rwanda's academic institutions. In Kosovo, those present were expelled from Pristina during the systematic ethnic cleansing campaign by the Serbian military in 1999, and they returned after the NATO bombing ended Serbian occupation. They were all part of a remarkable underground university system that had survived for a decade before 1999 during the Serbian occupation. One senior scholar had even set aside his academic career and joined the Kosovo Liberation Army (KLA) as a commander during the worst stage of the war. In Nepal, most of those around the table had played an active part in both the 1990 demonstrations and civic activism for democracy and the subsequent 2005–6 mobilization for peace and republicanism. Many were directly involved in the peace negotiations, in which the lead author played a key role.

The country consultations unveiled some of the challenges for the responsibility to protect in a variety of country settings. Skepticism and even suspicion of the so-called international community surfaced everywhere, but those present nonetheless expressed their palpable enthusiasm about the character of this project. One younger woman captured the mood of the skeptics in Nepal by noting that the UN would need to win back the faith and trust of populations before it could move toward implementing the responsibility to protect. Some participants questioned the dichotomy and categories of "North" and "South." However, this research project generally struck a sympathetic chord, especially the effort by the editors to break the pattern of Western scholars writing chapters based on brief interviews with local interlocutors.

Each consultation unveiled the distinctness of each country's context as relevant to R2P, with diversity and contrasts among the three cases. Yet, they also uncovered some areas of similarity. For example, the combination of support for the norm and its underlying principle of protection based on solidarity and humanity rather than self-interest resonated everywhere with values and traditions. Yet, participants expressed reservations about the UN's patent inability to apply such principles in a dispassionate and even-handed way, about the politics that surround UN decision making and the bitter disappointments suffered by all three countries in their own recent histories.

Culture and tradition often play a supportive role as society is rebuilt although they are often overlooked by international peacebuilders. A spontaneous movement has emerged in each of the three countries that aimed to restore cultural foundations, with varying degrees of governmental and international support. In post-conflict Rwanda, for example, several traditions are being revived and adapted, the most well known being *gacaca* courts to adjudicate justice for the innumerable *génocidaires* through community means and *torero* or initiation of the young into values and traditions, as well as solidarity or community work to help one other.

Kosovo's long cohabitation within the Socialist Federal Republic of Yugoslavia created a secular and liberal society imposed upon a deeply traditional, patriarchal, and provincial one. Yet, even the contemporary intellectual and largely secular elite notes the continuing importance of the ancient *Qanun* or traditional customary law and traditional values such as *besa* or honor in keeping one's word. Indeed, they are being revived as a new national identity is being forged or imagined for the new political entity of Kosovo.

Nepal is deeply stratified socially, ethnically, culturally, and religiously. Yet, notwithstanding the Maoist uprising that opposed repressive and sexist cultural traditions, mutual tolerance and respect among different religions, castes, and ethnic groups have largely prevailed. Many see tolerance and respect as the most enduring cultural characteristics of the Himalayan country.

Exclusion and marginalization create groups of haves and have-nots who resort to violence and atrocities, respectively, to maintain their positions or change them, as witnessed in all our case studies. In Rwanda, the stratification of Hutu and Tutsi that had once been loose and fluid became reified under Belgian colonization and then was deliberately manipulated by Hutu nationalists who came to power with independence. In Kosovo, despite the solidarity and lack of ethnic identification that marked Yugoslavia under Tito, Kosovar Albanians felt a growing sense of inferiority and discrimination within the republic, which was accentuated by the increasing encroachment on their autonomy and finally by Serbian occupation. In Nepal, discrimination and marginalization based on caste, ethnicity, and gender have been major factors in the war and violence—for instance, a majority of Maoist fighters are from discriminated castes and ethnic groups.

What was also apparent across the cases was the deep and self-conscious reflection about the causes of a societal collapse that had resulted in grisly violence. Each country has had to grapple with the painful puzzle of why its people were able to engage in mass atrocities and how its culture, traditions, and history abetted the violence. In all the cases, solidarity and mutual help were frequently cited as distinct values, and participants in project consultations regretted their erosion and breakdown with the onset of modernity and the outbreak of violence, war, and mass atrocities. The responsibility to protect evoked a probing discussion of historic notions and practices of the meaning of "responsibility" and "protection" within each country.

Everywhere there was some finger pointing at "outsiders" or "neighbors" or the "international community" with their purported or actual vested interests as the real cause of local problems. At the same time, there was a widespread realization of the need to look closer to home and engage in serious soul-searching about the local causes of violence as well as the local sources of healing.

During spring and summer of 2010, second consultations were held in Kosovo, Nepal, and Rwanda to discuss the drafts of the case studies;

insightful feedback on R2P from both scholars and students informed subsequent chapter revisions. Additionally, a seminar and student conference in Mexico discussed drafts of the book's thematic chapters. Scholars provided insights from their disciplinary perspectives and personal experiences. In Kosovo, for example, everyone had personally experienced the violent events of 1999, and in some cases of 1989 as well when Albanian professors were dismissed from their university posts. In Rwanda few professors had lived through the country's genocide, but many had experienced it in exile and returned thereafter.

A rich segment of the second round of conversations came from the candid and challenging inputs by students. Having been very young during the mass atrocities, they concurred that cultural values and practices had played a key role in mediating violence. Nonetheless, some raised concerns about culture's double-edged sword, manipulated to foment or justify violence as well. They also observed the weakening of these values and practices in their societies. In Rwanda a student noted that modernization, Westernization, and technological change made it challenging to return to or preserve valuable cultural values. In Kosovo students noted the strong solidarity that had accompanied the upheavals of 1999, but which evaporated once the threat passed. The main recommendation emerging from the consultations in Kosovo coincided with the core theme of the book—namely, that the international community of states must react earlier in the conflict cycle and identify a range of interventions rather than responding to violence with violence. In Nepal, where students have been at the forefront of political activism for democracy and peace since the 1950s, participants were as skeptical as Rwandan students about their bittersweet UN experience and about the possibility that R2P could be implemented without double standards and vested interests.

Despite a level of enthusiasm in principle for the application of the responsibility to protect across the three countries, youth fundamentally remained more doubtful than their elders that the UN and its member states would be able or willing to protect vulnerable populations without concern for economic and political interests. This was particularly the case for major powers, and even more particularly for the permanent members of the Security Council.

Conclusion

The contents of this book reveal that "culture" indeed is complex and requires careful articulation and deconstruction. However defined, culture is by no means static and should not be treated as such. It evolves continually; different cultures have different and varying degrees of resilience to pressure. Avowedly, aspects of culture often have been oppressive and have been co-opted to justify violence; however, it is grossly inadequate to only study this negative aspect of culture within mass atrocities. Even under the most repressive and violent conditions, when culture and traditions seem dormant or extinct, core values and practices subsist. Even in the face of mass atrocities, including genocide, when culture and traditions may appear to have disappeared and be inconsequential, they influence the ways that people respond to and cope with violence and repression. They also have an impact on the ways in which individuals and communities seek help and shape expectations of and responses to attempts to protect them.

As editors, we are aware of the intellectual and political limitations of a single publication. It is our hope that the current volume can contribute, however modestly, to ensuring a less violent future and to rethinking how future research in the humanities and social sciences could help protect people.

The gamble that we wagered—in undertaking this ambitious multidisciplinary effort with scholars located in far-flung countries—was vindicated. There is a clear value-added in listening closely to and hopefully understanding what the subtitle of this book calls "Cultural Perspectives in the Global South"—for advancing both the norm of the responsibility to protect as well as its implementation. The value-added is the subject for the final chapter.

Despite the challenges in commissioning such research in contrast to simpler approaches that rely on "the usual suspects" (i.e., primarily Western or Western-based scholars), our fledgling endeavor should be extended by others to examine the interplay of other contested or controversial principles, norms, and practices with political realities on the one hand and cultural contexts on the other. Funders should support and policymakers should give attention to the findings from such analyses by scholars from the global South where the majority of mass atrocity crimes continues to erupt.

In a context of skepticism and ambivalence toward "internationalism" and "multilateralism," there is profound value in embedding research within differentiated cultural contexts. Doing so helps to address at an early stage the suspicion and reticence that surround the emergence of new international principles and norms. They can appear to those directly affected or to diplomats and officials as having emerged from the netherworld—or worse, from the West with its apparently vested national interests. Research can help to overcome such suspicion before it hardens and takes on a life of its own. Beyond this, exploring rich and diverse cultures unearths a wealth of time-tested practices with echoes from the wisdom of the past that can be adapted to current needs in implementing such international norms as the responsibility to protect.

It has been deeply rewarding to undertake the globally spread but locally embedded initiative that resulted in this book, and to work with the gifted and committed contributors. We hope that this book proves as eye-opening and perspective-shifting for you as readers as it has been for us as editors.

Notes

1 *2005 World Summit Outcome*, UN document A/60/1, 24 October 2005, paras. 138–40.

2 See, for example, Ian Smillie and Larry Minear, *The Charity of Nations: Humanitarian Action in a Calculating World* (Bloomfield, Conn.: Kumarian, 2004); Peter J. Hoffman and Thomas G. Weiss, *Sword & Salve: Confronting New Wars and Humanitarian Crises* (Lanham, Md.: Rowman & Littlefield, 2006); Michael Barnett and Thomas G. Weiss, eds., *Humanitarianism in Question: Politics, Principles, Ethics* (Ithaca, NY: Cornell University Press, 2008); Alain Finkielfraut, *In the Name of Humanity: Reflections on the Twentieth Century* (London: Pimlico, 2000); Joanna Macrae, ed., *The New Humanitarianisms: A Review of Trends in Global Humanitarian Action*, Humanitarian Policy Group Report 11, 2002.

3 International Commission on Intervention and State Sovereignty, *The Responsibility to Protect* (Ottawa: International Development Research Centre, 2001). See also, Thomas G. Weiss and Don Hubert, *The Responsibility to Protect: Research, Bibliography, Background* (Ottawa: International Development Research Centre, 2001).

4 See, for example, Francis M. Deng *et al.*, *Sovereignty as Responsibility: Conflict Management in Africa* (Washington, DC: Brookings Institution, 1996); and Roberta Cohen and Francis M. Deng, *Masses in Flight: The Global Crisis of Internal Displacement* (Washington, DC: Brookings Institution, 1998). This history is analyzed by Thomas G. Weiss and David A. Korn, *Internal Displacement: Conceptualization and Its Consequences* (London: Routledge, 2006).

5 For interpretations by commissioners, see Gareth Evans, *The Responsibility to Protect: Ending Mass Atrocity Crimes Once and For All* (Washington, DC: Brookings Institution, 2008); and Ramesh Thakur, *The United Nations, Peace and Security: From Collective Security to the Responsibility to Protect* (Cambridge: Cambridge University Press, 2006). See also Alex J. Bellamy, *Responsibility to Protect: The Global Effort to End Mass Atrocities* (Cambridge: Polity Press, 2009); and Thomas G. Weiss, *Humanitarian Intervention: Ideas in Action* (Cambridge: Polity Press, 2007).

6 Evans, *The Responsibility to Protect*, 21.

7 High-level Panel on Threats, Challenges and Change, *A More Secure World: Our Shared Responsibility* (New York: United Nations, 2004), para. 203.

8 Kofi A. Annan, *In Larger Freedom: Towards Development, Security and Human Rights for All* (New York: United Nations, 2005).

9 *Implementing the Responsibility to Protect, Report from the Secretary-General*, UN document A/63/677, 12 January 2009.
10 Ibid.
11 See Global Centre on the Responsibility to Protect, "Implementing the Responsibility to Protect—The 2009 General Assembly Debate: An Assessment," August 2009, available at: globalr2p.org/advocacy/index.php.
12 See Global Centre for the Responsibility to Protect, "'Early Warning, Assessment, and the Responsibility to Protect': Informal Interactive Dialogue of the General Assembly held on 9 August 2010," September 2010, available at: globalr2p.org/advocacy/index.php.
13 *Early Warning, Assessment and the Responsibility to Protect: Report of the Secretary-General*, General Assembly document A/64/864, 14 July 2010.
14 Ramesh Thakur and Thomas G. Weiss, "R2P: From Idea to Norm—and Action?" *Global R2P* 1, no. 1 (2009): 22.
15 "An Idea whose Time Has Come—and Gone?" *The Economist*, 23 July 2009.
16 "Statement by the President of the General Assembly, Miguel d'Escoto Brockmann, at the Opening of the 97th Session of the General Assembly," 23 July 2009, available at: www.responsibilitytoprotect.org/index.php/component/content/article/35-r2pcs-topics/2493-general-assembly-debate-on-the-responsibility-to-protect-and-informal-interactive-dialogue.
17 Shannon D. Beebe and Mary Kaldor, *The Ultimate Weapon is No Weapon: Human Security and the New Rules of War and Peace* (New York: Public Affairs, 2010).
18 See Michael Barnett and Thomas G. Weiss, *Humanitarianism Contested: Where Angels Fear to Tread* (London: Routledge, 2011).
19 David Rieff, "A False Compatibility: Humanitarian Action and Human Rights," *Humanitarian Stakes Number 1*, MSF Switzerland, September 2008, 41.
20 Oscar Arias, "Culture Matters," *Foreign Affairs* 90, no. 1 (2011): 2–13.
21 See Peter Van Ness, ed., *Debating Human Rights: Critical Essays from the United States and Asia* (London: Routledge, 1999), which analyzes official US, Chinese, Indian, and other Asian positions.
22 Alison Dundes Renteln, *International Human Rights: Universalism versus Relativism* (London: Sage, 1990); Xiaorong Li, *Ethics, Human Rights and Culture: Beyond Relativism and Universalism* (Houndsmills, Basingstoke, UK: Palgrave Macmillan, 2006); Jane K. Cowan, Marie-Bénédicte Dembour, and Richard A. Wilson, eds., *Culture and Rights: Anthropological Perspectives* (Cambridge: Cambridge University Press, 2001).
23 Norman Fiering, "Irresistible Compassion: An Aspect of Eighteenth Century Sympathy and Humanitarianism," *Journal of the History of Ideas* 37, no. 2 (1976): 195–218.
24 M.A. Mohamed Salih, "Islamic NGOs in Africa: The Promise and Peril of Islamic Voluntarism," in *Islamism and its Enemies in the Horn of Africa*, ed. Alex de Waal (London: Hurst, 2004), 146–81.
25 See, for instance, Ina Friedman, "Jewish Soft Power," *Jerusalem Report*, 24 July 2006, 11–12.
26 See Ephraim Isaac, "Humanitarianism Across Religions and Cultures," in *Humanitarianism Across Borders: Sustaining Civilians in Times of War*, ed. Thomas G. Weiss and Larry Minear (Boulder, Colo.: Lynne Rienner, 1993), 13–22.

27 Eknath Easwaran, trans., *The Upanishads* (Tomales, Calif.: Nilgiri Press, 1987), 143, 149.

28 See, for example, Michael Battle and Desmond Tutu, *Ubuntu: I in You and You in Me* (New York: Seabury Books, 2009); and Mfuniselwa J. Bhengu, *Ubuntu: The Global Philosophy for Humankind* (Cape Town: Lotsha Publications, 2006).

29 Greenberg Research, *The People on War Report* (Geneva: ICRC, 1999), xvi.

30 Antonio Donini, Larry Minear, Ian Smillie, Ted van Baarda, and Anthony C. Welch, *Mapping the Security Environment: Understanding the Perceptions of Local Communities, Peace Support Operations, and Assistance Agencies* (Medford, Mass: Feinstein International Famine Center, June 2005), 53.

31 "Country Ownership of Peacebuilding through Parliaments, Other Institutions Crucial to Success, Says Secretary-General in Message to New York Parliamentary Hearing," SG/SM/10735, DEV/2603, 13 November 2006, available at: www.un.org/News/Press/docs/2006/sgsm10735.doc.htm; Statement by Mark Malloch Brown, UNDP Administrator to the Security Council United Nations, New York, 6 October 2004, available at: content.undp.org/go/newsroom/2004/october/mmb-security-council.en?categoryID=593045& lang=en.

32 Jean-Marie Guéhenno, "Preface," in *United Nations Peacebuilding: Establishing Rule of Law: Recommendations from the Field* (UN Association of America and The Project on Justice in Times of Transition of Harvard University, September 2004), 4.

33 For example, see Beatrice Pouligny, "Local Ownership," in *Post-Conflict Peacebuilding: A Lexicon*, ed. Vincent Chetail (Oxford: Oxford University Press, 2009), 174–87; and Annika Hansen and Sharon Wihata, *The Transition to a Just Order: Establishing Local Ownership after Conflict. A Policy Report* (Stockholm: Folke Bernadotte Academy, 2007).

34 John Paul Lederach, *The Moral Imagination: The Art and Soul of Building Peace* (Oxford: Oxford University Press, 2005); and Lisa Schirch, *Ritual and Symbol in Peacebuilding* (Bloomfield, Conn.: Kumarian Press, 2005).

35 See, for example, Vesselin Popovski, Gregory M. Reichberg, and Nicholas Turner, eds., *World Religions and Norms of War* (Tokyo: UN University Press, 2009).

36 See Kevin Avruch, Peter W. Black, and Joseph A. Scimecca, eds., *Conflict Resolution: Cross Cultural Perspectives* (Westport, Conn.: Praeger, 1991).

37 See, for example, Alexander Laban Hinton, ed., *Annihilating Difference: The Anthropology of Genocide* (Berkeley: University of California Press, 2002); Yueh-Ting Lee, *The Psychology of Ethnic and Cultural Conflict* (Westport, Conn.: Praeger, 2004); Tony Vaux, *The Selfish Altruist* (Sterling, Va.: Earthscan Publishing, 2001); and Arthur Kleiman, Veena Das, and Margaret Lock, eds., *Social Suffering* (Berkeley: University of California Press, 1997).

38 For example, a recent critique of the misunderstanding of culture in liberal peace building is S. Kappler, "The Romanticisation of the Local? Welfare, Culture and Peacebuilding," paper presented at the International Studies Association's 50th Annual Convention, New York, February 2009.

39 David Kualemu, "Beyond Contemporary Exclusivist Traditionalist Culture in Building Peace and Development," in *The Struggles After the Struggle: Zimbabwean Philosophical Studies 1*, ed. David Kualemu (Washington, DC: Council for Research on Values and Philosophy, 2008), 127–56, quote at 128.

Part one

Reflections in religion, philosophy, and art

1 Religion, spirituality, and R2P in a global village

Mutombo Nkulu-N'Sengha

- **What is religion and its social function?**
- **Overview of religious and spiritual traditions in the global South**
- **African religions and R2P**
- **Specific religious concepts with relevance for R2P**
- **Conclusion: where do we go from here?**

The aim of this chapter is to explore the contribution that religion can bring to bear on the development and implementation of the responsibility to protect (R2P) norm. To those aware of the long history of religious violence[1] and theocratic justifications for tyrannical regimes or the manipulation of divine authority to oppose human rights, the idea of a positive contribution of religion to R2P may seem far-fetched or even counter productive. Yet this chapter maintains that if religious beliefs and worldviews are overlooked, R2P can neither be well understood nor successfully implemented.

This view becomes evident when we take into account the overwhelming power of religions and their role in shaping human identity, consciousness, and ways of thinking and being in the world. Some scholars estimate that 10,000 religions are practiced across the globe. Christianity, for instance, comprises 39,000 different denominations, 900 of them in the United States alone. Christianity accounts for almost 33 percent of the world population, followed by Islam (22 percent), Hinduism (15 percent), and Buddhism (6.5 percent).[2] Moreover, because these major religions developed in a world where they drew some elements from older religions, and because some people still hold traditional beliefs even when converted to Christianity or Islam, it has been asserted by some scholars that "indigenous religions are the majority of the world's religions."[3] Most importantly, nowadays a significant number of people are returning to their "traditional religion," or engaging in both "indigenous" and another, newer religion.

It should be noted, however, that the power of religion cannot be reduced to the sheer volume of the followers. Rather its pivotal role resides in its incredible ability to shape the lives and thinking of the vast majority of the world's population.

The relationship between R2P and religion can be understood only when we better grasp the nature of religion and its function in society and in the personal lives of individuals. An exploration of R2P through a spiritual lens can shed light on some fundamental questions such as whether religion can challenge the sacrosanct notion of state sovereignty, and whether it condones the overthrow of violent tyrants responsible for mass atrocities. Indeed, the notion of R2P, and especially the concept of foreign intervention to stop mass atrocities that lies at its core, is hampered by the modern doctrine of state sovereignty and by understandable local resistance to outside interventions, especially in countries with a deep historical memory of colonialism, neocolonialism, and imperialism. This chapter argues, however, that R2P finds legitimacy in most cultures because of deep-seated religious beliefs in the common origin of humanity and the religious ethic of global solidarity that transcends the boundaries of states, kingdoms, tribes, and clans.

Despite the "high-minded foolishness" of some religious actors and the lurid grotesqueness of religious irrationalities, fanaticism, and obscurantist superstitions, religions remain, for good and for ill, an essential element of cultures and shape the way people think and act on various social issues and how they relate to one another and to human institutions. As Emile Durkheim asserted, "[I]t may be said that nearly all the great social institutions have been born in religion … [R]eligion has given birth to all that is essential in society … "[4] The African theologian John Mbiti pointed out that a human being "cannot live by the bread of science and politics alone; he also needs the vitamins of ethics and morals, faith and hope, love and security, comfort and attention in the face of death and misfortune; because it offers these elements religion plays a crucial role in the human quest for identity and security and provides a foundation and a direction of life for societies."[5]

The point of departure here is that religion can provide a rationale for the norm of the responsibility to protect. Indeed, the resurgence of religion in the last three decades and the fact that 80 to 90 percent of the world's population describe themselves as "religious" suggest that religion be taken into account in a meaningful development of the norm. Even in the West, where secularism and agnosticism have a strong hold, religion is still part of the life of a significant portion of the population, and Western religious structures and their network of missionary activities are still powerful.

This chapter intends to articulate this religious foundation of R2P through an analysis of the wisdom of world religions, with particular emphasis on the religions practiced in the global South. Moreover, instances of genocide and other mass atrocities in such places as Rwanda and the Democratic Republic of the Congo (DRC), as well as the long history of the slave trade, colonialism, neocolonialism, and dictatorship, require special attention to the role of African religions and spirituality in furthering the normative development of R2P.

Given the extraordinary complexity and ambiguity of the phenomenon in human history, religion can be an ally or a foe in the development of R2P; thus, two caveats are mentioned. First, while acknowledging the phenomenon of "sacred violence" (i.e., hatred, discrimination, and wars motivated by religious zeal) and violence beneath the surface of all cultures, a meaningful discussion of the contribution of religion to R2P requires a focus on those religious values that are commensurate with peacemaking and coexistence. This chapter thus explores the ways in which world religions have contributed and can still contribute more to peacemaking. Religions and local cultures in the global South can become major assets in the construction of a global civilization that manages to limit conflicts and promote a wider R2P consciousness.

Second, the contribution of religion to R2P requires a broad vision and a grand narrative to be meaningful. Yet, all such efforts run the risk of oversimplification, inevitable in light of the complexity of world religions and differences among cultures. The task of describing religion is even more complicated because every religion is dynamic, and what is said of one epoch may not be valid for another. However, the complexity of the task should not be an excuse for paralysis in developing the R2P norm.

This essay explores some common threads among religions and cultures in order to articulate a more meaningful discourse on the responsibility to protect. People who are victims of mass atrocities cannot be saved by endless theological disputes or absolutist claims of cultural uniqueness. Rather, they appreciate life-saving succor regardless of the cultural, ethnic, or religious ideologies of the helper.[6]

In this chapter, religions of the global South refer to the religious worldviews and traditional values produced by ancestral spiritualities that for centuries have fashioned cultural identities in Africa, Asia, and Latin America. We also include in the religions of the global South the major world religions—Christianity, Islam, and Buddhism—which, in many regions, have been "inculturated" and reinterpreted through the grids of traditional religious worldviews. However, given that this chapter intends to articulate the specific contribution of the global

South to R2P, we shall not dwell extensively on those widely known teachings of Christianity and Islam. Rather we shall highlight those religious elements of the global South that may be unfamiliar to many analysts.

This discussion of religion and its impact on R2P proceeds in five steps. Part one examines the nature of religion and its five dimensions, and the crucial roles that religion and spirituality play in society. Part two provides an overview of the religious and spiritual traditions of the global South. Part three explores a specific case study, namely the potential contribution of African religions and spirituality to human ethical development. Part four examines four specific religious and spiritual beliefs and practices that are relevant to R2P: the golden rule, sovereignty, nonviolence, and just war doctrine. Several historical examples from Africa are cited in which these tenets were applied in practice to protect the oppressed and oppose tyranny. Part five concludes with why humans should adopt R2P and provides recommendations on ways that religion can help shape the R2P norm. This chapter uses sources from sacred texts, oral tradition, and world history; it endeavors to cite literature produced by scholars from the global South.

As well as being interdisciplinary and multicultural, this chapter is grounded in the "epistemological privilege of the poor" and first-hand experience. Born and raised in the DRC, I grew up under the ferocious regime of Mobutu Sese Seko and experienced two civil wars. Moreover, this region has suffered the after-shock of the Rwandan genocide and endured a calamitous armed conflict in which some 5 million people have perished since 1997. The Democratic Republic of the Congo—the land immortalized by Joseph Conrad as the proverbial heart of darkness and also the country of Patrice Lumumba, the Congolese independence leader and the first legally elected prime minister of the Republic of the Congo after independence from Belgium in June 1960—constitutes an essential case for voices in the global South that oppose or call for the implementation of R2P.

What is religion and its social function?

"Those who say religion has nothing to do with politics," wrote Gandhi in his autobiography, "do not know what religion means."[7] In 1938, in his address to a group of missionaries, he made an explicit point that clarifies the connection between R2P and religion: "I could not be leading a religious life unless I identified myself with the whole of mankind and that I could not do unless I took part in politics. The whole gamut of man's activities today constitutes an indivisible whole … I do not know of any religion apart from activity. It provides a moral basis to all other activities without which life would be a maze of sound and fury signifying nothing."[8] Although religion is complex and lived in myriad forms, the notion that religion has a "political dimension" and an ethical dimension is critical to our understanding of the role that religion can play in the promotion of R2P. So, what is religion and what is its purpose? Is there any difference between religion and spirituality?

Traditionally, spirituality as what pertains to the life of the spirit has been associated with religion, deities, the supernatural, and belief in the afterlife. However, nowadays, in a world dominated by a growing secularism, the opposition to the pitfalls of "organized religions" has introduced in some milieux a distinction between religion and spirituality. In the United States, there is a growing number of people who adhere to "non-denominational" Christian churches and people who define themselves as "spiritual but not religious." For this type of believer, religion implies what is false in religion, the man-made rules and regulations, rigid structures, the external, social, public, and even political dimension of religion, while spirituality implies the interior mode of relating to the divine, the private and personal relationship with God. Religion is then equated with laws, external rituals, social institutions, and cultural customs, while spirituality is associated with love and with the soul or the heart. Some would view religion as the form and spirituality as the content of the same reality. Still others believe that spirituality is not limited to religion, for even atheists can be spiritual. It is not the aim of this study to solve the conundrum of these arcane and casuistic disputes. Suffice it to mention that this typically Western way of dealing with religion is not universal. In the world, religion is practiced and defined in a variety of ways. In the context of the global South, which is less shaped by secularism and atheism, the terms "spirituality" and "religion" can be used interchangeably since most people around the globe approach religion as a comprehensive and holistic way of life. This is in fact what we learn from the very nature of religion as understood in its primordial development. Since time immemorial, religion has had two dimensions, one visible and the other invisible.[9] While the visible aspect of religion is composed of cult, rituals, and institutions, the invisible aspect of religion is characterized by the principles of love, law, and justice, and transcends all attempts of institutionalization. This being said, a brief examination of the nature of religion will clarify this chapter's approach to the topic at hand.

Religion is a Western concept of Latin origin.[10] It emerged in the context of the Roman Empire and has evolved continually since. Aware of the "pagan origin" of the term, some Church fathers were even reluctant to apply this word to Christianity in the beginning. Outside of Europe, many languages do not have the term "religion." In Asia, people referred to their religious practices as "the way," as in Taoism or Shintoism (Shen-Tao). Semantics aside, peoples around the globe have a set of beliefs and practices that exhibit some similarities across cultures and that can rightly be called "religion." Scholars have defined religion in a variety of ways. This chapter relies on those definitions that help illuminate R2P.

For most theologians, "religion is an explanation of the ultimate meaning of life, based on the notion of the transcendent, and how to live accordingly."[11] It is a faith that commands a concrete way of being and interacting. Religion is at once a way of praying, thinking, and acting. Max Weber pointed out that "religion starts with the metaphysical needs of the human mind to understand the world as a meaningful cosmos and to take up a position toward it."[12] The quest for meaning has consequences. Religion calls for action, as Clifford Geertz wrote: "Religion is a system of symbols which acts to establish powerful, pervasive, and long-lasting moods and motivations in men by formulating conceptions of a general order of existence and clothing these conceptions with such an aura of factuality that the moods and motivations seem uniquely realistic."[13] Moreover, Emile Durkheim observed that religion is inseparable from the church as an institution and thus "is eminently collective."[14] Marx certainly understood the power of religion in shaping society: "Religion is the general theory of this world, its encyclopedic compendium, its logic in popular form, its spiritual *point d'honneur*, its enthusiasm, its moral sanction, its solemn complement and its universal basis of consolation and justification … [It] is the sigh of the oppressed creature, the heart of a heartless world and the soul of soulless conditions."[15] Indeed, as illustrated in the Buddhist *ahimsa* or nonviolence doctrine, and echoed in the Christian beatitudes and many other religions, the protection of life is the bedrock of religious laws and practices. It is the sine qua non for joining safely the village of the ancestors, for gaining salvation, achieving *moksha*, attaining *nirvana*, or achieving Buddhahood.

Religion is pertinent for R2P as it enables people to assess human behavior and political regimes and to decide what kind of behavior is abhorrent and should not be tolerated. The relevance of religion for R2P is even clearer from the five fundamental dimensions present in various forms of religion captured by the five "Cs" theory: creator, creed, code of behavior, cult, and community structure or church. Every religion begins with a body of knowledge about the origin of the world, the meaning of life, and the afterlife. This theoretical dimension of religion provides knowledge and understanding that shapes human conduct. The conduct or practical dimension of religion is defined by rituals of worship and ethical rules. Finally religion has a collective dimension: believers live their faith as members of a community, and thus have the duty to treat one another as brothers and sisters, according to the will of God. This approach involves the injunction to protect life, not only in one's own family or country but also in the global village. The religious ethic clearly condemns mass atrocities, motivates people to fight passionately against oppression, violence, and various forms of social injustice, and demands peaceful coexistence among people.

What Jan Assmann said about the ancient African religion of the Nile Valley reflects one of the fundamental characteristics of religion in general.[16] Religion entails not only pleasing the gods (cult), but also administering justice. However, religious law is more than a mere set of legalistic rules. It entails love, compassion, harmony, order, and most importantly that fundamental social order known as "justice." Hence, the most important distinction that religion establishes is not the contrast with the secular, nor between the sacred and the profane, but rather between order and disorder. It stands for order as opposed to all forms of disorder, and violence is the epitome of disorder or chaos. The purpose of religion is to expel chaos or disorder, which has direct implications for the raison d'être of states and governments. The traditional notion of kings as "God's sons" meant that the creator had placed the ruler on earth not to pursue self-aggrandizement but rather to bring justice, truth, order, and love, and to expel injustice, lies, chaos, and violence. Such is the meaning of divine law in the Torah of Judaism, the Dharma of Buddhism or Hinduism, the Tao of Chinese religions, and the Maat of ancient Egypt. Religion teaches that rulers must obey the great king and owner of the universe and that those who condone or perpetrate mass atrocities are opposed to the will of God and thus forfeit their right and legitimacy to govern.[17]

Overview of religious and spiritual traditions in the global South

Although this study intends to emphasize the contribution of ancestral spiritualities from the global South, a genuine approach to R2P should not overlook the fact that Christianity and Islam are now part and parcel of the spiritual and cultural identity of millions of people in the South. Moreover, Christianity and Islam are growing at a rapid pace in the South while their power is also increasing, due in part to the spread of modernity and globalization. Indeed, one of the fundamental characteristics in Africa is the distinct mixture between ancestral spiritualities and the monotheistic religions brought by colonialism, notably Christianity and Islam. To some extent, Asia too shares with Africa the history of being colonized by powers from Europe and the Islamic world. Subsequently, although the large majority of the population is shaped by Buddhism, Confucianism, Hinduism, and substantial numbers follow Jainism, Sikhism, traditional folk religions, and a variety of other traditions, there has been for many centuries a powerful impact of Islam and nowadays an estimated 5 to 10 percent of the Asian population practice Christianity. Moreover, based on the sheer volume of the population, the People's Republic of China is the third largest Christian nation in the world and India ranks seventh. In Africa about 20 percent of the population is shaped by traditional or ancestral spirituality, whereas 40 percent practice Christianity and the other 40 percent belong to Islam. In Latin America the overwhelming Christian presence has produced a new spirituality heavily influenced by Native-American spirituality and the African traditional religions brought during the slave trade and present-day migrations. The followers of Santeria and other religions of African descent are estimated at almost 100 million in the Americas, most of them in Latin America, and between 500,000 and 5 million in the United States.[18]

While the West is considered Christian, in 2005 the list of the 10 largest Christian countries in the world was, in descending order, the United States, Brazil, China, Mexico, Russia, the Philippines, India, Germany, Nigeria, and the DRC. Projections for 2050 show the total absence of North America and Europe from this list, which will include four African countries (Nigeria, the DRC, Ethiopia, and Uganda), three Asian countries (China, India, and the Philippines), and two countries from Latin America (Brazil and Mexico). In 1900 Europe and North America accounted for 82 percent of all Christians. However, in 2005 they counted only for 39 percent, while 60 percent of all Christians were found in the global South.[19] In 1900 white people accounted for 81 percent of all Christians, but in 2000 they had dropped to 43 percent. Christianity is growing in the South while declining in Western countries. In the West, roughly 7,500 people stop being Christian every day, but in Africa roughly double that number become Christian. Kenya has the second largest Yearly Meeting of Quakers in the world, and more Anglicans attend Church in Uganda than in England.[20]

In 2007, of 2 billion Christians worldwide, almost 400 million were in Africa, some 325 million in Asia, and over 500 million in Latin America. Likewise, of 1.2 billion Muslims in the world, almost 900 million were in Asia and 350 million in Africa.[21] Thus, a substantial population in the South is guided in approaching R2P by the principles and worldviews of Christianity and Islam, but the impact of traditional religions has led to new interpretations as well as hybrid spiritualities. Since this study intends to focus on the uniqueness of the South, we shall limit ourselves to outlining a brief summary of the salient elements that Christianity and Islam bring to R2P.

Christianity and Islam share some characteristics as monotheistic religions. Their contribution to R2P stems from some of their fundamental principles. At the heart of monotheistic worldviews is the notion of revelation, which relativizes human institutions and the power of human rulers, for the world belongs to God who is the true king of humankind. Christianity and Islam stipulate that God created the universe and that all humanity constitutes one single family in which humans are their brothers' and sisters' keepers. In this context, R2P appears as a mandate of heaven, for it is sinful for an individual to not intervene to save lives, according to the teaching conveyed by the "good Samaritan" principle and the notion of "sin by omission." Among the most significant religious beliefs relevant to R2P, we find: a common origin and course of life; a common bond of humanity; human equality; the unity and interconnectedness of everything (what happens to one person affects everyone, and atrocities committed against some people diminish the humanity of all); the sacredness of life; the distinction between good and evil; the golden rule and other ethical stipulations to protect life; judgment and punishment of those who mistreat other human beings (karma, hell); true worship or genuine faith are not about rituals and sacrifices but rather loving and compassionate acts; and the soteriological criterium of entrance into the kingdom of heaven or paradise, which teaches that one's afterlife depends on the treatment of others in this world.

The Christian contribution to R2P can be found in the following specific beliefs and values: the creation story; the *imago dei* doctrine (human beings are created in God's image); *imitatio Christi* (the injunction to imitate and emulate the life of Christ: be perfect as your heavenly father); the prophetic tradition of social justice; the ten commandments; the golden rule; the virtues of peace and nonviolence in the sermon on the mount; and the ethical criteria for entering the kingdom of God, the last judgment. Together they establish the foundation of R2P.

For Christians God has supreme authority over the universe; therefore, the power of mortal kings and principles of sovereignty are not absolute. Although Christianity justified theocracy, it also articulated the vision of a paradigmatic Christian king who should govern with kindness according to the example of Jesus. Christianity has elaborated the *bellum justum*[22] doctrine as well as the regicide doctrine,[23] which call for liberation from oppression and evil rule. Most importantly, the Hebrew prophets and Jesus articulated the denunciation of oppressors and evil rulers. The famous Mosaic statement, "Pharaoh, let my people go," and the liberation narrative of the Book of Exodus continue to inspire a great many people around the globe in their struggle against oppression. This biblical prophetic voice found one of its most powerful expressions in Latin America in the contemporary Christian struggle against ubuesque dictators articulated by liberation theologians such as Gustavo Gutierrez, Jon Sobrino, Leonardo Boff, Ignacio Ellacuria, Juan Luis Segundo, Dom Elder Camara, Oscar Romero, Paulo Freire, and Jose Pallares Cardenas.[24] In the lexicon of liberation theologians, mass atrocities refer to the notion of "crucified people" and include notions such as colonization, conquest, impoverishment, marginalization, oppression, exploitation, domination, and *paupérisme anthropologique.* Here the Christian concept of sin is not viewed as a metaphysical construct or a purely private matter of heart; it is viewed in structures of sin, which include economic and political structures of domination, oppression, exploitation, marginalization, and extermination. The Bible is read as a tool of liberation of the "crucified people" who struggle for equality and dignity, for full humanity and full citizenship in their own land, for the liberation of peasants assassinated by paramilitary squads, and for the poor whose land is robbed by the powerful. From liberation theology we learn that mass atrocities can occur in a variety of ways, for there are indeed economic and political structures that condemn millions of people to desperation and sub-human existence, to a form of alienation and estrangement that kills the souls and the minds of people and drives them to despair.

Likewise Islam is replete with teachings that expressly prohibit mass atrocities and call for a model of society based on peace and universal solidarity. Islam offers a foundation for R2P in two ways. On the one hand, it teaches the vision of a God of compassion and mercy who rejects violence and evil. This God commands resistance to evil rulers, especially those who condone or are responsible for mass atrocities. Moreover, through the doctrine of *jihad,* Islam offers a vision of self-defense that commands resistance to evil doers and evil political regimes.

Like Christianity, Islam has a history of colonialism and violence, but also has a spirituality that calls for global solidarity and places peace at the very core of its faith and practices. Indeed, the very name "Islam" means peace. The Koran repeatedly asserts that God hates aggressors and maintains that the most important attributes of God are love and compassion.[25] Islamic theologian Al-Ghazali tells us in his elaborate "99 names of God" that Allah is essentially Al-Mumin and Al-Salam (the author and giver of peace), and Al-Rahman or Al-Rahim (the merciful one). He is also Al-Malik, the sovereign par excellence to whom all the universe belongs. As such, Allah is not merely the holy (Al-Quddus), just judge who abhors evil, he is also the protector of people against oppressors and evil spirits.

The Koran goes even further to link mass atrocities to the killing of a single human being: "Whoever kills a human being shall be regarded as having killed all humanity, and whoever saves a human life shall be regarded as having saved all humanity."[26] Even self-defense is put into question by the Koran, which calls for forgiveness in many texts and explicitly declares: "Even if you stretch out your hand against me to kill me, I shall not stretch out my hand to kill you. I fear Allah, the Lord of the World."[27] Conversion by force, moreover, is expressly rejected by the Koran; it clearly states: "Let there be no compulsion in religion."[28]

Although Islam shares with Christianity and Judaism some characteristics of monotheistic exclusivism, there is another trend that posits a religion of global solidarity. The Koranic creation story teaches the common origin of all humanity. This doctrine led to an affirmation of equality: "All people are equal, as equal as the teeth of a comb. There is no claim of merit of an Arab over a non-Arab, or of a white over a black person, or of a male over a female, only God-fearing people merit a preference with God."[29] Muslims see themselves as part of the same spiritual tradition of Judaism and Christianity, and some mystics extended such solidarity to all other religions and cultures. Rumi explicitly maintains that a genuine man of God is not limited to the boundaries of his religion, but rather a follower of God is beyond religion and infidelity. He even proclaimed: "I am neither Muslim nor Christian, Jew nor Zoroastrian."[30] Continuing this same spirit, Ibn Al-'Arabi insists magnificently that love beyond borders and global solidarity are the hallmarks of genuine spirituality: "My heart has opened unto every form … I practice the religion of Love; in whatsoever directions its caravans advance, the religion of Love shall be my religion and my faith."[31]

The common threads from the teachings from Christianity and Islam were integrated in the global South partly because people found in them the reflection of the same religious wisdom already taught by their ancestors. However, other religions contain supportive elements as well.

In Japan, Shintoism is based on the pursuit of *makoto no kokoro* or *magokoro* (true heart, pure heart, heart of truth, sincerity, uprightness). It is understood that evil hearts in rulers or people can generate social disequilibrium and even produce imbalance in nature. The goal of pure heart is to find balance and harmony between people, between the ruler and the people, and between humans and nature. Shinto precepts clearly condemn mass atrocities that introduce chaos in society. Hence, Shintoism also could be a potent ally in disseminating and strengthening the R2P norm.

In China, 500 years before the birth of Jesus, Mo-Tzu preached a message of universal love stating explicitly that "partiality should be replaced by universality."[32] Moreover, in Chinese religions we find the same quest for peace, harmony, and balance encapsulated by the yin-yang philosophy of Taoism and Confucianism. The Chinese vision of *tien* (heaven), *Tao* (the Way), *wen* (the art of peace), and *wu-wei* (the art of inactive action) all call for peace and harmony. With an elaborate system of moral virtues that praise the genuine human being as a person of *dao* or a *shun-tzu* (gentleman), whose heart is in harmony with "the way of Heaven," a virtuous ruler or citizen is essentially a person of peace who rejects mass atrocities as a betrayal of the will of Heaven.

Buddhism, Hinduism, and Jainism have traveled from India to the entire world via the doctrine of *ahimsa* or nonviolence, and the interconnectedness of all things in Brahman (the Divine), which rejects violence and mass atrocities as vices that bring about negative karma to those who commit them. Native-American religions and other shamanistic religions are also based on the fundamental pursuit of balance and harmony that radically reject violence and mass atrocities.[33] An in-depth examination of Africa permits us to illustrate the relevance of this general view of religions of the South.

African religions and R2P

Africa has experienced mass atrocities for centuries, stemming from the slave trade, colonialism, neocolonialism, apartheid, dictatorship, and international and domestic armed conflicts. At the same time Africa, the cradle of humankind, has played a crucial role in the historical development of world religion and world spirituality. Africa is thus the crucial Petri dish for R2P.

As the American scholar Robert Baum pointed out, "If archaeologists are correct in believing that the first human beings came from Africa, then it stands to reason that the first religions also originated there … It is possible that, as the earliest humans slowly migrated to other continents of the world, they carried with them religious ideas and practices that originated in Africa."[34] The continent is thus one of the fundamental sources of moral values that are relevant to R2P. By values we do not mean ethnic violence, female genital mutilation, polygamy, or vulgar claims of absolute power by African ubuesque kinglets. As Jacques Maquet and some other postcolonial scholars have acknowledged, African wisdom is not a myth or a construct. It is not merely a convenient expression by some desperate souls in need of romanticizing African tradition, but rather it is something that exists; it is "a collection of unique precepts that enable the people of traditional Africa to settle as harmoniously as possible the disputes that mar human relationships."[35] Indeed, as Roger Bastide and others have observed, there is in Africa "an entire civilization of spirituality" comparable to that of Africa's finest wood carvings or its bronzes of Benin.[36]

A careful exploration of African spiritualities reveals that, contrary to some entrenched scholarly mythologies, a great many values found in "monotheistic religions" are not antithetical to the spiritual and moral values of African ancestral traditions. In fact, if Africans have easily adopted Christianity and Islam despite the involvement of these religions in slave trade and colonialism, it is precisely because many recognized in the positive values of Christianity and Islam the echo of ancestral wisdom.

Unlike Christianity and Islam, African traditional religions have not been centralized. However, as one speaks only with limited accuracy of "the West" or "the Arab world" or even "Hinduism," there still are common features among African cultures and religious worldviews that can be captured meaningfully for purposes of this chapter and moving forward the articulation of the R2P norm. The most relevant similarities of African traditional religions can be found in their creation myths, in visions of the raison d'être of governments and political power, and in the history of resistance movements and rebellion against abusive or violent political regimes. Most importantly, it can be found in the African vision of moral values and in the *bumuntu*[37] concept which defines the criteria of genuine personhood in Africa. These spiritual values are explicitly articulated in proverbs, prayers, songs, and sapiential teaching and folktales.

At the core of African spirituality is the notion of Shakapanga, the supreme creator of all life. Because life comes from the creator through ancestors and parents, any form of violence that hinders humans from flourishing stands against the will of the ancestors and brings upon its perpetrators a divine curse. Moreover, because all human beings are *bantu ba Vidye Mukulu* (God's children), even kings are not allowed to abuse people. The common origin of humanity establishes the sacred principle of solidarity and hospitality and calls for the rejection of mass atrocities.

Universal brotherhood is enshrined in creation myths and is explicitly expressed in the traditional Meru prayer of Kenya, which goes as follows:

> Kirinyaga [God], owner of all things,
> I pray to Thee, give me what I need,
> because I am suffering, and also my children,
> and all the things that are in this country of mine.
> I beg Thee, the good one, for life,
> healthy people with no disease.
> May they bear healthy children.
> And also to women who suffer
> because they are barren, open the way
> by which they may see children.
> Give goats, cattle, food, honey,
> and also the trouble of the other lands
> that I do not know, remove.[38]

This universal prayer is a powerful manifestation of global consciousness and solidarity. By begging God to remove the trouble of other nations, even unknown ones, the Meru link explicitly love and compassion for one's family and nation to love for all other nations. The religious consciousness of the Meru is not an isolated exception but an expression of a dominant pattern of global solidarity that stands at the core of African spirituality. In fact, thousands of miles away there is a similar vision in West Africa. According to the Yoruba creation myth, God as father of the universe created black and white people, albinos and hunchbacks, the Yoruba people and other nations as well.[39] Consequently, the Yoruba regard everyone as kin, so much so that most prayers and invocations offered in Ile-Ife are deemed incomplete until prayers are offered for the people of the entire universe (*agbala aye gbogbo*).[40] Meru and Yoruba religiosity point to the centrality of solidarity as a distinctive mark of an authentic spirituality. This solidarity emerges from the principle of unity stemming from the idea of the common origin of humanity so well exemplified in various creation myths.

Unity, solidarity, and charity emerge as fundamental pillars of world spirituality that constitute the religious foundation of the responsibility to protect. These notions can be captured with four terms from African lexicon: *umoja* (unity), *ujamaa* (solidarity, family spirit), *bumuntu* (genuine humanity, authentic personhood), and *mucima muya* (pure or good heart). Elsewhere concepts such as *imago dei*, *shun-tzu*, *yin-yang*, "the man of Tao," *atman-Brahman*, or Buddha nature are used to express comparable notions of the divine origin and interconnectedness of all humans and determine the nature of moral values that govern human conduct and attitudes toward life.

Another way of grasping religious values relevant to R2P is to analyze the nature of human beings. The evolving norm fundamentally depends on our understanding of the nature of humanity and the nature of both the individual and society. The African conception of the nature of human beings can be gleaned from African proverbs, creation myths, taboos, moral precepts, marriage and family institutions, kingship, and many other customs and traditions. For Africans, as for other peoples in the global South, human beings have a divine origin. As an Akan proverb asserts, "All humans are children of God, no one is a child of the earth."[41] This divine origin has implications for the way each person ought to behave and the way a person should treat fellow human beings.

The concept *bumuntu* encapsulates the essence of humanness. The term stems from the lexicon of Bantu languages. A human being is referred to as a *muntu* in Kiluba language (with *bantu* as the plural). While it comes originally from the Kiluba language, it is widespread in regions that speak Bantu languages, from some areas of West to Southern Africa where *bumuntu* has different linguistic variants including the more familiar term *ubuntu*, popularized by Archbishop Desmond Tutu. The opposite of a genuine *muntu* is *kintu* (a thing), a term that is used to refer to a human being without moral content, a person who has lost his *bumuntu* through immoral conduct. As the Yoruba religious teaching has it:

> If you have children, money, house, clothes,
> all the good things of life, but you lack good character,
> they belong to someone else.
> Iwà, Iwà is what we are looking for …
> I do not have any wickedness
> Iwà lèsin, good character, is the essence of religion.[42]

Bumuntu is the African vision of a noble individual, a holy person, a saint, a *shun-tzu*, a follower of *dao*, an embodiment of Brahman—in short, a genuine human being. The *bumuntu* is characterized by nonviolence, self-respect, and respect for the life and dignity of other human beings. *Bumuntu* is the embodiment of all virtues, especially peace, hospitality, and solidarity. They are expected from family members, and a genuine *muntu* is expected to extend these virtues to the global village. The highest expression of *bumuntu* is found in the treatment of those who cannot be expected to reimburse a favor: strangers, children, and the most marginalized segments of society (especially the handicapped, the sick, the poor, and beggars). In other words, one is genuinely human only when one honors humanity everywhere. The Meru believe that a believer must pray not only for oneself but also for the welfare of humanity.[43] The Bulsa treat strangers, orphans, the disabled, beggars, and lepers with kindness because of their belief that their ancestors visit them in these forms.[44] The Fang people of Gabon believe that an ancestor passes by in the person of a stranger, and therefore a stranger should always be accorded kind and warm treatment.[45] As M.P. Moila pointed out, most African communities believe that unexpected guests are the embodiment of ancestors and are thus given the ancestors' food.[46] Such hospitality goes beyond simple courtesy. It is the manifestation of *bumuntu*, or the African understanding of "good character."

This concept occupies a central role in the African understanding of the art and path of becoming humane, as the Yoruba of Nigeria put it explicitly: "Good character, good existence, is the adornment of a human being." Such goodness of character is inconceivable without hospitality and respect for the stranger and people with disabilities. Thus, in the Congo a Luba proverb commands people to treat an alien guest with care and respect due to deities, for "your guest is your God." As for those with disabilities, another Luba proverb warns: "Do not laugh at a crippled person, God is still creating" (*Koseha lemene Vidye muntanda ukihanga*). Another Luba proverb recalls that the only true or worthwhile knowledge is to know how to live in harmony and loving relationship with our fellow human beings. In this African model of society, altruism and appreciation for the community are not viewed as antithetical to self-love, for as an Akan proverb from Ghana has it, "If you do not let your neighbor have nine, you will not have ten."[47] This vision of the humane mode of being is extended to political power, and thus a Luba proverb reminds the ruler who has a penchant for tyrannical behavior that "power is the people." Likewise in Southern Africa, the tyrant is reminded that "one is a King only as long as he is acknowledged as such by the people."[48]

It should be noted that Africans make a distinction between a real or authentic human being and an empty one who is regarded as a "non-human." From the west to the south of Africa, a widespread belief exists that people of bad character are not truly human. In Nigeria the Yoruba say: "He/she is not a person." In South Africa we find the same expression. The Baluba people of Central Africa say, "He is a dead body walking." From an African standpoint, a vicious dictator, for instance, is not merely regarded as a "bad ruler," but as non-human. The same is said about any person whose behavior is oppressive to others. According to the Luba, every human being swings on a pendulum between two categories, good and bad.

Moreover, a human being can lose his humanness and shift to the category of things or an animal state. This transformation depends on a person's thought patterns and behavior. A person of good thought, speech, and deeds is a genuine *muntu*, a person of *bumuntu*. The person of evil thought, speech, and deeds loses his humanity and becomes a thing, a *kintu*. In African society, the perfect person is someone with a good heart, who has learned the art of living and promoting the essential harmonies of life. Such a person must have acquired fundamental *bumuntu* virtues, and the whole traditional process of education in the African family and in school consists of inculcating these virtues. The most important are: respect for and protection of life, hospitality, solidarity, compassion, love, self-control, politeness, moderation, humility, friendship, goodness, and kindness. It is worth noting here that the ethical language of Kintu does not mean that people with bad behavior should be treated like animals. Quite the contrary, as an African proverb put it clearly, "if a child burns the house we do not throw him in the flames." The life of the immoral person is still sacred in virtue of its origin from the creator Shakapanga and the ancestors. As such, the "kintu-person" remains sacred and should be treated with the reverence of forgiveness. Traditional religion was keenly aware of the wisdom of "hating sin but not the sinner." This is why it praised the virtue of forgiveness. In fact, traditional society discouraged the development of the "prison industrial complex." Because of the belief in the interconnectedness of the circle of life, it was believed that a community was not whole as long as a member was exiled or excluded for bad behavior or crime. Therefore, rituals of purification or reparation were performed to reintegrate in the community the malevolent characters. The "muntu-kintu" dichotomy is therefore intended not in the ontological sense, but rather as a metaphor used to emphasize the necessity of high moral standards in the process of becoming humane.

The African vision of personhood has a specific understanding of the individual and collective dimension of personhood, which bears directly on R2P. This vision of personhood was well captured in the *fadenya-badenya* paradigm, to borrow the language of the Mande people of West Africa. Each person is made up of two forces, which explains the constant tension between individuality and respect for the community.[49] *Fadenya* or "father-childness" is the centrifugal force of individualism that paves the way to individual greatness. It orients people toward heroic actions and a defense of personal dignity and honor that stimulates resistance and rebellion against oppressive traditions, debilitating conventions, and the status quo. The search for personal fame, however, can easily lead to self-aggrandizing passions, selfish pursuit of self-interests, and anti-social behavior. Thus, *fadenya* is feared as a force of social disequilibrium, a force of envy, jealousy, abuse of power, competition, and self-promotion. The individual can find equilibrium only with the intervention of a counter-power, the centripetal force known as *badenya* or "mother-childness." This force pulls the child back home, to the mother's womb. It is a conservative force of submission to authority, stability, cooperation, and dependency on others. From *badenya* arises social solidarity, benevolence, altruism, and hospitality. *Fadenya* corresponds to the Promethean impulse as restless, heroic, rebellious, revolutionary, individualistic, and innovative, as well as eternally seeking freedom, autonomy, change, and novelty.[50] *Badenya* represents the Saturnian impulse as conservative, stabilizing, and controlling, as that which seeks to contain, sustain, order, and repress bad behavior.[51] *Fadenya* and *badenya* stand as two sides of the *bumuntu* within every *muntu*.

What the *fadenya-badenya* paradigm indicates is that a healthy mode of being requires a harmonious balance between individualism and altruism. *Fadenya* is a revolutionary power that stimulates rebellion against forces of oppression. It provides the spiritual drive to protest against dictators and to protect the life of others, to intervene when a child is being mistreated, or to intervene in distant lands to halt mass atrocities. At the same time, the *badenya* dimension of humanity curbs the drive to exploit others and to commit crimes. It provides a feeling of revulsion against mass atrocities.

Hence, both in the biblical passages and African proverbs, good moral behavior is not merely a requirement to go to heaven but also a means to enhance one's humanity. In this context, the responsibility to protect is not a matter of charity but a genuine path of self-empowerment, of becoming an authentic human being. By assuming the responsibility to protect, one reconciles with one's true nature, with one's authentic being. R2P has its foundation in the very nature of human beings, in their *fadenya-badenya* structure, in their divine origin, and moral imperative.

In 1978, in one of the first systematic elaborations of an African liberation theology, Monsignor Bakole wa Ilunga observed, "If our ancestors could return and see what is going on in our society, they would not believe they were in Africa, nor would they recognize their descendants." Why? Bakole explains, "We are far from being true

Africans … There is nothing authentic about the way in which the masses and the leaders of society, especially in the cities, are living today … That shows how far we have lost our grasp of deeper meaning and of the values that supported the life and ways of our real ancestors."[52] He concludes with an appeal to rediscover traditional values, most importantly the vision of power for the people (*bulohw i bantu*). The sum of these African values can be found in one overarching concept, *bumuntu*, produced by the wisdom of African traditional religions. Bakole's perspective reflects the vision found elsewhere in the global South. Notwithstanding the erosion of values with modernity and postcolonial struggles for power, the global South brings a unique spiritual experience and an alternative religious vision that need to be taken into account in the further development of the responsibility to protect norm.

Specific religious concepts with relevance for R2P

In his public addresses and autobiography, Gandhi was firm in his conviction that religion was not separate from politics.[53] Rather a religious life, according to Gandhi, necessitated being involved in political activities, given the indivisibility of human existence and endeavor. Religion serves as a moral foundation for human activities and gives meaning to life.[54] It thus has very direct significance for R2P's normative development as well as its implementation.

The fundamental religious values common to both monotheistic and traditional religions—including love, compassion, forgiveness, the notion of creation and a common origin of humanity, the unity and equality of human beings, solidarity, hospitality to foreigners, the prohibition of killing, lying, or stealing, and the responsibility to care for one another—are relevant to the responsibility to protect. They carry religious injunctions to not harm and to protect both neighbors and distant strangers. Here the four most essential tenets are examined because they have the most direct pertinence for the implementation of the R2P norm: the golden rule, sovereignty, nonviolence, and just war doctrine. A final section illustrates cases in African history for which these principles were put into practice, and particularly where religious justification or divine intervention was sought to oppose or overthrow tyrants and protect the oppressed.

The golden rule

The core of a global religious ethic can be found in the universality of the golden rule.[55] Writing on Christian morality, the liberation theologian

Leonardo Boff pointed out that Christ did not come to bring a new morality; he rather brought to light what people knew or ought to have known, but because of their alienation were unable to see, comprehend, and formulate.[56] Far earlier, of course, Saint Augustine promoted the ideology of one true religion (*De Vera Religione*), but acknowledged the universality of morality. In *Retractationum* he made the oft-cited statement: "The substance of that which today is called Christianity was already known to ancient peoples, nor was it absent from the beginnings of the human race to the time when Christ came in the flesh. Since that time, the true religion that already existed began to call itself the Christian religion."[57] Jesus summarized his moral teaching in the golden rule recorded by Luke and Matthew in the New Testament. In the former we read: "Do for others just what you want them to do for you."[58] In Matthew the golden rule is not only stated but also said to be the essence of religion itself: "Do for others what you want them to do for you: this is the meaning of the Law of Moses and of the teaching of the prophets."[59] In this text Jesus teaches his contribution to Mosaic law, but the passage nonetheless was very well known in the Hebrew Bible and was well established in Jewish tradition.

The Torah teaches in Leviticus (written around fifth century BCE) that "[y]ou shall love your neighbor as yourself,"[60] and states in the book of Tobit (written around 200 BCE) that "[n]ever do to anyone else anything that you would not want someone to do to you."[61] Outside the written Torah, Rabbi Hillel—the major founder of Rabbinic Judaism, who lived about a generation before Jesus and was the teacher of Saint Paul—saw the golden rule as the summary of religion much like the Yoruba and the prophet Muhammad. At the time of King Herod, a "pagan" said to Rabbi Hillel: "I will accept Judaism on condition you tell me all the law while I am standing on one foot." Hillel answered: "Do not do unto others whatsoever you do not wish them to do unto you. The law consists in this. All the rest is commentary. Go and learn!"[62]

This Judeo-Christian wisdom is found in numerous other ethical traditions. In Africa, there is a clear common ground between traditional wisdom and biblical wisdom. The Baluba, for example, summarized the golden rule in the single concept of *bumuntu*, discussed earlier. This is made explicit in the proverb, *Bwino bonso ke bwino, bwino I kwikala biya ne Bantu* (the only true knowledge is to live in harmony with our fellow human beings). Likewise, a Yoruba proverb teaches the golden rule metaphorically, stating that "one going to take a pointed stick to pinch a baby bird should first try it on himself to feel how it hurts."[63] This is rendered in another expression, *iwa lesin* (good character is the essence of religion), which evaluates good character according to the way a person behaves toward his fellow human beings.

This Yoruba expression beautifully echoes the prophet Muhammad, who maintained that the golden rule was "the noblest religion." This is expressed in two ways in the Hadith: "Noblest Religion is this—that you should like for others what you like for yourself; and what you feel painful for yourself, hold that as painful for all others too"; "[n]o man is a true believer unless he desires for his brother that which he desires for himself."[64]

In China, well before Jesus' birth,[65] a disciple asked Confucius (551–470 BCE) if a norm existed that could be followed throughout life. He replied: "Love of the neighbor. Whatever you do not desire for yourself, do not do unto others."[66] In another version Confucius stated: "What I do not wish others to do to me, that also I wish not to do to them."[67]

During the sixth century BCE in India, Siddhartha Gautama Buddha taught: "Comparing oneself to others in such terms as 'Just as I am so are they, just as they are so am I,' he should neither kill nor cause others to kill."[68] In another version he declared: "Here am I fond of my life, not wanting to die, fond of pleasure and averse from pain. Suppose someone should rob me of my life ... If I in turn should rob of his life one fond of his life ... how could I inflict that upon another?"[69]

This Buddhist teaching itself stood in the line of a more ancient Hindu wisdom, which was well expressed in the national epic poem, the Mahabharata (dating between 400 BCE and 400 CE): "Learn the highest point of the law and when you have learnt it, think on it: Whatsoever you hate, do not do unto others." Like Hillel, Jesus, the prophet Muhammad, and the Yoruba sages, Hindus also have maintained that the whole Dharma or even the whole religion of Hinduism consists in the golden rule: "Vyasa says: Do not to others what you do not wish done to yourself; and wish for others too what you desire and long for yourself—this is the whole of Dharma; heed it well."[70]

This golden rule powerfully echoes across all major religious and ancient spiritual traditions. It forms the first pillar of the normative foundation for R2P.

Sovereignty

The norm of R2P, and especially the component of outside military intervention to halt mass atrocities, is hampered by the doctrine of state sovereignty. However, from a religious standpoint, states are a human invention, and God remains the real sovereign above all earthly rulers. Although traditional societies have known kingdoms and empires, creation myths generally talk of a universal creator and view human beings as belonging to God rather than to mortal and thus transient rulers. By claiming an authority above human rulers, religions establish a fundamental critique of political regimes that diminishes any claim to absolute and unaccountable power by any human ruler. Moreover, because God is the creator of the universe, borders are irrelevant; for a believer, the community of brothers and sisters requires no visas or passports. Far from standing in the way of intervention to protect people from mass atrocities, religions would *ipso facto* justify as a categorical imperative the right of intervention to come to the rescue of strangers.

Furthermore, religions are at pains to outline the duties of the sovereign, to define clear limits to sovereign authority, and to exhort the correction or removal of tyrannical sovereigns. Three factors are of great pertinence to the current conception of sovereignty and the erroneous belief in its inviolability.

First, religions have developed a doctrine of sage king. Plato's ideals of a good ruler—embodied in the philosopher king of his utopian city-state Kallipolis in *The Republic*—and revealed in the Christian king who imitates the example of Jesus, were preceded by similar aspirations and inspirations in the global South. It is found clearly in the Chinese *tien ming* (mandate of heaven) as well as in Buddhism with the example of King Ashoka's enlightened rule and the "ten duties of the king" known in Pali as "*dasa-raja-dhamma*": the king must be of high moral character (*sila*), nonviolent (*avihimsa*), gentle and kind (*maddava*), patient and tolerant (*khanti*), free from hatred or enmity (*akkodha*), generous (*dana*), honest (*ajjava*), willing to sacrifice everything for the good of the people (*pariccaga*), austere (*tapa*), and not opposed to the people's will (*avirodha*).[71]

The notion of divine kingship was essentially a call to the king to be pure like God and act accordingly. Many religious traditions have articulated a countervailing power to tyranny and explicitly reject violence and mass atrocities as repellent to the gods. Second, religions have delimited sovereignty. Although many despots have cited divine powers to justify abhorrent behavior, the notion that the power of the king comes from God simply cannot be interpreted as a justification of tyranny. Writing on an African kingdom that he visited in about 925 CE, Abu al-Hasan al-Masudi observed: "The Zanj people considered their ruler as a king of kings and gave him the title Waqlimi which means supreme Lord. But they could not tolerate any violation of their rights … Once he becomes tyrannical and departs from the rules of justice, they cause him to die and exclude his posterity from succession to the throne."[72] This widespread African attitude toward bad rulers was recognized even by Hegel. Despite his Eurocentric disdain for all things African, he observed, "Africans remove bad rulers from power."[73]

Third, the history of humankind is replete with resistance movements that found in religion an inspiration for rebellion against evil regimes. The Hebrew Bible offers countless examples of prophets challenging kings and denouncing their evil rule. Most importantly, the narrative of the Hebrew liberated from Egypt has become a potent source of inspiration for other liberation theologies. In the global South, people have found in their faith the power to resist home-grown tyrants and centuries of foreign colonial domination.

Nonviolence

In world history two important traditions have well defined the response provided by religions to the problems of aggression, war, violence, mass atrocities, and foreign invasion: nonviolence and the just war doctrine. The responsibility to protect human beings from mass atrocities finds additional moorings in the strict prohibition of murder.

"Thou shall not kill!" is a universal religious law found not only in the Judeo-Christian Decalogue, but also in Hinduism, Buddhism, and many other religions. This injunction rejects mass atrocities and other forms of political violence as evil. The tradition of nonviolence is well exemplified in Gandhi's response to the British Empire and in the response of Jesus to the Roman Empire. Gandhi waged a vigorous nonviolent campaign that led to the collapse of British colonialism in India, after having begun a similar struggle in racist South Africa. Jesus's nonviolence is well articulated in the Gospel of Matthew: "You have heard that it was said, 'An eye for an eye and a tooth for a tooth.' But I say to you, do not resist an evildoer. But if anyone strikes you on the right cheek, turn the other also."[74]

If Gandhi and Jesus did not create an army of rebels against empires, they did not condone brutality. In fact, they vigorously preached against injustice. In the second half of the twentieth century, the tradition of Jesus and Gandhi was followed in South Africa by Desmond Tutu and others in their struggle against apartheid. Of course, there was also the massive civil rights movement led in the United States by Martin Luther King, Jr., who was inspired by Jesus and Gandhi.

Just war doctrine

Nonviolence is not the only path offered by religion to mass atrocities. Often when principled nonviolent opposition to tyranny was ignored or violently suppressed, just war theory provided the religious rationale for the adoption of violent means to achieve liberation from oppression. While religions prohibit killing, we also find in many religious teachings the notion of a "just war" that compels people to rebel against violent and oppressive regimes and, under some circumstances, to go to war for self-defense.

The long-standing and best known just war tradition comes largely from Saint Ambrose, Saint Augustine, and Saint Thomas Aquinas. The Christian view of just war finds its foundation in sacred scriptures and its clearest expression in Augustine's writings where war itself is presented as an expression of Christian love in so far as it is waged with the intention of securing peace, punishing evil-doers, or uplifting the good.[75] Various Christian leaders and thinkers found in Paul's letter to Romans and in some mysterious statements of Jesus himself one of the most explicit biblical foundations of just war theology.[76] Indeed, the criteria originally spelled out by the International Commission on Intervention and State Sovereignty (ICISS) and later approved by the September 2005 World Summit contain virtually all the elements of Christian just war doctrine: just cause, proportionality, likelihood of success, and right authority.

Theologians also developed the regicide theory. In Islam, Muhammad made a distinction between greater *jihad* (struggle against oneself in order to achieve holiness) and lesser *jihad* (a self-defense war). This notion of just or holy war applies also to the protection of the weak, which was relevant for R2P as President Barack Obama emphasized in his Nobel lecture in December 2009.[77]

War can be waged on humanitarian grounds and its legitimacy is rooted in the sacred scriptures or sacred oral tradition of many religions. Although well articulated in Christianity and Islam, the theology of just or holy war is also found in other religious traditions as well, exemplified by the history of resistance movements against tyranny, the slave trade, colonialism, imperialism, and postcolonial dictatorships. It was manifest also in the historical instances in Africa.

African illustrations

Historical instances of religiously motivated—what we could call "R2P-like" interventions—in Africa are numerous.[78] Over the last five centuries religion has often served as a powerful countervailing power to tyrannical regimes. Africans turned to traditional religions[79] and to Christianity to find inspiration in their struggle against local dictators and foreign colonists. Traditional religion, Africanized Christianity, and Africanized Islam spearheaded the "art of resistance" against both the slave trade and colonial oppression. Various prophets and prophetesses preached a kind of "social gospel" or "liberation theology."

At the outset of the eighteenth century in the Kongo Kingdom, a young prophetess, Kimpa Vita (1684–1706), who was also known as Dona Beatrice or Jeanne d'Arc du Congo, fomented a rebellion against Portuguese slave traders.[80] Later, in 1921, another prophet, Simon Kimbangu (1887–1951), waged a revolt against Belgian colonialism and against the particularly alienating version of Christianity brought to Central Africa by European missionaries.[81] During the colonial era, traditional religions and their priests and diviners played a crucial role in formulating a liberation theology that provided moral legitimacy to resistance and even outright wars of liberation.

The role of African traditional religions in liberation theology was twofold. First, religion established the principle of just cause, thus providing legitimacy and a powerful motivation for struggle against oppression. Second, the principles of divine intervention and ancestor assistance played a role during wars of liberation. In many cases, religious rituals of "blessed water" were performed to invite the spirits and the ancestors to bestow strength, invulnerability, and even invisibility upon the warriors on the battlefield.

The Maji Maji uprising—the most serious challenge to colonial British rule in East Africa—drew on African traditional religion and the power of its "magic." In their colony of Tanganyika, the Germans faced the powerful prophet Kinjikitile Ngwale who relied on traditional religious worldviews when he preached that the war of liberation was ordained by God and that the ancestors would return to life to assist the African people. God and the ancestors, he added, wanted the unity and freedom of all African peoples and desired that they fight their German oppressors. Kinjikitile himself was captured and hanged by the Germans. Undeterred, his brother picked up his mantle, assumed the title of *nyamguni*, one of the three divinities in the region, and continued to administer *maji*, a religiously blessed water aimed at rendering the warrior invulnerable.[82]

Given the tendency, particularly prevalent in monotheistic religions, to relegate women to a subordinate role, the preeminent role of women leaders and prophetesses in resisting tyranny and protecting the weak in African history deserves mention. Women's role in African traditional religions brought them to the forefront in resistance movements. In the Zambezi Valley, for example, Shona mediums instigated the famous rebellions of 1897, 1901, and 1904. Along with Kimpa Vita, in the Congo there is the notorious case of Mwanana-Mukaya, the warrior princess in the Luba empire who opposed Belgian colonial rule for many years. In 1916 Maria Nkoie instigated the Ikaya rebellion, which lasted for five years. Many other women have played a crucial role in the struggle for freedom from slavery and from colonialism.[83]

Almost all wars waged by Africans against Western conquest were backed by religious beliefs in justice and just cause.[84] Enslaved Africans crossed the Atlantic carrying with them a liberation theology that would have repercussions in the Haitian revolution (1891–1903) and various slave rebellions in the United States and Latin America.[85] The spirit of traditional religions continued to have an important impact even after various charismatic figures converted to Christianity. For example, Simon Kimbangu and Kimpa Vita challenged not only colonial governments but also Western Christianity, which gave moral and spiritual legitimacy to foreign tyranny.

In the postcolonial era, African churches often have served as a fundamental countervailing power to entrenched dictators. A phenomenon known as the *conférence nationale souveraine*[86] emerged in the 1990s that gave political power to some bishops to lead parliaments and facilitate the transition from dictatorship to democracy. The violent repression of Christian nonviolent marches in the DRC led to the creation of what people refer to as *martyrs de la démocratie.* Meanwhile, bishops and theologians published numerous pastoral documents denouncing human rights violations and calling for democracy. Among the most influential was the 1990 "Memorandum des Evêques du Zaïre au Chef de l'Etat," and various documents issued between 1975 and 1993 that denounced the tyrannical tendencies of the president, the terror of the military and police forces, and the economic exploitation of the people.[87]

In brief, traditional religions generated a particular brand of liberation theology that was based on four basic principles. First, African political theology is built on the notion that life is the central gift from ancestors and the creator. In virtue of its transcendent origin, life is regarded as sacred and people's attitude toward life is the fundamental ethical criterion for distinguishing virtues from vices, good rulers from bad ones, liberation from oppression. Second, the raison d'être of government is to ensure welfare by protecting life and providing people with adequate means of existence. Third, as the representation of divinity on earth, civil authority is not absolute, for God remains the ultimate authority and judge of government actions. Fourth, a ruler is accepted as ruler only in so far as he conforms to the will of the ancestors and the creator.

The ancestors who established civil authority for the good of society and for the transmission of life and beneficence of divinity to the people are the ultimate overseers. When a civil authority ceases to be a transmitter of the graces and benefits of divinity, it forfeits its validity. To paraphrase paragraphs 138–9 of the *World Summit Outcome*, sovereignty is suspended when a state is unwilling or unable to protect its own people, or worse is the perpetrator of abuses. According to African traditional religion, such a forfeiture of validity by the king means an extrication of the people from his authority and rule. If such an illegitimate government refuses to resign, then it becomes the "abomination of desolation" standing in the ancestral shrine, a hindrance to people's access to divinity. The ruler must then be impeached or face capital punishment.

Conclusion: where do we go from here?

The notion of discussing the contribution of religion to R2P is a departure—certainly for social scientists and international lawyers—and this chapter has taken small strides toward uncovering rich materials embedded in the world's modern and ancient religions. They provide a possible foundation for building a global consensus around both the norm and its implementation. The choice can be formulated *mutatis mutandis* in Shakespearian terms: "R2P or not to be," or perhaps better "solidarity or chaos." Given the interconnectedness of the contemporary globalizing world, many communities are unable to fight successfully against powerful and often violent forces that draw support from local as well as external actors. Global solidarity is often necessary to combat mass atrocities.

From a religious standpoint, R2P reflects the fundamental spiritual values of universal solidarity, love, and compassion that are widespread in ancient African and other indigenous spiritual traditions as well as in monotheistic religions. While public international law provides an underpinning for concrete actions needed for the protection of life, religions provide that *firma mentis*, the mindset or habit of the mind that gives humanity the conviction of doing the right thing. While politics provides a framework for action, religions provide "inner laws" or moral compasses that govern hearts and minds and deal with the very roots out of which actions emerge. Despite its pitfalls, religion remains essential to the health of human societies; the comprehensive and more harmonious development of the R2P norm cannot overlook the contribution of religion and spirituality.

Religion is not merely the worship of God or a way of praying, it is also a way of minding the world, a way of thinking, seeing, and understanding humanity, and indeed a way of taking position vis-à-vis governments and political regimes. Religion is eminently political! It enables people to understand the world as a meaningful cosmos and provides a meaningful answer to the question, "Why and how should humans assume the responsibility to protect?" In so doing, religion addresses the fundamental political question of law and order, and the question of whether one should obey or disobey unjust laws and evil political regimes.

Religion, as this chapter has argued, contributes to R2P in three fundamental ways: by providing a critique of oppressive regimes and rendering them illegitimate by virtue of their violation of divine laws that command the respect and protection of life; by calling upon conscience to resist evil; and by providing legitimacy to rebellion against regimes that perpetrate mass atrocities. As Gandhi has shown in "The Duty of Disloyalty," a tyrannical state is one in which "sedition itself becomes a religion."[88] For many religions, loyalty to a corrupt and violent state is a sin, while disloyalty in this case is celebrated as a virtue. However, for religion to be not a farce but a force of genuine liberation from atrocities, it has to be itself liberated from distortions and the folly of harmful dogmas. How should religion, with its complexity and paradoxes, be reinterpreted as an ally rather than an obstacle to R2P? Three recommendations contain answers to that question and correspond to the three stages of R2P originally identified by ICISS, namely prevention before mass atrocities; active protection during the perpetration of atrocities; and post-conflict peace building.

This chapter discussed at length the golden rule as the abiding and ubiquitous principle that is the bedrock of all ancient and modern religions, a necessary foundation for human society and hence for the responsibility to protect. In our modern nation-states, politics is often shaped by tacit Machiavellianism, the free market ideology of competition, self-interest and ill-defined individual freedom, and by the doctrine of "national interest," and "national security," which, in some cases, foment insecurities for other nations, while protecting within a nation the interests and security of a dominant minority class against the welfare of the majority of the citizens. The "self-interest" worldview can easily foster selfishness and greed and lead to the "survival of the fittest" mentality, which is the breeding-ground of mass atrocities. The "self-interest" model should be replaced by the ethic of solidarity and universal brotherhood (*ujamaa*), grounded in the vision that we are all interdependent. One of the strongest recommendations from this comparative study of religion is the necessity of establishing the golden rule as a sine qua non of international relations and, more specifically, as the basis for the first pillar of R2P, namely the responsibility to prevent mass atrocities. Some differences among religions are irreconcilable, especially on doctrine, but there is no dispute about the real bottom line: our common humanity and the teaching of love and compassion.

Despite the discussion of the ways in which religions can bolster the R2P norm and its application, we know all too well how often and easily religious sentiments can be manipulated to exhort and justify mass violence. During the protection stage—or the international responsibility to react in the eye of an atrocity storm—the key recommendation is to balance faith with reason.

Despite dogmatic claims to the contrary, all religions are to some degree "man-made." Sacred texts offer us the word of God through the fallible words of human authors. As such, religions bear the limitations of the human imagination. No religion and no religious law can be taken for granted. History offers abundant evidence of the danger of theocracy, fundamentalism, and scriptural literalism. In Africa religious taboos, female circumcision, and witchcraft accusations illustrate well the need for critical thinking to save humanity from problematic manifestations of religious beliefs. In the Hindu tradition, the notions of karma, *sati* (the burning of widows), and the caste system have led to practices that harm individuals and societies. In Christianity the crusades, Inquisition, witch-burning, and various forms of outright religious persecution have shown the most problematic aspects of *extra ecclesiam nulla salus* (outside the church there is no salvation) ideology.

Religions themselves call for discernment and critical thinking. For example, Jesus and Buddha were harsh critics of received wisdom who challenged pseudo-religiosity and obsolete religious laws, hypocritical devotions, and tyrannical religious leaders.[89] They provided alternative visions and new modes of being religious that are relevant for R2P. Most importantly, all religions are susceptible to corruption, and this is why their history is constantly punctuated by reform movements. Religion needs to be rescued from the merchants of death, and to be purified of unholy superstitions, delusion, hysteria, obscene patriotism, nationalism, imperialism, sexism, racism, tribalism, self-worship, hypocrisy, partiality, and the drive to exploit people economically and politically in the name of God. Consequently, faith always should be tempered with reason, commonsense, discernment, and critical thinking, most especially in times of social crisis or war when it is easy to confuse "the voice of God" with one's anxiety and self-interests. Only then can it be useful for the international responsibility to react and halt mass atrocities.

For post-conflict peace building, the key recommendation is to make greater use of interreligious dialogue to cement peace and heal the wounds of violence.[90] Interreligious dialogue is an essential ingredient for strengthening the R2P norm, and fostering the global agreement that mass atrocities are not only conscience-shocking but also evil and unacceptable anywhere on the planet. In addition to the mobilization of political will, religious outrage could be an important contributing factor if "never again" is to be more than a slogan. Dialogue among religions is indispensable in order to identify an ethical common ground that enables agreement on how and when to operationalize R2P across different cultures and countries. Moreover, interreligious dialogue can help prevent and reduce religiously motivated violence. Here African and Asian religious traditions provide their greatest contribution to R2P because of their long tradition of religious tolerance and their fundamental vision that God and truth can be found in various religions, and that all humans are God's "chosen people." Given the particular social situation of many countries of the global South, where religion permeates all aspects of social life, the majority of the people still live in villages, and newly created modern nations are still fragile, interreligious dialogue should include intercultural dialogue and most importantly interethnic dialogue. Since independence, most conflicts in Africa over government representation and access to national wealth have had ethnic overtones. In the DRC, for instance, such dialogue is being attempted with government structures known as "Le dialogue inter-Congolais" and "La conférence nationale souveraine," which include the participation of religious leaders.

This chapter is a prelude for such a dialogue. It begins to uncover and expose the extensive diversity, wealth, and yet common ground in the values that underpin both ancient and modern religions. Through interreligious dialogue it should become clear that a global ethic is not the precinct of any religion but emanates, with distinctly different echoes and emphases, from all spiritual traditions. The myriad hues of the proverbs of African spiritualities, the parables of Christ, and the Hadiths of Islam, all have resonance for the ethics and practices that must underpin R2P.

The emerging norm of R2P can draw strength from the history of human rights, which faced opposition from religions before being accepted and championed by them. Pope Pius VI regarded the 1789 French Declaration of the Rights of Man and Citizens as madness, and he condemned it in 1791, and several popes following him were equally inimical to human rights until the twentieth century.[91] This opposition found its best expression in the Vatican's "anti-Modernism" documents. After centuries of opposition, the Christian church embraced human rights as reflecting the will of God. The theologian Walter Kasper summarized the paradigm shift since that time: "Today more than ever, indeed, the bearing witness to the Gospel in a credible way is only possible by commitment to the rights of man."[92] This view was predicated upon a fundamental belief so well summarized by Saint Irenaeus, that the "glory of God is the human being fully alive!" (*Gloria dei vivens homo*).[93] In 1994, during the first African Synod of Catholic Bishops held in Rome, those present explicitly pointed out that human rights are an integral part of the mission to proclaim the Gospel of Jesus in Africa. Cardinal Bernard Yago, archbishop of Abidjan, stated: "The promotion of people, their integral blossoming, the respect for their dignity and rights, and the establishment of justice and peace are basic parts of evangelization. They are the signs by which we may recognize that the kingdom of God has arrived."[94]

In Islam, extremism and intolerance found a powerful counterpower in the theology of Ibn Al-'Arabi (1165–1240), who proclaimed a vision of religion that is certainly echoed by Hinduism, African religions, and many other traditions:

> My heart has opened unto every form.
> It is the pasture for gazelles,
> a cloister for Christian monks,
> a temple for idols,
> the Ka'ba of the pilgrim,
> the tablets of the Torah and the book of the Koran.
> I practice the religion of Love;
> in whatsoever directions its caravans advance,
> the religion of Love shall be my religion and my faith.[95]

More than 1,000 years earlier, an African playwright, Terence, captured in a secular language the same spirit of "global solidarity" when he popularized in the Roman Empire the expression, *Homo sum, humani nihil a me alienum puto* (I am a man and nothing human is alien to me). This feeling of oneness with the entire human race commands the responsibility to protect all life. In African traditional religions, life (*bumi*) is the sine qua non of genuine spirituality. Evil is what destroys life, and good is what enhances human empowerment. True knowledge and true spirituality is to know how to live in harmony with our fellow human beings. Or in the eloquent wisdom of Yoruba religion, *iwa lesin* (good character is the essence of religion). The fundamental virtue of good character is respect for all life. In this, Africa joins the wisdom of other religious traditions of the global South, as well as that of the dominant spiritualities of Christianity, Islam, and Buddhism.

By promoting the responsibility to protect, religions can reconcile with their authentic nature. They can thereby become a potent and natural ally of like-minded governments as well as intergovernmental and nongovernmental organizations in ongoing efforts to protect humanity from the scourge of mass atrocities.

Notes

1 Among texts that sanction, or seem to sanction violence in the Bible, we find among others: Numbers (chapters 13 to 15, and chapter 33); Deuteronomy (chapters 6, 7, 8, 13, 17, 26, 32, 33); Genesis (chapters 11 and 12); Exodus (chapters 7 to 15, 20 to 23, and 31 to 34); Leviticus (chapters 12 to 15, 19, 20, and 25); 1 Samuel (chapters 14 and 15); 2 Samuel (chapter 22); Judges (chapters 5, 7, and 11); the entire book of Joshua; Isaiah 60: 11–12; and Psalms 109, 135, 136, and 139. Notorious cases in the New Testament are found in Romans 13: 1–7; Acts 5: 1–11; Matthew 10: 11–15; Titus 3: 1–3; 1 Timothy 2: 1–6; and 1 Peter 2: 13–20. To these texts could be added the plight of slaves in Ephesians 6: 5–8; Colossians 3: 22–25; 1 Timothy 6: 1–6; Titus 2: 9–10; Leviticus 25: 39–46; and those problematic texts on women found in Leviticus 12: 1–8 and 15: 19–31; 1 Corinthians 11: 1–16; 1 Timothy 2: 1–14; and Ephesians 5: 22–33. All biblical references in this chapter are drawn from Michael D. Coogan, ed., *The New Oxford Annotated Bible: New Revised Standard Version with the Apocryphal/Deuterocanonical Books* (Oxford: Oxford University Press, 2007). In the Koran, surah 8 and surah 9, among many others, have explicit violent statements about the "infidels," and the Dharma of Hinduism, and even Buddhism, have their own share of "sacred violence."

2 See for example, Mary Farrell Bednarowski, ed., *Twentieth-Century Global Christianity*, vol. 7 (Minneapolis, Minn.: Fortress Press, 2008), 32–33; and Philip Jenkins, *The Next Christendom: The Coming of Global Christianity* (New York: Oxford University Press, 2007), 193.

3 Graham Harvey, ed. *Indigenous Religions: A Companion* (London: Cassell, 2000), 4.

4 Emile Durkheim, *The Elementary Forms of the Religious Life* (Glencoe, Ill.: The Free Press, 1961), 48.

5 John S. Mbit, *African Religions and Philosophy*, 2nd edn. (London: Heinemann, 1989), 270.

6 Although we do not yet have a systematic reflection on R2P, African philosophers and theologians have articulated, in thousands of publications, a profound critique of dictatorship, tribalism, as well as colonialism and neocolonialism. This literature is useful for understanding African support for R2P. See for instance, Kaumba Lufunda, "Guerre et Paix au Coeur de l'Afrique," in *Philosophie et Politique en Afrique: Journées Philosophiques Canisius* (Kinshasa: Editions Loyola, 1997); and Metena M'nteba, "Démocratie et Participation en Afrique Noire," in *Philosophie et Politique en Afrique: Journées Philosophiques Canisius* (Kinshasa: Editions Loyola, 1997).

7 For an elaborate articulation of this Gandhian view, see Raghavan Iyer, *The Moral and Political Thought of Mahatma Gandhi* (London: Concord Grove Press, 1983), 41.

8 Iyer, *The Moral and Political Thought of Mahatma Gandhi*, 41.
9 See Thomas Luckmann, *The Invisible Religion: The Problem of Religion in Modern Society* (New York: MacMillan, 1967).
10 For a sophisticated history of the term religion, see Wilfred Cantwell Smith, *The Meaning and End of Religion* (Minneapolis, Minn.: Fortress Press, 1991).
11 Leonard Swidler and Paul Mojzes, *The Study of Religion in an Age of Global Dialogue* (Philadelphia: Temple University Press, 2000), 7.
12 Max Weber, *Economy and Society*, ed. Guenther Roth and Claus Wittich (Berkeley: University of California Press, 1978), 499.
13 Clifford Geertz, *The Interpretation of Cultures* (New York: Basic Books, 1973), 90.
14 Durkheim, *The Elementary Forms*, 62.
15 See Karl Marx, *A Contribution to the Critique of Hegel's "Philosophy of Right,"* ed. Joseph O'Malley (Cambridge: Cambridge University Press, 1970).
16 Jan Assmann, *Religion and Cultural Memory* (Stanford, Calif.: Stanford University Press, 2006), 33–34. For further development of this topic see Assmann, *Ma'at: Gerechtigkeit und Unsterblichkeit im Alten Ägypten* (Munich: C.H. Beck, 2001).
17 Among recent publications that address the theme of liberation from oppression in world religions, the following expounds insights that are relevant to R2P: Miguel A. De La Torre, ed., *The Hope of Liberation in World Religions* (Waco, TX: Baylor University Press, 2008). Written with the contribution of a great number of scholars from the global South, this book examines the teaching of African traditional religions, Native-American religions, Korean folk religions, Orisha religious traditions in the Americas, Daoism, Confucianism, Buddhism, Hinduism, as well as Protestantism, Catholicism, Judaism, and Islam.
18 Miguel A. De La Torre, *Santeria: The Beliefs and Rituals of a Growing Religion in America* (Grand Rapids, MI: Wm. B. Eerdmans Publishing Co., 1995), xiv.
19 Mary Farrell Bednarowski, ed., *Twentieth-Century Global Christianity*, vol. 7 (Minneapolis, Minn.: Fortress Press, 2008), 32–33.
20 Elizabeth Isichei, *A History of Christianity in Africa: From Antiquity to the Present* (Grand Rapids, MI: Wm. B. Eerdmans Publishing Co., 1995).
21 Warren Matthews, *World Religions*, 5th edn. (Belmont, Calif.: Thomson and Wadsworth, 2007), 275 and 321.
22 Just war doctrine (*bellum iustum*) with its components (*ius ad bellum* and *ius in bello*) was formulated by three of the most illustrious doctors of the Church: Saint Ambrose of Milan (340–97), Saint Augustine of Hippo (354–430) in his magnus opus *The City of God*, and Saint Thomas Aquinas (1225–74) in his *Summa Theologica*. This doctrine is repeated in the recent catechism of the Catholic Church (paragraphs 2,302–2,317). See www.vatican.va/archive/catechism/ccc_toc.htm. This doctrine emerged as a synthesis of the legal system of the Roman Empire, the philosophical speculation of the Roman thinker Cicero (who is largely quoted by Saint Augustine), and divinely sanctioned war in the biblical texts of the Old Testament.
23 See for instance, Henry Hadley Norris, *The Jesuits and the Doctrine of High Treason and Regicide* (Whitefish, Mont.: Kessinger Publishing, 2005); and Graham E. Seel, *Regicide and Republic: England 1603–1660* (Cambridge: Cambridge University Press, 2001).

24 Key works in this regard include among others: Paolo Freire, *Pedagogy of the Oppressed* (New York: Seabury, 1970); Gustavo Gutierrez, *A Theology of Liberation: History, Politics, and Salvation* (Maryknoll, NY: Orbis Books, 1971); Leonardo Boff, *Jesus Christ, Liberator: A Critical Christology for Our Time* (Maryknoll, NY: Orbis, 1978); Jon Sobrino, *The Bible of the Oppressed* (Maryknoll, NY: Orbis Books, 1982); Jon Sobrino, *Jesus the Liberator: A Historical-Theological View* (Maryknoll, NY: Orbis Books, 1993); Ignacio Ellacuria and Jon Sobrino, eds., *Mysterium Liberationis: Fundamental Concepts of Liberation Theology* (Maryknoll, NY: Orbis, 1993); Jon Sobrino, *Principle of Mercy: Taking the Crucified People From the Cross* (Maryknoll, NY: Orbis Books, 1994).
25 Koran 28: 77–78.
26 Koran 5: 31–32.
27 Koran 5: 28.
28 Koran 2: 257.
29 It is believed by many Muslims that these words are from a Hadith pronounced by the Prophet Muhammad. See Muhammad Abdul-Rauf, *The Islamic View of Women and the Family*, 2nd edn. (Cairo: The Supreme Council for Islamic Affairs, 1993), 13.
30 Quoted in Huston Smith, *The World's Religions*, 2nd edn. (New York: Harper Collins Publishers, 1991), 264.
31 Smith, *The World's Religions*, 264.
32 John M. Koller and Patricia Koller, eds., *A Source Book in Asian Philosophy* (Upper Saddle River, NJ: Prentice Hall, 1991), 463.
33 An interesting summary of Native-American spiritual values relevant to R2P can be found in Tink Tinker, "American Indians Religious Traditions," in *The Hope of Liberation in World Religions*, ed. Miguel A. De La Torre (Waco, TX: Baylor University Press, 2008), 261–72. See also the abundant publications of Vine Deloria, Jr., especially his famous book *God Is Red: A Native View of Religion* (Golden, Colo.: Fulcrum Publishing, 1994).
34 Robert M. Baum, "Indigenous Religious Traditions," in *A Concise Introduction to World Religions*, ed. Willard G. Oxtoby and Alan F. Segal (Oxford University Press, 2007), 15–17.
35 Georges Balandier, and Jacques Maquet, *Dictionary of Black African Civilization* (New York: Leon Amiel, 1974), 336.
36 Quoted in Dominique Zahan, *The Religion, Spirituality, and Thought of Traditional Africa* (Chicago: University of Chicago Press, 1983), 126.
37 The term *bumuntu* (the essence of authentic personhood) comes from the Kiluba language spoken in the Katanga province of the DRC. It is known in South Africa as *ubuntu*.
38 Laurenti Magesa, *African Religion: The Moral Traditions of Abundant Life* (Maryknoll, NY: Orbis books, 1997), 197–8.
39 Wande Abimbola, "The Attitude of Yoruba Religion Toward Non-Yoruba Religion," in *Attitudes of Religions and Ideologies Toward the Outsider*, ed. Leonard Swidler and Paul Mojzes (Lewiston, NY: The Edwin Mellen Press, 1990), 137.
40 Abimbola, "The Attitude of Yoruba Religion Toward Non-Yoruba Religion," 138.
41 Kwame Gyekye, *An essay on African philosophical thought: The Akan conceptual scheme* (New York: Cambridge University Press, 1987), 19.

42 Wande Abimbola, "Ifa: A West African Cosmological System," in *Religion in Africa: Experience and Expression* (London: James Currey and Heinemann, 1994), 114; and George Anastaplo, "An Introduction to 'Ancient' African Thought," in *The Great Ideas Today, 1995; The Great Books of the Western World* (London: Encyclopedia Britannica, Inc., 1995), 176.
43 Magesa, *African Religion*, 197–8.
44 G.I. Olikenyi, *African Hospitality: A Model for the Communication of the Gospel in the African Cultural Context* (Nettetal, Germany: Steyler Verlag, 2001), 105.
45 Olikenyi, *African Hospitality*, 105.
46 M.P. Moila, *Challenging Issues in African Christianity* (Pretoria: CB Powell Bible Centre, 2002), 3.
47 Kwame Gyekye, *An essay on African philosophical thought*, 17.
48 For Luba proverbs and other African proverbs, see Mutombo Nkulu-N'Sengha, "Proverbs and Teaching," in *Encyclopedia of African Religion*, vol. 2, ed. Molefi Asante and Ama Mazama (Thousand Oaks, Calif.: Sage, 2009).
49 See Charles S. Bird and Martha B. Kendall, "The Mande Hero," in *Explorations in African Systems of Thought*, ed. Ivan Karp, and Charles S. Bird (Washington, DC: Smithsonian Institution Press, 1987), 14–16.
50 Richard Tarnas, *The Passion of the Western Mind* (New York: Ballantine Books, 1991), 492.
51 Tarnas, *The Passion of the Western Mind*, 492.
52 Bakole Wa Ilunga, *Paths of Liberation: Third World Spirituality* (New York: Orbis, 1984), 17. Other works of significance to R2P in virtue of their reflection on the theme of liberation include: Engelbert Mveng, ed., *Spiritualite et liberation en Afrique* (Paris: l'Harmattan, 1987); Emmanuel Martey, *African Theology: Inculturation and Liberation* (Maryknoll, NY: Orbis Books, 1993).
53 For an elaborate articulation of this Gandhian view, see Iyer, *The Moral and Political Thought*, 41.
54 Iyer, *The Moral and Political Thought*, 41.
55 We rely here in part on the excellent Excursus of the Golden Rule in world religions summarized by Leonard Swidler, "Toward a Universal Declaration of a Global Ethic" in Leonard Swidler, ed., *For All Life: Toward a Universal Declaration of a Global Ethic* (Ashland, OR: White Cloud Press, 1999), 19–21. See also in Swidler and Mojzes, *The Study of Religion*, 182–85.
56 Leonardo Boff, "Jesus, a Person of Extraordinary Good Sense, Creative Imagination, and Originality," in *Third World Liberation Theologies: A Reader*, ed. William Deane Ferm (Maryknoll, NY: Orbis Books, 1986), 111.
57 Saint Augustine, "Retractationum," in *Patrologia Latinae*, ed. J.P. Migne (Paris: Garnier Frère, 1877). Also see Boff, "Jesus, a Person of Extraordinary Good Sense," 111.
58 Luke 6: 36.
59 Matthew 7: 12.
60 Leviticus 19: 18.
61 Tobit 4: 15.
62 See Leonard Swidler, "Toward a Universal Declaration of a Global Ethic," 21.
63 Andrew Wilson, ed., *World Scripture* (New York: Paragon House, 1991), 114.
64 Quoted in Swidler, "Toward a Universal Declaration," 21.
65 Elsewhere, we find similar views among Greek philosophers. Well before Socrates, Thales of Miletus (600 BCE) stated the highest rule of good living:

"Do not do the evil you find in others." Another Greek thinker, Isocrates (400 BCE), states the same truth: "Treat others as you would wish them to treat you."

66 Analects 12.2 and 15.23.

67 Analects 5.11.

68 Sutta Nipata v. 705.

69 Samyutta Nikaya v. 353.

70 Mahabharata, Anusasana Parva 113.8. Also see Mahabharata 5:1517.

71 The vocabulary of the Pali language is followed here. Buddha outlined the basic framework of Buddhist ethics for rulers. This text is available in various publications and internet resources. See, for instance, Bhikkhu Saranapala, "A Buddhist Perspective on Global Economic Meltdown," talk delivered at the Multi-faith Center Auditorium, University of Toronto, 19 March 2009, available at kinrarametta.org/my/?page_id=322.

72 Basil Davidson, *The Search for Africa: History, Culture, Politics* (New York: Times Books, 1994), 36.

73 G.W.F. Hegel, *The Philosophy of History*, Great Books of the Western World vol.46, 2nd edn. (Chicago: Encyclopedia Britannica, Inc., 1990), 208.

74 Matthew 5: 21–48. Paul's theology of nonviolence is formulated in Romans 12: 9–21.

75 The topic is treated in various sections of the book. See Saint Augustine, *The City of God*, Great Books of the Western World vol.16, 2nd edn. (Chicago: Encyclopedia Britannica, Inc., 1990).

76 Romans 13: 1–7. Also significant in this regard is 1 Peter 2: 13–17, and Luke 22: 35–38.

77 For remarks and full text see nobelprize.org/nobel_prizes/peace/laureates/2009/obama-lecture_en.html, and www.whitehouse.gov/the_press_office/Remarks-by-the-President-on-Winning-the-Nobel-Peace-Prize.

78 An excellent study of the role of religion in resistance movements in Africa is found in the eight volumes of the UN Educational, Scientific and Cultural Organization's (UNESCO) General History of Africa, especially the seventh volume. A. Adu Boahen, ed., *General History of Africa: Africa under Colonial Domination* (Berkeley: UNESCO and University of California Press, 1990). There are many other important works on the subject, such as Isidore Ndaywel è Ziem, *Histoire du Zaïre: de l'héritage ancient à l'âge contemporain* (Louvain-la-Neuve, Belgium: Duculot, 1997); Elizabeth Isichei, *A History of Christianity in Africa: From Antiquity to the Present* (Grand Rapids, MI: Wm. B. Eerdmans Publishing Co., 1995); John Bauer, *2000 and de Christianisme en Afrique: Une Histoire de l'Eglise Africaine* (Kinshasa: Filles de Saint Paul, 2001); Adrian Hastings, *A History of African Christianity 1450–1950* (Oxford: Clarendon, 1994), and *A History of African Christianity 1950–1975* (Cambridge: Cambridge University Press, 1979); Martial Sinda, *Simon Kimbangu, Prophete et Martyr Zairois* (Abidjan, Côte d'Ivoire: Nouvelles Editions Africaines, 1977). Various works on the history of African independent churches, books on the life of Nelson Mandela, and writings by Bishop Desmond Tutu and other South African theologians are also useful on this theme of resistance.

79 Centuries prior to the publications by Gustavo Gutierrez and Leonardo Boff, Africa had already generated a liberation theology movement that challenged the slave trade, colonialism, and local tyrannies. This led one

African theologian, Gabriel Setiloane, to argue that Africa has indeed its own traditional version of just war theory that could provide an important inspiration for the development of contemporary African theology. See Gabriel M. Setiloane, "Civil Authority from the perspective of African theology," in *Religious Plurality in Africa*, ed. Jacob K. Olupona and Sulayman S. Nyang (Berlin: Mouton De Gruyter, 1993), 145–65.

80 John K. Thornton, *The Kongolese Saint Anthony: Dona Beatriz Kimpa Vita and the Antonian Movement, 1684–1706* (Cambridge: Cambridge University Press, 1998). The perspective of a Congolese historian can be found in Isidore Ndaywel è Ziem, *Histoire du Zaïre: de l'héritage ancient à l'âge contemporain* (Louvain-la-Neuve, Belgium: Duculot, 1997). This religious resistance movement of Africans who claimed to be possessed by Saint Anthony developed during the seventeenth century. In the eighteenth century, Kimpa Vita emerged as its most prominent voice. See also Albert J. Raboteau, *Slave Religion: The "Invisible Institution" in the Antebellum South* (Oxford: Oxford University Press, 1978).

81 See Marie-Louise Martin, *Kimbangu: An African Prophet and his Church* (Grand Rapids, MI: Eerdmans, 1975).

82 See Adu Boahen, ed., *General History of Africa*, vol. VII, 80.

83 See Ndaywel è Ziem, *Histoire du Zaïre*, 94; and Adu Boahen, "Africa and the colonial challenge," in *General History of Africa*, vol. VII.

84 As shown in the history of African resistance movements and the dethroning of some kings, Africa has clearly its own version of *bellum justum* and regicide doctrine based on the principles of self-defense and the protection of life and common good.

85 See Mutombo Nkulu-N'Sengha, "African Religions and Resistance to Enslavement," in *Encyclopedia of African Religion*, vol. 2, ed. Molefi Asante and Ama Mazama (Thousand Oaks, Calif.: Sage, 2009). See also John Thornton, "African Roots of the Stono Rebellion," *American Historical Review* 96 (1991): 1101–13; John Thornton, "I am the Subject of the King of Congo: African Political Ideology and the Haitian Revolution," *Journal of World History* 4 (1993): 181–214. A brief synthesis of these studies is found in John K. Thornton, *The Kongolese Saint Anthony*, 2–3.

86 See Fabien Eboussi Boulaga, *Les Conférences Nationales en Afrique Noire: Une affaire à suivre* (Paris: Karthala, 1993).

87 An interesting collection of these texts is found in Léon de Saint Moulin and Roger Gaise N'Ganzi, eds., *Eglise et Société: Le discours socio-politique de l'Eglise catholique du Congo (1956–1998)*, vol. 1 (Kinshasa: Facultés Catholiques de Kinshasa, 1998).

88 See Iyer, *The Moral and Political Thought*, 257.

89 Christianity celebrates a long "faith and reason" tradition grounded not only in scholastic theology, but also in biblical texts such as 1 Peter 3: 13–17 and 2 Peter 1: 1–11, and in the examples of Jesus' challenge to the religion and religious leaders of his time, especially in the gospel of Matthew (chapters 5, 6, 7, and 23). According to his accusers, Jesus was killed for fomenting rebellion against political powers, insulting religious leaders, not respecting the Sabbath, not obeying the law of Moses, and for committing blasphemy against God. Technically, Jesus was accused of atheism for his radical opposition to the pseudo-religiosity of his time. Some scholars such as Cardinal Jean Danielou have maintained that Christianity is not a religion,

but rather a relationship with God: "The religions are a gesture of man towards God; revelation is the witness of gesture of God towards man. The religions are creations of human genius; they witness to the value of exalted religious personalities, such as Buddha, Zoroaster, Orpheus. But they also have the defects of what is human. Revelation is the work of God alone ... Religion expresses man's desire for God. Revelation witnesses that God has responded to that desire. Religion does not save; Jesus Christ grants salvation." See Jean Daniélou, "Christianisme et religions non-chrétiennes," *Etudes* 321 (1964): 323–36. Also cited by Francis A. Sullivan, *Salvation outside the Church?: Tracing the History of the Catholic Response* (New York: Paulist Press, 1992), 187.

90 We now have an abundant source of wisdom to draw upon in support of interreligious dialogue. Although all religions have their pitfalls and their forms of ethnocentrism, it is worth noting that historically indigenous religions seem to have been more tolerant than the three monotheistic religions with their absolutist claims of Divine revelation and their exclusivist view of salvation (*Extra Ecclesiam Nulla Salus*). A great deal can be learned from the spirituality of the global South in matters of interreligious dialogue. India gives us the excellent example of King Ashoka and many other teachers of religious tolerance. An excellent articulation of the traditional African wisdom of religious tolerance can be found in Wole Soyinka, "The Tolerant Gods," in *Orisha Devotion as World Religion: The Globalization of Yoruba Religious Culture*, ed. Jacob Olupon and Terry Rey (Madison: University of Wisconsin Press, 2008). Moreover, as the writings of Ibn Arabi show, there is some tradition of religious tolerance and openness to interreligious dialogue in Islam and the same can be said about Judaism and Christianity. In fact, using these overlooked traditions, some Christian scholars have introduced a paradigm shift in Christianity in support for interreligious dialogue. Between 1965 and 2000 important works on Christian support for interreligious dialogue have been published by theologians and religious scholars such as Leonard Swidler, Raimundo Panikkar, Jacques Dupuis, Cantwell Smith, John Hick, Paul Knitter, and David Krieger. These authors often find support in the Copernican revolution introduced by the Second Vatican Council (especially in "Nostra Aetate" and "Dignitatis Humanae"), and in the actions and speeches of Pope Paul VI and Pope John Paul II in favor of interreligious dialogue. On the Catholic side, one of the best and most comprehensive articulations of the various theological and biblical perspectives on interreligious dialogue is found in the book of the Jesuit priest Dupuis: Jacques Dupuis, *Toward a Christian Theology of Pluralism* (Maryknoll, NY: Orbis Books, 2001).

91 See Jean Comby, *Pour lire l'histoire de l'Eglise*, vol. 2. (Paris: Cerf, 1986), 93; Alf Tergel, *Human Rights in Cultural and Religious Traditions* (Uppsala: Acta Universitatis Upsaliensis, 1998), 164; and Leonard Swidler, "Human Rights: An Historical Overview," in *Human Rights: Christians, Marxists, and others in dialogue*, ed. Leonard Swidler (New York: Paragon House, 1991), 12. Needless to say, a history of opposition to human rights is also found in Judaism and Islam, as well as a shift in support of human rights.

92 Tergel, *Human Rights in Cultural and Religious Traditions*, 13.

93 Cited in Jacques Dupuis, *Toward a Christian Theology of Religious Pluralism*, 61.

94 Maura Browne, ed., *The African Synod: Documents, Reflections, Perspectives* (Maryknoll, NY: Orbis Books, 1996), 109.

95 Ibn Al-'Arabi, *The Tarjuman Al-Ashwaq*, poem XI, lines 13–15. English translation from Philip Novak, *The World's Wisdom: Sacred Texts of the World's Religions* (New York: Harper Collins, 1995), 325. Text also available in Muhyi'ddin Ibn Al-'Arabi, *The Tarjuman Al-Ashwaq: A Collection of Mystical Odes*, ed. Reynold A. Nicholson (London: Royal Asiatic Society, 1911), 67.

2 Philosophy, ethics, and R2P

Yolanda Angulo Parra

- **Philosophy and ethics as societal transformation**
- **Critical philosophy in the global South: overcoming injustice**
- **Latin American philosophy: the search for justice and freedom**
- **Philosophical concepts and ethical values relevant to R2P**
- **Preventing mass atrocities by expanding their scope?**
- **Conclusion: achieving (an imperfect) utopia—implementing R2P informed by philosophy and ethics**

Philosophy resembles the double-faced god Janus: since its emergence it has either placed itself at the service of domination or alternatively taken sides with the less fortunate, the weak, and the suffering. It has helped the latter to clarify, understand, and look for better ways of life and engage in societal transformation. Examples of what can be referred to as "critical philosophy" are: Epicurus in Ancient Greece, Seneca in Hellenism, Marx in modernity, the Frankfurt School, neo-structuralism, neo-Marxism, and the philosophy of liberation.

This chapter explores what philosophy, and specifically ethics, can contribute to clarifying and reinforcing the responsibility to protect (R2P) norm to aid people who have suffered or are about to suffer mass atrocities. It also examines how to shape R2P's future evolution by analyzing how mass atrocities are defined and responses to them specifically through the prism of philosophical perspectives from the global South. Focusing on Latin America, it highlights this region's specific contribution, through the philosophy of liberation, to shaping R2P. Although this is an overly ambitious task for a single chapter, an analysis of the variety of perspectives on the thorny question of "responsibility" itself—by whom, for whom, and under what circumstances—provides a starting point for a much longer and more detailed conversation.

Several factors should be taken into account as the argument proceeds. First, the so-called global South[1] is a vast region with both differences and similarities. Contemporary civil wars and mass atrocities, as currently conceptualized, are mostly located in Africa, Asia, and the Middle East. Although there are few internecine conflicts in Latin America, various countries in the region share with trouble spots elsewhere endemic forms of violence, not visible at first glance, but nonetheless insidious, constant, and cruel—and even potential precursors of mass atrocities. Among these are daily killings, kidnappings, and extortion of organized crime syndicates; institutionalized and widespread corruption; extreme poverty; poverty-induced forced migration; and inequality-induced crime.

The moral philosopher must detect and describe the conditions for the emergence of victims of mass atrocities, as well as the historical, political, and economic causes of extreme violence. R2P may even become an ethical obligation—as discussed below—not only to heal immediate suffering but also to redress the wounds of colonization, neocolonization, and repression. Regardless of whether this proposition is accepted or rejected, the question herein raised is how can the R2P norm be better shaped from an ethical point?

The first part of this chapter addresses how philosophy can provide a specific discourse to clarify concepts, grasp our time in words, and aid its transformation. The second part examines briefly the work of some Southern philosophers relevant to R2P and demonstrates through select examples how both ancient and contemporary philosophical traditions of the global South are directly pertinent. The illustrations not only demonstrate the resonance of R2P in diverse philosophical traditions but also help to sharpen and ground R2P's ethical values more deeply and shape effective implementation strategies. However, a cursory overview of contemporary Southern philosophers also indicates the extent to which recent historical experiences of slavery, colonization, and domination continue to influence Southern philosophy and breed public distrust of even benevolent or protective international actions. If R2P is to be relevant and resonant, its proponents must listen attentively to the calls for justice and liberation that are key underpinnings of contemporary Southern philosophy.

Due to the vast scope of philosophical traditions from the global South, the third part focuses on Latin America and its specific contribution to philosophy in general and to R2P in particular, through liberation philosophy. It analyzes pre- and post-Columbian philosophy, emphasizing discourses that best fit the purpose of providing ethical notions to inform the R2P norm. It outlines what can be considered the historical and contextual origins of liberation theology and later the philosophy of liberation in Latin America and their political influence and impact across the global South.

The fourth part addresses key philosophical and ethical concepts in order to shed light on how mass atrocities can be prevented or halted. It contains a philosophical analysis of moral responsibility, ethical obligation, victims, the value of human life, human rights, and the category of mass atrocities.

The fifth part looks toward the future and argues that the current notion of mass atrocity ultimately needs to be expanded to include less visible forms of violence. Although politically infeasible for the moment, nonetheless broadening the category would elevate the importance of the preventive and peace building components of R2P. Mass atrocities such as genocide receive media coverage because they are the result of highly visible violence perpetrated against a large number of people. Problems such as organized crime, governmental corruption, and forced migration—which often flourish in contexts of extreme poverty—are given less media attention. These, however, are often precursors of large-scale violence.

Finally, the conclusion summarizes the argument. It outlines the contributions that philosophy generally, and a genealogical Southern perspective of ethics specifically, could make to foster the development and implementation of the R2P norm.

Philosophy and ethics as societal transformation

Epicurus's extant prescription of philosophy is a good starting point for this study in the following way: "Vain is the word of the philosopher which does not heal any suffering of men. For just as there is no profit in medicine if it does not expel the diseases of the body, so there is no profit in philosophy either if it does not expel the suffering of the mind."[2] Two traditions characterize Western philosophy. The first emphasizes wisdom as the possession of true knowledge, and the second interprets wisdom as a constant search for better forms of living.[3] As noted at the outset, philosophy has served the less fortunate, the weak, and the suffering to question their lot in life.[4] It has helped them clarify, understand, and aspire to more dignified lives and engage itself in societal transformation, as Karl Marx expressed it in his 11th thesis on Feuerbach.[5]

There are, of course, many instances when philosophical discourse has been used to justify oppression—a few such cases are examined below. However, this chapter emphasizes philosophy placed at the service of life—mostly inspired by critical philosophy[6]—which is relevant for R2P and can be valuable in its elaboration and application. Thus, when Epicurus depicts philosophy as a discourse aimed to expel the mind's suffering, such utterance can be broadened to refer to human suffering as a whole. Philosophy is thus an activity the central purpose of which is to clarify propositions, to grasp our era in thought, and interpret the world in order to change it, in a constant search for happiness.[7] A few months before his death, Michel Foucault succinctly asserted: "In its critical dimension—understanding critical in a very broad sense—philosophy is a challenge to all phenomena of domination, notwithstanding their place or form: political, economical, sexual, institutional or others."[8]

Foucault's genealogical approach helps to diagnose our time (the ontology of the present) and understand the significance of contemporary cultural practices as well as their historical transformations. According to this philosophical tradition,[9] there is no human essence by itself that is merely "traveling" throughout history, or a subject of knowledge untouched by history. Each epoch develops forms of subjectivity from specific social practices and power relations and creates its own victims according to what is deemed "mass atrocities." Some main features of the genealogical approach are that concepts acquire a different sense according to the context in which they appear, allowing us to demystify any fixed concepts or categories; there is no transcendental subject that acts as the structure of meaning; subjects emerge under certain conditions; the human body is placed at the center of all struggles and forms of domination; and the philosopher has a social commitment to detect and fight any form of domination, violence, and suffering.

If the aim of philosophy is not only to understand the world but to change it, one of its most compelling branches is ethics, due to its practical or applied nature. Hence, the task of critical philosophy is to end domination (broadly understood as any form of enforced suffering, obviously including mass atrocities), and to expose it when it is invisible. In our case the application of critical philosophy would enable states, institutions, and organizations that have embraced the responsibility to protect to have more clarity as to why mass atrocities occur as well as their role and responsibility toward victims.

Critical philosophy in the global South: overcoming injustice

Since what is usually conceived as modernity,[10] philosophy in the global South can be broadly said to have been marked by two tendencies. The first follows European mainstream philosophy without questioning its scope, truth, values, and effects on economic, political, or cultural spheres; and the second is often critical of Eurocentrism[11]and in recent decades of Americanism.

Long before European modernity, however, Africa, Asia, and the Middle East, as well as Latin America and the Caribbean, had developed traditions of philosophical thought, worldviews, and moral values, with distinct methodologies, forms, and evolutions, addressing ontological, anthropological, and ethical problems, among others. In many of these ancient wisdom traditions can be found strong underlying justifications for both the R2P norm and its implementation in violent crises.

For example, Confucianism, with its distinct and diverse Chinese, Japanese, and Indian sources, is replete with such traditions. Confucius during the late sixth century BCE proclaimed an ethics of virtue that was similar to the one developed by Aristotle two centuries later, with happiness as its goal.[12] According to Confucian philosophy, someone who cultivates virtues may become a wise and good human. There are three levels of virtue: *li* consists of mutual respect, norms of conduct, rites, ceremonies, and good manners; *yi* is the virtue of justice—the art of giving to each one what he or she deserves; and *ren* is the equivalent of goodness, benevolence, the desire for the wellbeing of all people, and acting accordingly. The third embraces the golden rule, akin to many religious and philosophical traditions such as Christianity and utilitarianism: "do unto others as you would have them do unto you." *Ren* embraces love and respect for others as the supreme virtue, resulting in authenticity and autonomy. Unlike modern Western philosophy, however, autonomy is not a mere characteristic of the self but embraces everyone. In a society every person must have disinterested and altruistic attitudes.

The ethical notion of responsibility is, thus, the core of this level of virtue, for one must take responsibility not only for oneself but for others. Such ethics is also an ontology, for the personality is constituted in the interrelationship with others in society. Confucianism is thus a moral philosophy that seeks equilibrium between the individual and society, and the full development of both. Harmonious relations must be examined at every level: in the family; between those who govern and those who are governed; between father and son; between wife and husband; among siblings; and among friends. Confucian philosophical concepts are relevant to understanding, adapting, and balancing the tensions between human rights and current conceptions of state sovereignty and responsibility. Still relevant in China and influential far beyond, Confucian virtues provide an ancient but relevant ethical grounding for R2P in our times. The golden rule and justice provide the twin normative foundations for protecting the vulnerable; protective action would constitute virtuous conduct.

This section, however, focuses on contemporary Southern philosophy, where the themes of R2P have deep resonance. The vast regions of the global South that birthed great civilizations in ancient and medieval times have endured in recent centuries oppression, slavery, colonization, internal and external wars, neocolonialism, and dictatorship. Thus, it is not surprising that the ethical discourse of so many non-Western philosophers includes justice and liberation as the major objects of study, in many cases presenting and reviving historical and cultural traditions that have been buried or blurred by other cultures.[13]

Contemporary African critical philosophers and political activists, including Kwame Nkrumah, Leopold Senghor, Patrice Lumumba,[14] all of whom became their nations' leaders, as well as Frantz Fanon,[15] pursued cultural, political, economic, or social revolution to end colonialism and remove its vestiges. Fanon's book, *Les damnés de la terre* (*The Wretched of the Earth*), was especially influential on philosophers and activists interested in liberation movements against colonialism, in revolutionary and critical thought. Fanon considered that counter-terror and counter-violence to suppress colonial terror and violence were necessary to achieve independence. Liberation wars, moreover, have positive effects on those who fight, for they show gestures of solidarity around a common cause, national destiny, and collective history. Hence, the first step toward liberation is war or the destructive stage, and the second is the constructive stage of the struggle against poverty, illiteracy, and underdevelopment. Fanon stressed that the European wealth of diamonds, oil, silk, cotton, wood, and slave labor were stolen from underdeveloped continents; European aid is thus a "just reparation."

Although developed in the context of decolonization, this reflection is pertinent to R2P today: given the historical antecedents of most mass atrocities, the United Nations, and its most powerful members, might view timely protective action as a form of just reparation for the devastating past. The responsibility to protect, although not outlined as such, essentially undertakes a liberating task, akin to that of anti-colonial thinkers, who seek to emancipate the oppressed from their oppressors.

Another example from contemporary African philosophy is Burundian philosopher and poet Michel Kayoya, who explains the impact of colonialism in the Great Lakes region and attributes to Eurocentrism the series of massacres and periodic ethnic cleansing that occurred after Burundi's independence from Belgium in 1962. The 1972 genocide—in which 300,000 Hutu intellectuals as well as people who pronounced themselves as democrats were killed by the Tutsi army—was also a result of this colonial legacy, according to Kayoya. His philosophy and poetry can be construed as a critique of the mass atrocity crimes committed during colonial and neocolonial processes.

Mahatma Gandhi's philosophy of civil disobedience or resisting colonial domination and oppression with nonviolent means is an Asian alternative to Fanon's approach. Fanon was born in the Caribbean but honed as a philosopher-activist in Africa's anti-colonial struggles; and Indian-born Gandhi also found his political and philosophical cause on African soil, fighting racism in South Africa. Gandhi's philosophy is based primarily on the Buddhist and Hindu concept of *ahimsa*, or nonviolence, but it is by no means passive. Gandhi developed his philosophy over time on the front-lines of struggle, based on deep philosophical reflection and experimentation and drawing on numerous ethical and spiritual sources.[16] *Satyagraha*, or the path of truth, was uncompromising in its ethical principles, and its philosophical conviction that truth and justice would inevitably trump oppression and unjust power. The strategy of civil disobedience that Gandhi derived from it was equally unflinching in risking oppression to defend human dignity in the pursuit of liberation. The end of the British Empire in India provides a clear case in which ethically informed strategies of pacific resistance succeeded where violent protest often failed.

Gandhi provides a living example of the relevance of philosophy and ethics for practical political action, particularly in the face of crisis or oppression. It shows how philosophy can inform and shape an ethical approach, which in turn crafts a deliberate and universally applicable political strategy. This is of particular relevance to R2P today: philosophy and ethics could inform, especially, how R2P might be implemented more effectively at the preventive stage to protect both human dignity and lives, and thus avoid subsequent forceful intervention.

Turning to contemporary philosophers in Asia, a current influential tradition is that of Indian philosopher Arjun Appadurai. His work is especially pertinent because it sheds light on the constitution of modern subjectivity and helps to deepen our understanding of R2P. Appadurai finds electronic communications and media crucial in the constitution of an image of the self. Although throughout history migration has been a constant phenomenon, current immigrants are distinctive: they are not attached to a territory because, with electronic communication technology, they can, virtually, be in many places at the same time. People constantly imagine living and working in different places than those in which they were born; others are forced to change their locations of residence, as in the case of refugees; and finally, others migrate looking for work or opportunities unavailable in their current places of residence.

Whether through the push of war or the pull of economic opportunity, Appadurai analyzes different forms of migration and their accompanying diasporas of hope, terror, and despair. Migrants dream, imagine forms of life, most of which are provided and shaped by television, movies, radio—in short, electronic means of communication.[17] Appadurai's emphasis on migration captures the reality of much of the population of the global South today: they are trapped in poverty or insecurity and are dreaming of escape. His identification of the three categories of diaspora is relevant to the R2P norm and is discussed below with regard to the linkage between forced migration and atrocities.

In the Middle East, philosophers have also grappled with issues of colonization and oppression. Elizabeth Suzanne Kassab describes the colonial issue, and her work is worth citing at some length:

> The "ethnicization" of the mind outside Europe came in the first wave of response to the European colonial definition of the colonized. This definition emphasized the civilizational ineptitude of the colonized and served to justify the so-called "civilizational mission" of the colonizer. It took different forms in the different colonial regions. For instance, in Black Africa it claimed that the African mind was inherently incapable of logical and theoretical thinking and consequently incapable of producing an advanced culture. In Latin America European culture was to fill the civilizational gap that was created by the defeat of supposedly "uncivilized" local populations. Arabs, in turn, were seen to be captive of an oriental, religious worldview, intrinsically inimical to reason and progress. These definitions, imposed from a power position, carried the weight of an alleged scientific truth, coming from the scholarly and political authority of "superior" civilizations.[18]

The revolt against domination continues to shape contemporary thinking as a result of recent history in the Middle East. Iraqi contemporary philosophy, for instance, can be seen as an example of the disenchantment with the strength of discursive forms of changing the world. As contemporary philosopher Bassam Romaya points out:

> The ruthlessness of a past regime has not been eliminated, but doled anew by petrol-hungry "emancipators." The occupation-imperial globalization project ensures that nothing stands in the way of its profits, and any journalist who dares to challenge its actions will be dealt with accordingly—such is democratic reform à la Iraq. Perhaps we're better off siding with Plato's demonization of "democracy" (so eloquently captured in *The Republic*). Whatever so-called "free" thought may get from the occupation-imperial globalization project, it must be unfettered and genuine, surpassing all limits of thought control presently imposed upon the Iraqi intellectual subject by its master.[19]

This quotation reflects a sense of despair and skepticism in the South about both the hegemony of Western philosophical discourses and the actions or non-actions by the international community of states.

International peacekeepers risking their lives in deadly war zones, whether in Rwanda or Afghanistan, Haiti or the Democratic Republic of the Congo (DRC), are often bewildered by the hostility they soon encounter from the host populations they are ostensibly protecting. This brief review of some contemporary philosophical threads from Africa, Asia, and the Middle East suggests the lingering mistrust of long-humiliated and recently decolonized populations toward the seemingly civilizing and patronizing mission of their international interveners—however benevolent their intentions—is a reality that R2P has to confront. As Gareth Evans points out: "There has been a falling away of overt commitment to the norm in sub-Sahara Africa … and … increased skepticism in the Arab-Islamic and Latin American worlds." One critic in Sri Lanka even went as far as arguing that "the so-called responsibility to protect is nothing but a license given by the white man to himself [to] intervene in the affairs of dark sovereign countries, whenever the white man thinks it fit to do so."[20]

At the same time, this brief engagement of Southern philosophical traditions reveals how they provide fertile ground for deepening the understanding of R2P and seeking inspiration for its effective implementation in sometimes hostile territory. Past and recent bloody events and experiences of oppression in Africa, Asia, and the Middle East have provided ample subject matter for philosophical reflections in these societies. Southern philosophers in these regions show a deep concern with justice and liberation mixed with skepticism, strength, and optimism. UN officials could beneficially take into consideration the ethical and philosophical critiques emanating from these societies in crisis and from the global South more generally. They would also need to eschew rigorously and consistently actions that may be supported by interests alien to the responsibility to protect, in order to overcome hostility and distrust. Such an approach—guided by local philosophy and ethics and eschewing, to the extent possible, vested interests—would diminish skepticism and inculcate sympathy for R2P.

Latin American philosophy: the search for justice and freedom

The previous part introduced critical philosophy from Africa, Asia, and the Middle East; this one focuses specifically on its Latin American variants. A few historical remarks on Latin American philosophy and ethics are required to understand the emergence of liberation theology and the philosophy of liberation, and their political impact on the region. It takes inspiration from José Martí's advice: "It is necessary to make virtue fashionable."[21] As will be shown below, virtue is relevant to ethical judgments and actions, and it can link philosophy and the responsibility to protect. This section discusses the pre-Columbian period and colonial genocide as a prelude to the emergence of the predominant approach of the philosophy of liberation.

The pre-Columbian period, the Spanish Conquest, and accompanying colonial genocide

Many centuries before Europeans conquered and colonized pre-Columbian cultures, there were wise men among Mayans, Incas, Aztecs, and other peoples. In Mesoamerica, Nahua systems of thought were predominant until the sixteenth century. As Miguel León-Portilla[22] explains, Nahuas (indigenous peoples, such as Toltecs, Aztecs, and Teotihuacans from Mesoamerica) had a worldview that was expressed through myths and beliefs to understand the mysteries of creation and the universe. They also had a perception of the problem of the being of things and a rational questioning about the origin and end of the universe and human beings, about the sense and value and truth of life, existence after death, and other issues that go beyond myths and beliefs.

Two key books of that period are: *El coloquio de los doce* (*Formal conversation of the twelve*)[23] and *Huehuetlatolli* (*Discourses of the elderly*),[24] a series of doctrinal utterances and conversations to teach children and young Nahuas moral lessons. The former contains a passage with allusions to the new colonial order: "His kingdom enters; in our souls the Real God enters. Life is withered; and the heart is dead of its flowers. Those who pull everything until it breaks spoil and suck the flowers of others … There is no truth in the word of foreigners."[25] Such laments represent the feelings of defeated peoples whose societies had been completely destroyed.

It would be naïve to regard such ancient pre-Columbian cultures as the Aztecs or Incas as ideal societies—they too suffered from oligarchy, oppression, and exploitation by priests and lords within a specific tribe,[26] as well as wars and slavery among different tribes. Yet, the forms of domination changed with colonization. Before the arrival of the Spaniards in Mesoamerica, the Aztecs predominated and used several mechanisms of domination. The primary ones were truth discourses, such as myths of origin and of war; knowledge scenarios such as the Calmecac, Telpochcalli, and Cuilcacalli;[27] and spaces of power such as the distribution of cities according to the ontological conception of time, all of which resulted in new subjectivities, such as the conqueror-warrior subjectivity and the Aztec lordship subjectivity.[28]

Independent long before other regions of the global South, Latin America nonetheless has continued to struggle against the domination of Europe and subsequently the United States. In the New Spain, during the colonial period, new subjectivities emerged as a consequence of profound changes in social practices, power relations, and discourses of truth. The new dominant forces were mainly Spaniards and Creoles; the vast indigenous population, who had been transformed into different forms of subjects, remained dominated, together with the former dominant Mexica subjects.[29] Although colonization diminished the power of local elites, it certainly did not end intra-communal exploitation. Indigenous peoples were typically the least powerful.[30]

Western philosophy was imported by Spanish friars to places like present-day Cuba, Dominican Republic, Mexico, Guatemala, Peru, and Colombia; however, it was influenced also by local social practices. The evangelization process gave birth to a new philosophical discourse, partly in reaction to what was one of the greatest mass atrocity crimes in recorded history. Many ontological, ethical, religious, and political controversies arose: Were so-called Indians rational human beings, semi-humans, or beasts? Were they even capable of being evangelized? Had Spain not only the right but also the obligation to subdue and enslave those peoples and their territory for the Spanish Crown? Through the 1493 papal bull *Inter Caetera*,[31] Pope Alexander VI granted King Fernando and Queen Isabella almost full rights on the lands discovered by Castilians. The bull was used as a justification to dispossess, declare war, enslave, and kill indigenous peoples in order to occupy their territories.

The central polemic revolved around whether the conquest was an act of justice. To justify the cruelty of looting gold and silver from indigenous peoples, a so-called just cause for war and occupation was promptly found: Satan preyed on the indigenous peoples because they were not baptized. For some, indigenous peoples did not have the right to become Catholics because they had no soul or had one of a different kind. Juan Ginés de Sepúlveda put forward this argument to justify slaughter, which he based on the philosophy of Aristotle and the writings of Gonzalo Fernández de Oviedo (1478–1557), the Spanish writer and colonizer who considered indigenous peoples as homunculus.

Dominican friar Bartolomé de las Casas (1484–1566) defended indigenous peoples: "Indians are not barbarians, stupid or owners of a weak intelligence; on the contrary, they have great talent to learn and are willing to accept the Christian religion."[32] During the early sixteenth century in the New Spain, he was one of many friars who fought against the cruel methods used by the Spaniards to subdue indigenous peoples and erase their religion, customs, language, and any trace of their culture. Trying to understand the present in the light of the past without falling prey to anachronism or presentism, there are nonetheless aspects of a responsibility to protect in his "testimony of the destruction of the Indies" that are highly pertinent to this discussion. Bartolomé de las Casas wrote this well-known letter to Prince Felipe—son of King Carlos V of Spain, who was in charge of matters regarding the Indies—so that he could put an end to atrocities perpetrated against "Indian people, pacific, humble and docile, who offend no one."[33] Las Casas's defense of indigenous peoples against Juan Ginés de Sepúlveda is said to be the first Westernized ontological and ethical treatise of the New World. In particular, Las Casas defended the fundamentally human nature of indigenous peoples.

It was not easy to influence attitudes; and change was slow and painful. Las Casas estimated that 12 to 15 million people were killed in the New World between 1502 and 1542.[34] Before the arrival of Europeans in the Americas, there were between 90 and 112 million people. In 40 years the population in what is now Mexico diminished from 25.3 to 16.8 million, clearly one of history's starkest cases of mass atrocities. Professional soldiers slaughtered and dispersed pacific indigenous populations with no military strategies or modern weapons. As Las Casas vividly recounted:

> The Spaniards reached the villages and they left no old Indians or pregnant women without being cut in the stomach and torn to pieces. They played bets on who could open an Indian in half at one cut of a knife, or cut his head at one stroke. They took children from their mothers' breasts and threw them on the stones. They cut off the hands of men. Others were tied with dry straw and burned to death. They would stick a cane in their mouth to muffle their screams. To keep dogs trained to kill, they would bring chained Indians to be beaten and torn, so they could have public human flesh hunting. I have witnessed all of these and many other forms of cruelty never seen or heard of.[35]

Liberation arose during the eighteenth and nineteenth centuries as the core theme of independence movements promoted by Simon Bolívar and José Francisco de San Martín in South America, and José Martí in the Caribbean. Such liberators emerged from the particular conditions of mature colonized people who lived under new power relations and social practices. From a peculiar position between having a relatively privileged place in his own country and a very different one as a colonized subject, Martí conceived what is currently considered one of the precursors of international humanitarian and human rights law: "There lies in men the strength of what is just, and that is the first Rule of Law. When it is conceptualized in thought, justice is developed in formulas: this is natural Rights. And when formulas are fulfilled in life, they develop in application; the concurrence of rights creates special rights."[36]

More than a century before the Universal Declaration of Human Rights was adopted and proclaimed by the UN on 10 December 1948, Martí wrote about liberation in the following way: "Why must blood-painted means be resorted to, when not all means that illustrate with rights have been used?"[37] He was at the time advising the use of rights instead of force or violence to solve problems.

The emergence of the philosophy of liberation

From the perspective of contemporary Argentine-Mexican philosopher Enrique Dussel, one of the creators of the philosophy of liberation, the conquest of the Americas was among history's most bloody and vast mass atrocities. Latin America's philosophical tradition has not yet been able to free or distance itself from a history of cultural devastation, and economic and political oppression. Hence, philosophical discourse should aim to free peoples to stand as equals before Europe and the United States. After more than 500 years of oppression, liberation involves justice and freedom from any form of domination. In ontological terms, a human being should not belong to another and should be able to act on his or her own free will; while in ethical terms, an individual should be able to produce and reproduce his or her life and the lives of others:

> Those who function ethically and critically have recognized the victim as an autonomous human being, as the Other, as other than the norm, act, institution, ethnicity system, etc. whose possibility to live has been denied (completely or partially); the recognition of which simultaneously results in the recognition of a co-responsibility for the other as victim; a situation that obliges to take care of such victim in front of the system and to criticize the system (or aspects of the system) that cause such victimization.[38]

Twentieth-century traditions such as liberation theology and the philosophy of liberation were a response to contemporary situations of subjugation and abuse of rights across Latin America. But their roots lie in the liberation movements and thought, which date back to the Spanish conquest and colonial period. These traditions were also shaped by Christianity intertwined with Marxism. Such Catholic theologians as Gustavo Gutiérrez Merino in Peru and Leonardo Boff in Brazil confront the poverty, ignorance, and oppression suffered by most Latin American peoples. They applied some of Marx's philosophical categories and concepts with teachings from the Bible to help clarify the contextual realities of their people. Out of this intellectual fusion came a new theological and later philosophical perspective that sustained the Catholic movement that aimed to liberate Latin America. Liberation theology acquired a distinctly earthly face. The need to understand the causes of poverty and oppression gave rise to the philosophy of liberation.

Some of the key components of that philosophy have relevance for R2P:

- Philosophy is not only a specific knowledge but a practical wisdom; it is a kind of praxis related to *lebenswelt* (lifeworld). It is determined by praxis and by a non-transcendental subject shaped by history and social class.
- The philosophy of liberation binds itself to oppressed peoples through a dialectic method that critiques the totality of the system and not just specific aspects of reality. It is radical because it rejects reform or praxis that supports the oppressing system. A genuine philosopher must rid himself or herself of the fear of losing position or standing, or being expelled from a country and segregated from society. It is a weapon of the oppressed, an emblem of the ideological struggle against the dominant discourse and its hegemonic apparatus.
- Hegemonic classes in Latin America and officials from transnational corporations as well as some politicians and various civil society groups oppose the philosophy of liberation because it compromises their economic and political advantages. Nonetheless, First World philosophers can sometimes be allies of the philosophy of liberation by adhering to the critical-liberating discourse of the global South and applying it at home and abroad.

Liberation theology and the philosophy of liberation have had a crucial impact in the Americas. During the 1970s and 1980s in countries such as Brazil, Guatemala, Nicaragua, and El Salvador, many rebel and discontented groups embraced liberation theology and were inspired to struggle for better conditions for the poor and violently oppressed. Religious women and men as well as artists, poets, philosophers, and intellectuals aided liberation causes with their weapons of podium, paintbrush, and pen. A paradigmatic example was Monsignor Oscar Romero, the Catholic archbishop of El Salvador who was murdered while conducting mass because his ministry tirelessly defended human rights and denounced violence and military repression.[39]

Thus, liberation theology and the philosophy of liberation and the movements that they inspired can be seen as Latin America's particular contribution to Southern and global philosophy. As a response to mass suffering, they have had a major influence on academic and political events. Critical philosophy has a vital contribution to make in shaping and implementing new norms that respond to mass suffering and in influencing political action. Liberation philosophy is not a quaint "Third World" philosophy the time of which has passed with the ostensible end of colonization. Its core elements are directly relevant to R2P in helping to shape the norm's application. In expanding, deepening, and implementing R2P, it would be valuable to draw on liberation philosophy, normatively and practically. As José Martí observed, "One just principle from the depths of a cave is more powerful than any army."[40]

Philosophical concepts and ethical values relevant to R2P

As a general reaction to mass atrocities during the last few centuries, and following the Rwandan genocide and the ethnic cleansing in the former Yugoslavia specifically, the R2P norm not only emerged but also was formally adopted by heads of state and government at the 2005 UN World Summit. This new norm raises several philosophical and ethical questions. Is there a moral or ethical responsibility toward victims? Who needs protection and who is responsible for providing it? What are the fundamental ethical concepts and values that could generate the foundation of R2P? Finally, from both an ethical and pragmatic perspective, what can be deemed mass atrocities requiring concerted and preventive action?

At the outset, some key concepts should be clarified. Philosophical discourse is dynamic, and so its vocabulary varies over time and from one culture to another. To begin, the difference between ethics and morals should be distinguished. The word ethics comes from the Greek *ethos* (custom) and *êthos* (character). Moral comes from the Latin *mos, mores,* according to Cicero's translation of *ethos.* Thus in ancient Rome ethics and morals were synonymous and, in everyday language, some people still use them in the same way.[41] However, over time and among various traditions, these terms have acquired different meanings, so philosophers must clarify their conceptual use. Morals is usually understood nowadays as the series of norms, principles, and values established by a cultural group in order to shape or govern peoples' behavior in matters concerning right or wrong in their relationships with others. Morality is the realization of the subject's behavior in the everyday lives of people. In other words, it is the way people live and internalize morals. Ethics can be understood as the philosophical study of morals, which provides an analysis of the reasons for the norms, standards, principles, and values, and questions their origins and functions. Adolfo Sánchez Vázquez characterizes morals and ethics as follows: "If we are to understand morals as a number of norms and regulations of action devoted to rule the relationships among individuals in a certain community, the meaning, function and validity of them cannot stop being historically changed in the various societies."[42] "Ethics," he further explains, "is theory, investigation or explication of a certain type of human experience … or form of behavior: that of morals, but deemed in its totality, diversity and variety."[43]

Human rights are considered to be the foundation of the responsibility to protect. However, as Jack Donnelly mentions, "human rights should be understood as a political conception of justice around which an international overlapping consensus has formed over the past half century."[44] Human rights, together with an ethical investigation of specific cases, can be of great help in shaping R2P principles and procedures.

Article 1 of the Universal Declaration of Human Rights reads: "All human beings are born free and equal in dignity and rights. They are endowed with reason and conscience and should act towards one another in a spirit of brotherhood." This article encompasses several ethical concepts: freedom, dignity, reason, conscience, and solidarity. Without freedom, reason and conscience, morals or ethics would not be possible, for only free, rational, and conscious beings can be held morally responsible for their actions. The moral subject must act consciously on his or her own free will and assume responsibility for the consequences. The ethical concept of human dignity is useful to determine who can be deemed victims of mass atrocities, for not all people in distress need the help of outsiders—from another community or an international organization.

Dignity has been construed in many forms. For Kant, it refers to the ability of humans to create law and freely conduct their moral life. They may also use any means toward the achievement of goals, but always treating the other as an end and never as a means. Hereinafter the Kantian conception of human dignity will be used.

A few words on the concept of responsibility are necessary to understand its ethical scope. The noun "responsibility" and the adjective "responsible" are derived from the Latin term *respondere*, which means capable of responding, answering, being "morally accountable for one's actions" or for taking care of others, as free, conscious, willing, and rational human beings before other equal beings. Moral responsibility is attributed to individuals, who as moral subjects or agents act freely doing right or wrong; however, the same argument applies to institutions that are composed of human beings.

Dussel's concept of responsibility is relevant to our discussion of R2P, as it is not only moral but ethical. He uses indistinctly the terms "moral" and "factual morality" to refer to the current status quo, and "ethics" as the aim and struggle for a better future: a utopia of justice and liberation. Considering such liberation praxis as an ethical obligation, every human being must be responsible for preserving his or her own life; hence, life is the criterion on which he founds his material universal ethical principle,[45] according to which everyone who acts ethically must produce, reproduce, and develop the life of every human subject in a community. Ethical responsibility is thus invariably an act of solidarity for and between oneself and others: "Love moves us to assume the Other; to assume their joy and grief. Such mutual responsibility for the Others, what it is superiorly in itself, intertwined by intersubjectivity, constitutes the community."[46]

The ethical perspective of Dussel's philosophy of liberation may seem very different from the voices of other Western ethical discourses (who are his interlocutors) because his point of departure is that the history of poor countries is marked by conquest, colonization, oppression, exploitation, and plunder. The ethical conclusion facing such a scenario is the need to free those peoples putting forward philosophy as a weapon, so that justice can be achieved. In this context, justice occurs when the ethical attitude is to take responsibility for victims of injustice, who are incapable of defending their own rights and consequently cannot fulfill their life project. Being responsible for the Other is thus taking care of the victim's life project as if it were our own, in a total act of solidarity and justice.

The responsibility to protect goes beyond the political idea of justice.[47] It creates a relationship between victims as subjects of protection, on the one hand, and policymakers and other agents who directly take action, on the other. Thus, ethical responsibility is shared, with respective asymmetries.[48]

Rights are always linked to duties: one gives to a community and is compensated by the giving of others. Consequently, a country's legislature could pass laws, for example, to bind governments to aid communities in instances of natural or human-made disasters. However, from an ethical perspective, the question is whether it is possible to be just, to give, to be generous, and to aid our fellow human beings without a moral reason or a binding law and without the expectation of reward or praise. For Dussel that should be the sense of solidarity toward violated women, discriminated races, exploited social classes, seniors confined to asylums, the poor, the "wretched of the earth," and future generations who will inherit a devastated earth.[49]

Consequently, the ethical duty is to intervene in the qualitative progress of history by constructing a new order that eliminates oppression, exclusion, and genocide. Dussel's approach, based on the material principle of life, is opposed to formal ethics, which places the foundation of ethics in an abstract subject of knowledge instead of a real living and, in many cases, suffering corporal human being with real necessities. Justice means the instauration of a politics of justice—that is, the liberation of the poor. The ethical act, however, must go beyond a mere rational act or formal ethics and encompass responding to calls for help by those who are suffering. The concept of positive obligation is used here. It entails a strong bond between those who suffer and those who alleviate their suffering in a free, disinterested, and immediate response.

The word "obligation" derives from the verb "oblige" (from Latin *ob* = toward and *ligare* = bind), meaning to bind or be morally constrained toward others. Its negative dimension consists of not hurting others, but its positive dimension goes far beyond, for in order to be ethical, action must be taken to aid others, especially those in distress.[50]

In the pursuit of its positive dimensions, ethical obligation reunites with Kant's two antagonistic ways of being moral: autonomous and heteronomous. It is heteronomous because the victims of disaster cry for help (explicitly or implicitly), so the responsibility to protect comes from the outside, from someone alien to the subject's conscience. It is autonomous because the moral subject freely decides to *ob-ligate* him- or herself to engage in aid.[51] Ethically, it should not be a matter of helping others with the expectation of some kind of recognition, praise, or reward, or to take economic or political advantage of a situation. The ethical obligation is both an ethics of duty and an ethics of virtue and care because its final goal is justice, which in this context means to do everything in one's power to avoid massive human suffering.

It is now necessary to turn to the notion of "victim," which is directly related to responsibility and obligation. Based on the foregoing, two notions of victim are used here. One is Dussel's notion of a victim as someone who cannot obtain the required material means to develop and fulfill a dignified life; the other is John Caputo's notion of "victims of disaster," those who have lost the capacity to protect themselves because they have lost their guiding star.

Not all those who suffer can be labeled "victims." Dussel devoted considerable attention to the concept of victim as intimately related to his conception of ethics, and thus his depiction is particularly relevant to this discussion. He differentiates two kinds of ethical consciousness. The first is as an accomplice of the system with a theory of good and evil that implicitly supports the status quo. The second type of ethical consciousness is critical of the current order, its morals, institutions, and politics, which inaugurates a new kind of rationality from the perspective of victims, namely "those who cannot produce and reproduce their own lives, who have been excluded from discussion, who are affected by some death situation (at any level, there are many of different intensity and dramatism)."[52]

It is useful to circumscribe Dussel's conception of victim because there may be groups who are able to overcome their own calamitous situation (war, exclusion, ignorance, poverty) without external aid. Moreover, it is possible that they might even perceive certain kinds of protection or feelings of compassion toward them as offensive. Each state and civil society must create protection institutions or strengthen existing ones. Narrowing the criteria allows us to focus on those so helpless that the need for protection by others is imperative.

John Caputo's concept of "victims of disaster" is useful to narrow the category. Victims of disaster (*dis-astrum*) are those who literally have no star to light their path in life.[53] Their distress generates the ethical positive obligation of those who are able to provide protection. Caputo defines obligation as follows:

> Obligation is a feeling, the feeling of being bound (*ligare, ob-ligare, re-ligare*), an element of my feeling *befindlichkeit*, but I cannot get on top of it, scale its heights, catch a glimpse of its rising up. It comes at me, comes over me, overtakes me, seizes hold of me. As soon as I come to be I am already in its grasp. I have neither the will nor the means to deny it. When I am obliged I do not know by what dark powers I am held. I only know/feel/find myself caught up, in the midst of obligation, in its snare, in the scandal, in a panic—perhaps even blinded.[54]

He further elaborates:

> Obligation comes over us from the other whose transcendence shocks our freedom and autonomy. But they lay siege to us with a particular forcefulness in the case of what I will call disasters. A disaster … is a matter of being cut off from the star that protects us from misfortune (*dis-astrum*), a matter of running out of luck.[55]

> … A disaster is an economic notion. It refers to an unrecoverable loss. By irretrievable loss I mean a wasting of life. Something that cannot be incorporated into a "result," that cannot be led back into a gain. You cannot grow another body; you cannot regain wasted years … you cannot compensate someone who has spent the best years of his life in unjust imprisonment, or whose health has been irreparably destroyed, whose family has been killed. You cannot grow new flesh, new time.[56]

Not all people are in a position to respond to victims of disaster. The degree of moral responsibility varies among individuals, groups, and organizations that have the capacity to do so. What a common citizen can do to protect victims from a powerful individual or system is very different from what an international organization or foreign government or a coalition of the willing could. From this we can extrapolate that the rights of victims give rise to an ethical obligation on all actors with the means to provide protection. However, the ethical obligation falls more heavily on those individuals or states or organizations with the wherewithal—financial, logistic, diplomatic, and military—especially those with a specific mandate to protect victims.

In closing this discussion, it is worth referring to the genealogical perspective and Foucault briefly. Based on Foucault, it could be said that current victims are not the same as the ones of the sixteenth century discussed earlier,[57] because subjects are the product of power relations and social practices. If those practices and how they shape certain subjectivities are understood in their historical development, then current victims can be better understood. Foucault called such a project "ontology of the present." Thus, once we are able to describe the victim of a mass atrocity and the causes of its emergence, the next step is to ethically accept or reject it; if rejected, the task then is to look for the mechanisms to change existing subjectivities for better ones. An ideal goal for R2P and all those institutions and individuals who assume the ethical responsibility for the victims of mass atrocities would be "no more victims"—or the operational meaning of "never again," the cry that followed the horrors of the Holocaust.

Dussel's concept of responsibility resembles Caputo's concept of obligation, and they both are more comprehensive interpretations of responsibility than is generally the case for other analysts. Dussel lays ethical foundations for his concept of responsibility, while Caputo resorts to something more "instinctive."

What conclusions can we draw from this brief discussion of philosophical concepts related to R2P? The Marxist tradition, liberation theology, and the philosophy of liberation, as well as other Western and non-Western discourses, would all agree on Kant's categorical imperative to preserve human dignity and not treat humans as means to an end. In the face of mass atrocities, humans are denied their dignity, deprived of life itself, and used as a means to fulfill political or economic ends. A genocidal regime's pursuit in terrorizing or exterminating a targeted population clearly violates Kant's categorical imperative and generates an ethical responsibility to redress the situation. Thus, whenever human beings are treated as means instead of ends and the state does not respond with the means to restore dignity, fulfill human rights, and defend life itself, it is ethically right for these human beings to seek external help once other measures have failed.

Having examined some of the main ethical concepts and values, it is significant from a philosophical perspective that R2P as adopted by the World Summit is defined as a responsibility, but not strongly enough supported by member states to be conceived of as entailing a positive ethical or legally binding obligation or duty to respond. Whether deliberate or accidental, the result is weakness and the risk of non-implementation without a sense of ethical, moral, or legal obligation.

A pertinent conclusion emerges from this discussion for the application of R2P in its three stages. First, in order to determine in which cases people outside of a specific community or state have the positive ethical obligation to intervene, the preservation of life and the value of each individual human life from a philosophical perspective could be a strong and valid criterion to shape the R2P norm and compel protection during an active phase of mass atrocities. The value of each human life underlined in philosophy implies that attention has to be paid to protecting every single human life endangered during mass atrocities as not only a moral but an ethical responsibility. That is, it is imperative to act to save human lives during mass atrocities due to the ethical value of each individual life and the obligation to defend life. Second, in order to give ethical weight to the corollary obligations inherent in R2P to both prevent atrocities and to rebuild societies after atrocities have ended, the concept of a good quality of life provides philosophical justification. The ethical imperative of preserving a good quality of life would require attention to the preventive and capacity-building dimensions of R2P. In sum, responsibility neither begins nor ends with protection. It implies maintaining a good quality of life in the preventive stage to elude a descent into mass atrocities. It further requires restoring a good quality of life after the end of mass atrocities in the post-conflict peace building phase.

Preventing mass atrocities by expanding their scope?

In light of the ethical imperative that values each individual life and sees the defense of life as the highest objective, the very concept of mass atrocities should be the object of philosophical scrutiny. While the current legal and political limitations of R2P are clear, if we are to take this norm seriously, every individual human being has infinite value from a philosophical and ethical standpoint. Thus, all efforts should be made to avoid the suffering of each and every human being. Until now, however, proponents of R2P have concentrated on genocide, war crimes, crimes against humanity, and ethnic cleansing. The reasons for political realism are clear, but genealogically speaking the events of a mass atrocity have a history; they occur in a specific place and time and reflect the convergence of specific social practices, power relations, and discourses, along with their respective "truths."

The concept of mass atrocities varies from one cultural context to another. Thus, a few remarks could help situate the emergence of victims and mass atrocities in the Americas, the case covered in most depth in this chapter, and the global South more generally. Two forms of mass atrocities can be identified:

- Evident: These consist of genocide and widespread massacres, in which a visible and large number of innocent people are killed deliberately in one sole event or series of similar events.
- Veiled: These imply prolonged human suffering also resulting in death caused by other human beings to a considerable number of people, underpinned by structural factors (e.g., discrimination, inequality, lack of opportunity, domination, and other forms of injustice).

In both evident and veiled cases of mass atrocity, however, countless people suffer. As we have seen, the political consensus at the moment means that R2P applies only to proximate prevention and urgent measures to forestall or halt genocide, war crimes, crimes against humanity, and ethnic cleansing. However, the logic of philosophical inquiry and the application of ethics should, over time, push decision makers to consider the need to give more attention to the structural violence that affects millions of people daily and all too often results in the mass atrocities as agreed by the World Summit.

Moreover, the two kinds of violence are related. Structural or everyday violence, which is referred to here as "veiled" because it is less dramatic and visible, is almost always the precondition, precursor, and tell-tale indicator of impending and evident mass atrocities. As in Rwanda, genocide is preceded by cultural ethnocide. Each mass atrocity is also preceded by structural injustices, patterns of discrimination, marginalization, and systemic violence that create a permissive climate of hatred and political violence, and culminate in targeted mass atrocities.

In the first decade of the twenty-first century, countless deaths are being caused by organized crime and the structural systems that make some ordinary citizens live in constant terror and uncertainty. In Mexican cities that border the United States, about 3,000 to 4,000 people are murdered annually. In places like Juarez, thousands of people are killed yearly, presumably by organized crime, but many others are kidnapped or tortured, have their ears or fingers cut off, and many more are extorted, threatened, or lose their livelihoods. Structurally maintained poverty and inequality, as well as insecurity and violent crime, force thousands of poor people to migrate internally or to risk their lives by migrating across international borders in search of survival and a decent livelihood.

In their own countries migrants are victims of structural violence and constant violations of human rights. In other countries they are treated as criminals. Their rights to both life itself and a decent quality of life are denied. They are hunted and gunned down,[58] incarcerated, and forced to return to their places of origin with near-certain death from crime or poverty. Contrasting with such a way to treat migrants, Dussel constantly refers to the Hammurabi Code, and its recommendation of aiding foreigners, widows, and orphans. This ethical conduct and hospitality toward strangers is echoed in all philosophical and spiritual traditions, Judeo-Christian and non-Western alike.

To return to Appadurai's classification, the poor were lured to join the diasporas of hope in order to seek survival and livelihoods in the more prosperous West. Removed from the oppression, insecurity, and poverty at home, they are members of diasporas of terror and despair, deprived of rights and often of life itself. These cases constitute flagrant violations of human rights.

Ironically, before mass atrocities, systemic patterns of group targeting, discrimination, and marginalization compel members of these groups to begin migrating outward to guarantee their survival. However, because a mass atrocity has not yet occurred, these migrations are ignored or treated as ordinary economic phenomena rather than being interpreted as possible precursors of genocide or ethnic cleansing. Thus, the opportunity to act early and prevent them also is missed. So too, the increasing violence directed by ordinary citizens in host countries at migrant groups with overtones of racism and ethnocentrism has not as yet rung alarm bells among decision makers concerned with mass atrocities. Both the reasons that make migrants leave and the treatment that they receive in countries of asylum are potential reasons for paying closer attention to migration and migrants as ongoing cases of veiled atrocities and potential cases of evident mass atrocities.

More generally, recognizing the direct and indirect linkages between evident and veiled mass atrocities and addressing structural violence would be an effective way to implement R2P's preventive and capacity-building dimensions, which the UN secretary-general emphasized in his January 2009 report to the General Assembly.[59]

Conclusion: achieving (an imperfect) utopia—implementing R2P informed by philosophy and ethics

This chapter seeks to demonstrate how the application of philosophy and ethics is relevant for the advance of the R2P norm. The distinct philosophical perspective of R2P consists of viewing mass atrocities from the vantage point of both the victims and the moral subjects willing to assume the responsibility to protect them from harm.

The contributions of philosophy to strengthening the responsibility to protect are numerous. First, a genealogical approach to philosophy, which understands the importance of history and context, and considers philosophy as the pursuit of justice and human dignity, is the most relevant perspective for the development of the R2P norm. Non-Western philosophers in Latin America and elsewhere have been influenced by and in turn have influenced historic events. Non-Western philosophies were not merely intellectual currents, but they deeply influenced and mobilized individuals and shaped events, particularly in the struggle against colonization and dictatorship, and for liberty, independence, and democracy.

Second, philosophy is not merely an intellectual pursuit but has value-added in responding to contextual realities, especially to suffering and injustice. Indicating alternative and more desirable realities or "utopias" and influencing political and social outcomes are of the essence. The discussion of ethical concepts revealed that value for life, human dignity, and quality of life could provide foundations for fostering R2P before, during, and after mass atrocities. It called for a spontaneous feeling of solidarity and relationship between the victim of disaster and the respondents based on compassion and ethical obligation—that is, built on justice rather than charity, and eschewing vested interests or personal reward. In order to give weight to the preventive dimension, it argued for an expansion of how mass atrocities are conceptualized, recognition of the linkage between veiled and evident violence, and addressing the former in order to prevent deterioration into mass atrocities.

Ethical values such as dignity, liberty, justice, and life—all included in the Universal Declaration of Human Rights—must be constantly reviewed by philosophers because these concepts are mentioned but should be interpreted in their philosophical content or context. Working relationships between UN officials and critical philosophers would be helpful in security decision making, and specifically in reflecting upon and elaborating the criteria to decide where and how the R2P norm can and should be applied to prevent, react, or rebuild. If we agree that R2P and human rights are political, that dignity is their ethical foundation, and that moral concepts change over time and across societies, then the value-added of philosophy and ethics is to help shape strategies for developing and implementing the responsibility to protect.

However, good intentions are not and never have been enough: power relations that underlie both evident and veiled violence and cause mass atrocities should be analyzed and understood. To alter patterns of domination and asymmetrical relationships, the exercise of another form of power is necessary. Countries of the global South can contribute to the preventive phase of R2P by strengthening institutions to honor and promote human rights and human security, which can be achieved with actions such as struggling against governmental corruption, striving for educational quality and institutions, reducing inequality and eliminating discrimination, and teaching philosophy, ethics, and critical thinking.

In short, political action is fundamental in what is effectively a proposal for co-responsibility, as outlined below. While the moral responsibility and ethical obligations of sovereign states and their populations are key, ultimately individual change and co-responsibility will be decisive in ensuring that R2P is no longer a distant dream but a concrete reality. Each person should inject moral norms and values to constitute him or herself as a moral subject who is ultimately responsible for avoiding evil and promoting good even without external pressure. At the same time, the notion of "co-responsibility" is useful, the necessary efforts to identify and to find partners—be they local authorities or national governments, local or international institutions, associations, and organizations, civilian or military stake-holders at any level. The proverbial bottom-line amounts to taking responsibility upon oneself or one's polity and not washing one's hands and relying upon others to come to the rescue.

Dussel's category of political postulates is relevant because it resembles the notion of utopias: they are never completely realized but serve as a guiding light, as references to orient actions. Such was the function of Kant's perpetual peace. Postulates present perfect, ideal situations; regardless of their political impracticality, they serve a practical political function in imagining new horizons and possible institutions as well as motivating individuals and organizations to strive for change.[60] Horacio Cerutti, an Argentine/Mexican philosopher, describes the utility of utopias:

> My subject is thus the operating utopia in the current history of our America.[61] Namely, the one that studies the tension between what is desirable and the given, which mobilizes the collective memory and provides meaning to the eager searches for something better. The issue is, in the region that was *topos* for alien utopias, to vindicate the right for our own utopia.[62]

R2P seemed utopian only a few years ago, when it appeared impossible to break the status quo interpretation of absolute state sovereignty and the accompanying norm of nonintervention in the domestic affairs of states. The 2005 World Summit took a dramatic normative step forward, but now the next and perhaps more arduous step will be to translate this utopian norm into reality and thus actually prevent future and effectively halt ongoing mass atrocities. The paths on our unfinished journey toward the ideal will be challenging. Cerruti's advice is relevant:

> Does this mean that the new to emerge will be perfect and the definite solution to all humankind's problems? By all means no! It just means that the novelty—always perfectible—shall emerge from changes in the codes that rule the current system, from the structural transformation of such a system, from the instauration of what is unedited regarding the existing status quo. The root or matrix of the unedited is constituted by such daydreams and longed-for ideals, the relevance of which is feasible only on the condition of a profound structural transformation that allows us to break the petrified rules of coded social relationships.[63]

The moment is ripe for R2P to effect a profound structural transformation in human and international relations.

Notes

1 There are many terms for countries that are not included among the globe's advanced industrialized countries, such as Third World, undeveloped,

developing, non-Western, and Southern. None of these truly reflect the geographical, political, economic, or cultural status of these heterogeneous places. Nonetheless, this chapter uses the term "global South."

2 See Diogenes Laertius, *Lives and Opinions of Emminent Philosophers in Ten Books* (Cambridge, Mass.: Harvard University Press, 1925), Book X.

3 Richard Rorty finds in Plato's writings two different traditions: Plato's philosopher king and Socrates's cultural intermediary. In the first tradition, *episteme* means true knowledge. The philosopher king is apt to rule because he knows the essence (*eidos*) of all things and of concepts like justice, beauty, truth, and goodness. For the second tradition, true knowledge is a fallacy, for there are no essences, only dialogical relations from which truth emerges. Hence, philosophy places itself at the service of life, seeking better forms of living; such is the meaning of wisdom. Following Nietzsche, Richard Rorty speaks about a "joyful wisdom," not as knowledge, but as an aid for living, a joyful living. See Richard Rorty, *La filosofía y el espejo de la naturaleza* (Madrid: Ediciones Cátedra, 1979), 288–9.

4 Throughout history, dominating groups, acting as the philosopher king and based on the presumed possession of the truth, have committed all types of atrocities, such as discrimination, exclusion, extermination, and racism. The Socratic cultural intermediary tradition has been in favor of diversity, dialogue, conversation, and respect. Richard Rorty, *Philosophy and the Mirror of Nature* (Oxford: Blackwell, 1979), 317. Derived from Socrates, Rorty's ethical criteria is to follow the cultural principles of non-humiliation and non-cruelty: "The principal motive behind the new directions taken in scholarship in the United States since the sixties has been the urge to do something for people who have been humiliated—to help victims of socially acceptable forms of sadism by making such sadism no longer acceptable." Rorty, *Achieving Our Country: Leftist Thought in Twentieth Century America* (Cambridge, Mass.: Harvard University Press, 1998), 80.

5 See, for example, Marx's *11th Theses on Feuerbach*: "Philosophers have hitherto only interpreted the world in various ways; the point is to change it." Text available at: www.marxists.org/archive/marx/works/1845/theses/index.htm.

6 Examples include Nietzsche's vitalism, Foucault's search for different forms of subjectivities, and Dussel's aim for the liberation of Southern peoples from the vestiges of colonialism and the evil effects of globalization and Eurocentrism.

7 Readers familiar with philosophy will recognize Aristotle, Epicurus, Hegel, Marx, Wittgenstein, and Foucault in this characterization of philosophy.

8 "An interview with Michel Foucault by Raul-Fornet-Betancourt, Helmut Becker and Alfredo Gomez-Muller," in *Hermenéutica del sujeto* (Madrid: Ediciones de la Piqueta, 1987), 142. Text also available at: jingshenfengxi.blogspot.com/2009/11/entrevista-michel-foucault.html (author translation from Spanish to English).

9 Genealogical refers to philosophical traditions with an historical approach, many of them heirs of Nietzsche's *Genealogy of Morals*. See Michel Foucault, "Nietzsche, Genealogy, History," in *The Foucault Reader*, ed. Paul Rabinow (London: Penguin, 1991), 83.

10 Enrique Dussel has a different thesis regarding modernity. In his view, modernity began in Medieval towns in 1492, when Europe confronted "the

Other," defeated and controlled it, and could define itself as a discoverer, conqueror, and colonizer. See Enrique Dussel, *1492. El encubrimiento del otro. Hacia el origen del mito de la modernidad* (Madrid: Nueva Utopía, 1992).

11 International Commission on Intervention and State Sovereignty, *The Responsibility to Protect* (Ottawa: International Development Research Centre, 2001). See also, Thomas G. Weiss and Don Hubert, *The Responsibility to Protect: Research, Bibliography, Background* (Ottawa: International Development Research Centre, 2001).

12 Aristotle, "Ética nicomaquea," in *Obras* (Madrid: Aguilar, 1986).

13 As an example of these traditions in African culture, Eugenio Nkogo Ontó asserts that it was in Africa that the first graphic systems of humanity were developed 3,000 years BCE on Egyptian papyrus. Although African as well as all other philosophies are usually deemed as emanating from Western thought, Nkogo argues that in Africa religion and philosophy as myth were invented long before the pre-Socratics in Greece. He explores African thought and categorizes it as philosophical, looking for the recognition of Africa's primacy and influence on Greek philosophy. See Eugenio Nkogo, *Síntesis sistemática de la filosofía africana* (Barcelona: Ediciones Carena, 2005).

14 In his book, *Síntesis sistemática de la filosofía africana*, Eugenio Nkogo mentions that Lumumba was killed in front of the United Nations Blue Berets and humiliated.

15 Fanon was born in Martinique and thus was not African by birth.

16 Mohandas Karacham Gandhi, *An Autobiography: The Story of My Experiments with Truth* (Boston: Beacon Press, 1983).

17 See Arjun Appadurai, *La modernidad descentrada* (Mexico City: Fondo de Cultura Económica, 1998).

18 Elizabeth Suzanne Kassab, "Contemporary Arab Critique of Islamicization," in *Re-ethnicizing the Minds? Cultural Revival in Contemporary Thought*, ed. Thorsten Botz-Bornstein and Jürgen Hengelbrock (Amsterdam: Rodopi, 2006), 323.

19 Bassam Romaya, "Iraq and the Question of Philosophy," in *Re-ethnicizing the Minds?* 354.

20 Gareth Evans, *The Responsibility to Protect: Ending Mass Atrocity Crimes Once and For All* (Washington, DC: Brookings Institution Press, 2008), 53.

21 Excerpts from Carlos Ripol, *Marti Thoughts/Pensamientos*, available at: www2.fiu.edu/~fcf/marti.pensamientos.10797.html.

22 I will not enter here into the polemic of whether cultures such as African, Mayan, Hindu, Islamic, Chinese, or Náhuatl developed their own philosophy, which is irrelevant, as long as we recognize and respect other forms of thought, regardless of their name. Ancient Mesoamerican cultures, such as the Mexicas, posed questions regarding the beginning and end of life, and the order of the universe, similar to Western philosophical thought. Miguel León-Portilla's work *La filosofía Náhuatl* (Ciudad Universitaria, Mexico: Universidad Nacional Autónoma de México, 1979) is devoted to demonstrating that Nahuas developed a philosophical system. Regarding this issue, León-Portilla states that, "if we recognize among prehispanic nahuas, the existence of individuals concerned about 'problems' in those things that others lived and accepted ordinarily, then it is possible to say that all these 'discoverers of problems' about the world and men had found the way to philosophical wisdom." See León-Portilla, *La filosofía Náhuatl*, 5. Alfredo

López Austin's work is also a must to study Mesoamerican thought, especially religion. One interesting work is: *Cuerpo humano e ideología* (Ciudad Universitaria, Mexico: Universidad Nacional Autónoma de México, Instituto de Investigaciones Antropológicas, 1996).

23 This is a manuscript written in 1524 that recorded the conversation of the last *tlamatinime* or Aztec wise men and Franciscan friars. See Miguel León-Portilla, *Coloquios y doctrina cristiana, con que los doce frailes de San Francisco, enviados por el papa Adriano VI y por el emperador Carlos V, convirtieron a los indios de la Nueva España, en lengua mexicana y española. Los diálogos de 1524, dispuestos por fray Bernardino de Sahagún y sus colaboradores* (Mexico City: Universidad Nacional Autónoma de México, Instituto de Investigaciones Históricas, 1986).

24 See, *Huehuehtlahtolli, Testimonios de la Antigua palabra* (Mexico City: Secretaría de Educación Pública, Fondo de Cultura Económica, 1991). From a genealogical point of view, Osiris González considers that "*Huehuetlahtolli* were related to 'disciplinary mechanisms' that ensure the continuity of cultural values, moral rules and educational institutions. Most of the time they were reserved for special occasions like births, religious rituals, weddings, war speeches, and funerals. The *huehuetlahtolli,* recompiled by Andres de Olmos, show the importance attributed to education, in the moral formation of pre-Columbian people." Osiris González, "Ethical issues in Nahuatl pre-Columbian thought: A genealogical approach," (2010), available at: www.estudiosgenealogicos.com/Publicaciones/ArchivosCege/ETHICAL_ISSUES_IN_NAHUATL_PRE-COLUMBIAN_THOUGHT[1].pdf

25 "Entra su reino, entra en nuestras almas el Verdadero Dios. Marchita está la vida; y muerto el corazón de sus flores. Los que lo estiran todo hasta romperlo, dañan y chupan las flores de los otros ... No hay verdad en la palabra de los extranjeros." Translated from Nahuatl to Spanish by López Portillo. Author translation from Spanish to English. See jamillan.com/para_blat.htm.

26 See Enrique Dussel, *Historia de la Iglesia en América Latina* (Mexico City: Editorial Nova Terra, 1974), 3.

27 Among the Nahuas, noble families (*pipiltin*) sent their young boys to the *Calmecac* (house of tears), where they received an intellectual education, preparing them to be priests, governors, or learn the art of war; the rest of the population (*macehualtin*) sent them to the *Telpochcalli* (house of the young boys), to learn arts and crafts, as well as the use of weapons. Girls received their education at home. *Cuilcacalli* (house of chant) was a place where adolescents went to sing and dance.

28 Marcelo Méndez, "Formas de dominación mexica," available at: www.estudiosgenealogicos.com/Publicaciones/ArchivosCege/FORMAS%20DE%20DOMINACIN%20MEXICA.pdf.

29 For a discussion on the emergence of new forms of subjectivities, based on the Foucauldian genealogy, see Yolanda Angulo Parra, "Latin America Between Horror and Beauty: A Critical Approach to the Effects of Globalization," in *Re-ethnicizing the Minds?*, 81–98; and Yolanda Angulo "Therapeutic Philosophy: A Counseling Alternative for Women in Prison," July 2006, available at: www.globaljusticecenter.org/papers2006_name.htm.

30 See Michel Foucault, *Society Must Be Defended: Lectures at The College De France 1975–1976* (New York: Picador, 2003).

31 See the full text of the papal bull *Inter Caetera* translated into English at: www.kwabs.com/bull_of_1493.html.
32 Lewis Hanke, *La humanidad es una* (Mexico City: Fondo de Cultura Económica, 1973), 100.
33 Bartolomé de las Casas, *Tratados I* (Mexico City: Fondo de Cultura Económica, 1965), 11.
34 In his letter to Prince Felipe, Bartolomé de las Casas mentions that Spanish soldiers killed "mil cuentos de gentes," which means 1,000 million people. Las Casas, *Brevísima relación de la destrucción de las Indias* (Mexico City: Fondo de Cultura Económica, 1985). Although his figures may be exaggerated, there is no doubt that mass killings, death, torture, and slavery occurred. Indirect causes of deaths were the appearance of diseases unknown in America before the arrival of the Spaniards and changes in the mode of production. The controversy regarding the number of deaths and the methods of the conquest still remain, with some defending the Spanish Crown and others denouncing the cruelty against the indigenous peoples. Leaving the issue of figures aside, this can be interpreted as a real case of action produced by the philosopher king attitude, for some of the main reasons used to justify the bloody conquest were universal and ahistorical "Truths" regarding God, religion, and the nature of human beings. Forty years after the arrival of Spaniards, Las Casas clearly depicts the true motives for those "unjust, cruel, bloody and tyrannical wars": gold and other riches (21).
35 Las Casas, *Brevísima relación de la destrucción de las Indias*, 25.
36 José Martí, "Oral Lessons," *Revista Universal* 6, no. 18 (1875): 234.
37 Quoted in: Hubert Jerez Mariño, *El cantar de Martí* (Plantation, FL: Jerez Publishing Inc., 1999), 171.
38 Enrique Dussel, *Ética de la Liberación en la era de la globalización y la exclusión* (Mexico City: Editorial Trotta, 1998), 376.
39 For an overview of the first decades of liberation theology, see Roberto Oliveros Maqueo, "Historia Breve de la Teología de Liberación (1962–90)," available at: www.servicioskoinonia.org/relat/300.htm. See also excerpts from Leonardo Boff and Clodovis Boff, *Introducing Liberation Theology: History, Politics and Salvation* (Maryknoll, NY: Orbis Books, 1987), available at: www.landreform.org/boff2.htm.
40 See Lillian Martinez, "Jose Marti: Cuban Statesman, Poet, and Journalist (1853–95)," available at: www2.fiu.edu/~fcf/marti.pensamientos.10797.html.
41 For a precise discussion of the genealogy of these concepts, see Ernst Tughendhat, *Lecciones de ética* (Barcelona: Gedisa, 1997), 35–36; and Yolanda Angulo, *Ética y valores 1, enfoque por competencias* (Mexico City: Editorial Santillana, 2010).
42 Adolfo Sánchez Vázquez, *Ética* (Mexico City, Editorial Grijalbo, 1969), 33.
43 Vázquez, *Ética*, 20.
44 Jack Donnelly, "Human dignity and Human Rights," *Protecting Dignity: An Agenda for Human Rights* (2009), 82, available at: www.udhr60.ch/report/donnelly-HumanDignity_0609.pdf.
45 Such a statement has been refuted by Karl-Otto Apel, for he considers life to be a point of departure but not the founding concept of ethics. For a discussion of life as the foundation of ethics, see Enrique Dussel, "Foundation of ethics? Human life: from Porfirio Miranda to Ignacio Ellacuría,"

Andamios 4, no. 7 (2007): available at: www.scielo.org.mx/scielo.php?script=sci_arttext&pid=S1870-00632007000200007&lng=en&nrm=iso.

46 Dussel, "Foundation of ethics?" 17.

47 "Critical is when the politician has left behind the ingenuity of thinking that the in-forced system, for being such, is already just. When the system is seen from the perspective of those oppressed and excluded by the same, the politician acquires a 'critical' deconstructive consciousness and is willing to transform whatever is necessary." Enrique Dussel, *20 tesis de política* (Mexico City: CREFAL, Siglo XXI, 2006), 157. (The author's translation from Spanish to English.)

48 Both the exercise of power and the degree of responsibility are asymmetrical.

49 See Enrique Dussel, *Reconstrucción del Concepto de "Tolerancia" (de la Intolerancia a la Solidaridad)*, available at: www.pucp.edu.pe/eventos/congresos/filosofia/programa_general/viernes/plenariamatutina/DusselEnrique.pdf.

50 See Tughendhat, *Lecciones de ética*.

51 In my interpretation, there are two forms of heteronomy, namely, the Kantian one, according to which one cannot be an ethical human being if the motivation to act well comes from the outside. Following Caputo, I have argued that not all "outsides" are equal. Thus there is another kind of heteronomy that attends, hears, and acts in favor of those who are effectively victims of disaster. See Yolanda Angulo, *Ética y Valores 1* (Mexico City: Editorial Santillana, 2004), 34–37.

52 Dussel, *Ética de la Liberación*, 299.

53 See John D. Caputo, *Against Ethics* (Bloomington: Indiana University Press, 1993).

54 Caputo, *Against Ethics*, 27.

55 Caputo, *Against Ethics*, 27.

56 Caputo, *Against Ethics*, 29.

57 According to Foucault, there are "three modes of objectification that transform human beings into subjects." 1. "The modes of inquiry that try to give themselves the status of sciences," such as in philology, linguistics, economics, and biology, etc. 2. "Dividing practices," that is, drawing distinctions, for example, between criminals and good people, the sick and the healthy, and for our purpose, the victim and the aggressor. 3. "The way a human being turns him or herself into a subject." See Michel Foucault, "The Subject and Power," *Critical Inquiry* 8 (Summer 1982): 777–95.

58 Recently, in the border between Juarez and El Paso, Texas, a young boy was shot and killed by a US migration officer. Such a flagrant crime inflamed US, Mexican, and international public opinion. Arizona Senate Bill 1070 is another example of xenophobic acts, which has provoked reactions and resistant movements against it. According to the bill, "A law enforcement officer, without a warrant, may arrest a person if the officer has probable cause to believe that the person has committed any public offense that makes the person removable from the United States." For further information, see Senate Bill 1070, available at: www.azleg.gov/legtext/49leg/2r/bills/sb1070s.pdf.

59 *Implementing the Responsibility to Protect, Report from the Secretary-General*, UN document A/63/677, 12 January 2009.

60 Enrique Dussel, *Política de la liberación*, vol. II (Mexico City: Trotta, 2009), 357–8.

61 "Our America" is a term coined by José Martí, to refer to Latin America.
62 Horacio Cerutti, "Lo utópico operante en la historia como núcleo motriz de la praxis," in *El Saber filosófico*, vol. 3, ed. Jorge Martínez Contreras and Aura Ponce de León (Mexico City: Asociación filosófica de México y Siglo XXI Editores, 2007), 51.
63 Cerutti, "Lo utópico operante en la historia como núcleo motriz de la praxis," 52.

3 Creation amidst destruction

Southern aesthetics and R2P

Rama Mani

- **Art, aesthetics, and the global South: universal origins, specific orientations**
- **ARC: artistic responses to crisis**
- **Artistic responses to mass violence across the global South**
- **Art in the three stages of R2P**
- **Conclusion**

> Art offers an opening for the heart.
> True art makes the divine silence in the soul
> Break into applause.
>
> Hafiz[1]

> I have two goals in my paintings. First to show all that happened to people [during the Cambodian genocide]. Second to prevent this from happening again.
>
> Vann Nath, Tuol Sleng, S 21 torture camp, Cambodia, 2009[2]

This chapter examines the significance for the responsibility to protect of a hitherto largely overlooked phenomenon in almost all contemporary societies that have experienced mass atrocities—the burgeoning of artistic expressions and the revitalization of aesthetic traditions. They may be expressions of resistance, protest, demands, alternatives, cries for help, manifestations of hope, pathways to reconciliation, signs of a renaissance, or victims' memorialization. Sometimes such art carries messages that are specific to the principle, values, and practices implicit in the nascent norm of the responsibility to protect (R2P). For example, they may directly appeal for international solidarity and assistance to save threatened lives. They may depict outrage at action taken by local, regional, or international actors, or conversely at their inaction or apathy. They may depict alternative courses of action or desirable outcomes.

Why is it essential to examine art in its manifold forms as a vibrant but subtle gauge of affected populations during mass atrocities? An understanding of aesthetic expressions in societies that experience mass atrocities can help shape the development of the R2P norm and its application in preventive, protective, and post-atrocity phases. Such art may express itself through music, theater, dance, visual art, poetry and literature, sculpture, handicrafts and folk art, and other culturally or contextually specific media; it may include contemporary and conceptual art, film, and photography.

A few preliminary clarifications are in order. First, this chapter argues that the outpouring of artistic expressions during mass atrocities is a universal phenomenon, common to North and South, but focuses on the global South, as does this book. Further, this chapter offers only an indicative and selective sampling of the sheer breadth of artistic expressions that have appeared across Southern countries during wars and mass atrocities; this is not an exhaustive listing.

Second, despite the variety, wealth, and history of artistic traditions in the South, it is under-examined in academic literature. As Michael Robinson observes, "Most people … still see the 'Orient' through western depictions of its 'otherness' through appropriation and often misappropriation of (Asian) art. Perhaps more importantly, they are still blissfully unaware of the contribution non-western artists have made to civilization, and the influence they have had on western culture."[3] Artists and art critics writing about Africa and Latin America echo this view.[4] There is an even greater paucity of writing on Southern aesthetics and art *by* Southern scholars writing within their own societies, to provide an embedded and contextualized perspective, for reasons partly explained by Nigerian artist/art theorist Krydz Ikwuemesi: "The greatest problem facing artists and scholars in Africa has been the dearth of books, research, and charismatic and committed scholarship occasioned by a progressive intellectual desertification that is a by-product of the inverted value syndrome."[5] Academic publishing in the South is underfunded, often dependent on the commercially driven Western publishing industry, and art books are in low demand. This chapter aspires to stimulate its further development by Southern scholars.

Third, the absence of published materials and theorizing about artistic expressions as specific responses to mass atrocities is noteworthy. Greater support should be provided to studies, projects, and doctoral dissertations undertaken by artists and scholars in social sciences.

This study draws on various primary and secondary sources to supplement academic literature. The main primary sources that most significantly inspired this chapter were in-country interviews by the author with artists and citizens in the three case study countries in this project, Rwanda, Kosovo, and Nepal, as well as in Afghanistan, Peru, Cambodia, and Bosnia. Additionally, observations and experiences over the past decade by the author and other peace builders in several war-torn societies such as Somalia, South Africa, Kenya, Guatemala, Haiti, Sri Lanka, and Mali were included. Secondary sources include newspaper reports, electronic journals, websites of artists, art galleries, and libraries.

This chapter has deliberately sought to identify and cite as much of the existing documentation and ongoing projects on this subject as possible. Among initiatives documenting Southern art during conflict, "The Power of Culture" website in the Netherlands is the most comprehensive. Others are The Hemispheric Institute at New York University, which focuses on art in the Americas; the Virtual Resource Center of Brandeis University's Slifka Program on Coexistence; and a completed research project titled "Re-imagining Peace After Massacres," based in Paris at the Institut de Sciences Politiques and the Centre d'Etudes sur les Relations Internationales.[6] All four are based in the global North because of available funding, human resources, and information technology. Even these are tenuous: the "Power of Culture" website, for example, was suspended due to lack of funding in July 2010.[7] Art communities in several countries emerging from atrocities and war try to convene national, regional, or global art festivals but are severely constrained—for example, Zimbabwe's Harare International Arts Festival or Rwanda's Arts Azimuts Theatre Festival. It is hoped that this study's analysis and collation of sources will assist Southern researchers and artists, and stimulate generous funding.

The chapter proceeds in four parts. The first provides a sketch of the history of art with a more detailed depiction of Southern art and aesthetics. The second part offers a characterization of the aesthetics of crisis: artistic expressions that emerge in Southern societies experiencing mass atrocities and violent conflict; it seeks to theorize this under-examined, episodically reported phenomenon. The third part examines specific artistic expressions that have emerged across countries of the global South in response to political violence or mass atrocities. "Global South" refers to Africa, Asia, Latin America, and the Middle East; the former Yugoslavia, particularly Bosnia and Kosovo, are included in this discussion because of their role in the R2P debate. The fourth part illustrates specific instances where aesthetic responses have actually influenced events during, or shaped the reaction to, mass atrocities or acute political violence; the distinct functions served by these artistic responses are categorized according to the three stages of the R2P norm. The conclusion contains recommendations on possible ways that artistic responses could shape the norm and its implementation before, during, and after mass atrocities.

This chapter represents as much an academic and political as a personal journey. As a scholar-practitioner of peace building, I've personally witnessed the burgeoning of art in war zones the world over. My dual aim here was to subject this edifying and humanizing phenomenon to both critical enquiry and robust policy analysis, thus rendering it relevant to practitioners, policymakers, and scholars. I aspire thereby to enable peace builders to notice, decipher, and be guided by these aesthetic messages amidst the conundrums of violent crisis, in order to strengthen our collective capacity to forestall mass atrocities and build peace.

Art, aesthetics, and the global South: universal origins, specific orientations

This section briefly surveys the origins of art and the specificities of Western, feminist, and Southern aesthetics to provide a rudimentary basis for the subsequent analysis.

Art in human history

Art originated with the appearance of *homo sapiens*.[8] Art is a biological need the denial of which is a vital deprivation, according to eminent art historian Ellen Dissanayake: "Art is a normal and necessary behavior of human beings that like other common and universal human occupations and preoccupations such as talking, working, exercising, playing, socializing, learning, loving, and caring should be recognized, encouraged, and developed in everyone."[9] Art is linked intrinsically to human nature and evolution, in all cultures and across all regions. Noel Carroll argues that the universality and diversity of art cannot be explained by a single source but rather by their adaptive, evolutionary, and societal purposes, which means that, "culture, art and human nature are, in consequence, indissolubly intertwined, and will continue to be until and unless evolution takes a radically different turn."[10]

Artistic and cultural representations have been found across the world dating back to Neolithic and pre-Neolithic times, and they have emerged to reflect specificities of culture, geography, and history.[11] The full gamut of forms of artistic expressions and the diversity of aesthetic traditions is ever-expanding and constantly evolving. While some artistic traditions have remained hermetic over centuries, such as Coptic crosses of Ethiopia or *kora* music of West Africa, others have traveled extensively, since the earliest years of trade, and similarities or parallels emerge surprisingly in different contexts.

As apparent and expressive forms of culture, the arts have played a central role in the evolution of history and society. Hegel observed: "in works of art the nations have deposited their richest inner intuitions and ideas, and art is often the key, and in many nations the sole key, to understanding their philosophy and religion."[12] Although Hegel disparaged Southern and African art, his observation characterizes Southern as well as European art. Narrative forms of art—poetry, music, and storytelling—were fundamentally important in transmitting a society's myths, history, and cultural norms intergenerationally, even in the absence of written traditions. Art also depicted societies' central personalities, values, and religious or secular customs.

Western aesthetics

Aesthetics generally refers to the study of beauty, taste, and arts. Leading Western philosophers have theorized on aesthetics through the ages, including Aristotle, Kant, Hegel, Heidegger, and Danto, among others.[13] Hegel noted in *Aesthetics: Lectures on Fine Arts* that the term "aesthetics" is unsatisfactory as "aesthetics means more precisely the science of sensation, of feeling."[14] He preferred the term "philosophy of art."

In the Western philosophical tradition, art usually is considered non-utilitarian and distinct from craft or technology. Aesthetics is associated with the objective or detached contemplation of an object and refers to both the formal qualities of the object and the qualities or attitudes aroused by its perception. Kant asserts that aesthetic perception and judgment is free of all concepts,[15] a social phenomenon and a mark of civilization. He believed that "[w]ith no one to take into account but himself, a man abandoned on a desert island would not adorn either himself or his hut, nor would he look for flowers, and still less plant them, with the object of providing himself with personal adornments. Only in society does it occur to him to be not merely a man, but a man refined after the manner of his kind (the beginning of civilization)."[16]

Art and aesthetics were initially considered by Western philosophers to be entirely European. Hegel and Heidegger considered non-European arts to be in their infancy. The exclusiveness and disregard for non-European art inherent in these traditional Western views have been squarely criticized by postmodernists, feminists, and Southern scholars. Contemporary philosopher Arthur Danto observes that this exclusion was due to the determination by a narrow art elite of what qualified as art.[17]

Recently Western philosophers and artists have gone beyond these narrow confines. Contemporary artists reject geographical parameters. Further, since the emergence of pop art in the 1960s, beauty, a defining trait of Kantian aesthetics, is irrelevant to or deliberately absent from art.[18] Kathleen Marie Higgins observes that "judgments that beauty is inappropriate underlie the decision to forego beauty in much contemporary art."[19] Much contemporary art is engaged, political, or activist art, and "beauty seems at odds with political activism as it is not a directly practical response to the world."[20]

Many scholars also challenge the characterization of Western art as non-utilitarian and contemplative. Carroll, for example, observes, "One reason for this rejection is the observation that this theory does not encompass all the objects and performances that *we* are prepared to categorize as art in our own culture. For even in our own culture, we are happy to classify works designed, intended and used for their practical purposes as art works."[21] Despite such critiques and contradictions, the Kantian and Hegelian characterization of Western aesthetics remains influential and largely unchanged.

Feminist aesthetics

Feminist aesthetics radically critiques the fundamental premises of Western aesthetics. First, it links the domains of the personal and cultural to the domain of art. Feminist scholars insist that art is gendered and embedded in culture,[22] that it is impossible to separate the individual artist from her culture and community, and that art may emerge as much from scholarship as from experience. This approach is pertinent for the global South where art is not viewed or lived as a distinct, hermetic, elite activity separated from the general community. Second, feminist aesthetics differentiates "matriarchal" or "gynecentric" from "patriarchal" art. Heidi Gottner-Abendtroth identified nine characteristics of matriarchal aesthetics that include: participants as simultaneously authors and spectators, the creative process as more important than the actual product, and total commitment.[23] Third, it rejects the detached, rational individual contemplation of Western aesthetics. Art encompasses the cultural, spiritual, and emotional in feminist aesthetics. Finally, art in the feminine aesthetic is fundamentally transformative—the artist's vision tends toward the utopian. Renee Cox develops the "gynecentric aesthetic" based on art forms that emerge in societies where women enjoy higher social status: "[A]esthetic activity would function to integrate the individual and society. Intellect, emotion and action would combine to achieve a synthesis of body and spirit."[24] The vision is of a society in which art is not separate from life.[25]

It hardly needs repeating that for centuries in the West, women artists were strenuously discouraged, their artworks disparaged and often plagiarized by their husbands or patrons, leaving us mere vestiges of female artistry until the late nineteenth century. The feminist aesthetic re-establishes art as a vital human phenomenon beyond gender, and brings us closer to the reality of Southern aesthetics.

Southern aesthetics

The diverse ancient art traditions of Africa, Latin America, Asia, and the Middle East were denigrated by Western aesthetics for centuries. Southern artwork was considered unfit for aesthetic consideration by Western scholars and art collectors and treated as mere ethnological artifacts. Furthermore, Southern artworks were destroyed by European missionaries and colonialists as pagan, or pillaged by adventurers, as has been well documented by art historians and anthropologists.[26] Only recently have Southern arts been understood and given their rightful status.[27]

The Southern aesthetic is well encapsulated in Ananda Coomaraswamy's depiction of Asian art as representing "not merely another species of art, but an art generically different from what we have come to understand by 'art' in modern times."[28] This section primarily draws on African aesthetics to develop a broader characterization of Southern aesthetics.[29] In African aesthetics, it is not possible to conceive of art for art's sake but "art for life's sake," according to Nigerian philosopher Dele Jegede.[30] "African art has been maligned in the writings of Western scholars who have failed to understand its source and origin … African art responds to an Afrocentric framework instead of to a European-centered notion of the artistic."[31]

One view describes Southern aesthetics as utilitarian. The Nigerian-British philosopher Antony Appiah observes that art objects in Africa were conceived not for contemplation but for utilitarian purposes, while "European art is supposed to be opposed to science and to utility."[32] Coomaraswamy echoes this attitude in Asian art: "The Asiatic work of art has always been produced upon occasion, that is to say to supply a specific human requirement."[33]

The utilitarian view provides a factual but partial description, which seems to vindicate the Hegelian rejection of African art as merely functional and prehistoric. Coomaraswamy pointed out that the second function of traditional art beyond its functionality was symbolic and used to preserve and transmit moral values and spiritual teachings.[34] A closer analysis of the "functionality" attributed to African or non-Western art reveals a deeper relationship between life and beauty in the Southern aesthetic. Dating back to the oldest civilizations thousands of years ago, we observe the persistent closeness between daily life and beauty or art. Art is not a part of life simply because it is useful, but almost all aspects of daily life, however routine, are embellished by artistic acts and expressions of beauty. Ordinary daily objects like combs, pots, and beds, as much as magnificent pyramids, temples, and mosques have always been canvases for superb art work in ancient Southern civilizations. Retracing European history, the same practice existed across the European continent in premodern days; however, with industrialization, the veneration of the ordinary through beauty was discarded. An impoverishment of the creative spirit did not accompany the economic decline of the South.

In non-Western art, there is no wall separating beauty from daily life. Even in the simplest rural habitat in Burkina Faso, the freshly built walls of huts are painted elaborately with cultural symbols by women; in rural and urban India women still create sacred designs with white flour on the earth in front of their homes at sunset that will disappear overnight. Both the cow that tills the land and the bullock cart that carries produce to the market are rendered beautiful by peasant farmers, however modest their means. Daily tasks are given attention, importance, and respect; their centrality in sustaining life is acknowledged.

In the Southern aesthetic there is no need to go to a separate space—a king's palace, a concert hall, or a museum—to contemplate art because it is ever present in daily life in both mundane and festive moments. Coomaraswamy expressed this pithily: "Neither the existence of museums nor of rich collectors can be said to prove the love of art in modern society. Necessary as they may be, the very necessity for museums goes far to prove the absence of any genuine artistic activity in the community; for they exist to preserve such things as were once but common articles of commerce."[35]

Nor is Southern art the preserve of an elite and intellectual class; it is more ubiquitous and democratized. There are indubitably master artists in a category all their own: Pablo Neruda, Miriam Makeba, Wole Soyinka, and Rabindranath Tagore. The urbanized elite in the South may sometimes be estranged from ancient aesthetic traditions as are their Western counterparts. Notwithstanding maestros and urban elites, the predominantly democratic and inclusive character of Southern aesthetics is defined by three elements: art and beauty are intrinsic parts of daily life; art belongs to all members of society; and all members of the community can and sometimes must partake in artistic production. The learning of certain art forms has always been integrated into the education of boys and girls, which often forms a part of initiation rituals and rites of passage. Even urbanized elites often return to their cultural and aesthetic traditions to mark significant life stages of birth, adolescence, marriage, and death.

This interpretation of Southern aesthetics resembles the depiction of Leopold Senghor, who is considered Africa's first art critic. As Senegal's president and patron of the arts, he believed that functionality or utility was only one of art's many roles. For him, the essential characteristics of Negro-African arts are: the generic activity of humans; functional; interdependent; collective, notwithstanding the existence of professional artists; and engaged. He underlined, "The artisan poet is situated, and he engages with himself, his ethnic identity and group, his history, his geography."[36] Nobel laureate Wole Soyinka underlines this artistic engagement emphatically: "The artist has always functioned in African society as the record of the mores and experience of his society *and* as the voice of vision in his own time."[37] Thus African aesthetics views art as participatory, collective, committed, and transformative.[38]

This discussion does not presume that Southern art is static and invariably fulfills the characteristics described here. Continental and linguistic boundaries that kept Southern artists isolated from the Western art world have eroded with the increasing global mobility of artists.[39] Some Southern scholars today would reject Senghor's and Wolinka's engaged, visionary, and societal view of art. Ola Balogan, Allasane Ndaw, and Raoul Lehuard arduously defend the existence of the Kantian "disinterested beauty" in African art. Contemporary art has emerged across the global South with repudiations of standard tenets of beauty, as in the West. Many individual Southern artists would define their work as conceptual and expect to be categorized as part of the global art world and not simply branded as Asian or African. Publications, biennales, and websites trace and critique the contemporary art of the Southern continents and attest to their rapid expansion and popularity: FESPACO, the biennial African Film Festival held in Burkina Faso since 1969, Art Radar Asia, and Africa/Contemporary, or Dak'art, the Biennale of African Contemporary Art in Dakar initiated in 2002.[40]

There is not always a clear break between traditional and contemporary; apparently stark differences belie a common source within age-old tradition and symbolism. Even in cases where contemporary artists work with abstract and culturally neutral or a-cultural forms, it is often their conscious attempt to transcend and expand their cultural aesthetic traditions. Moreover, modern Southern artists influenced by European artists or trained in Western aesthetics combine external influences with a grounding within their own cultures. As Michael Kerrigan notes, "For modern (Asian) artists, their rooting in their cultural heritage has been a springboard for renewed creativity."[41]

Southern art is not restricted to the traditional but constantly adapts to changed circumstances.[42] "In African artistic creation, new sociological conditions appeared since independence, and they will continue to appear constantly, without any doubt," writes Babacar Mbaye Diop. "New forms of art and new movements appear and will appear which will demand decisions on the part of the interested as to the question of whether the concept of art should be extended or not. Ethnologists, anthropologists and aesthetic scholars may well align conditions of similitude, but never the conditions that are necessary and sufficient for the correct application of the concept."[43]

Southern art and aesthetics is defined in this study, based on the preceding discussion, as both the process of creation and the outcome of that process with (most or all of) the following characteristics: it is embedded within a culture, community, and context; it is participatory, inclusive, and transformative; it encompasses the political and personal, the social and spiritual. Such art is often but not exclusively collective. Even individual art is not divorced from the collective but in dialogue with community. Southern aesthetics is the participation in and study of this artistic process, which is, necessarily, as passionately committed and personal as the art itself.

ARC: artistic responses to crisis

Here "artistic responses to crisis" or "art in crisis" is characterized as the phenomenon of artistic and creative revival during and despite crisis. Individual life crises may generate apathetic despondency or, contrarily, unprecedented creativity. Renowned artists and lay individuals alike have stumbled upon their own unearthed artistry during crisis. So too, in collective societal crises of war, creativity is unleashed amidst suffering and despair. Like an "arc," artistic responses to crisis permit individuals and communities to bridge over from current suffering to alternative imagined futures; to convert apathy into action; to transcend from despair to hope.[44] In its transformative capacity, it resembles Southern and feminist aesthetics. This phenomenon is accessible to all humans and all cultures, although this chapter focuses on mass atrocity situations in the global South, where it is particularly evidenced and serves multiple functions relevant to R2P.

A paradoxical dual reality is observed in the theatre of mass atrocities and violent conflict. Art is destroyed, and artists are targeted and exterminated precisely because they are seen as dangerous expressions of freedom or revolt. Yet simultaneously, creativity blossoms defiantly; art forms arise from the ashes of destruction, and artists become central organs of protest, civic expressions of defiance, hope, and freedom. Collin Sekajugo, founder and director of Kigali's Ivuka Arts Studio, asserts: "All arts create freedom. When you paint, you are healed at the same time. And art creates equality."[45]

The manipulation and instrumentalization of art and artists by ruling regimes or opposition forces to spread messages of hate and foment violence is well known. Hate songs were composed and chanted across Rwanda well before the tragic 1994 genocide, just as propaganda art was used by Nazi and Soviet regimes among others.[46] Jean-Marie Kayishema observes, "Every genocide is preceded by a systemic cultural ethnocide."[47] Before the onset of violence against targeted groups, genocidal regimes systematically denigrate and demolish symbolic and artistic representations and representatives of their culture.

The destruction of art during violent conflict and mass atrocities can take different forms, of which three are noted here. First is the deliberate targeting, incarceration, and elimination of selected artists whose work is considered inflammatory or unbearable by ruling authorities or armed movements. For example, Palestinian poet laureate Mahmoud Darwich faced harassment, house arrest, and imprisonment at the hands of Israeli authorities for his poetry and political activism. In Algeria, innumerable poets and writers were assassinated during the civil war for both defying military rule and rejecting Islamist extremism.

Second is the systematic destruction of works of art for ideological, political, and symbolic reasons. In Afghanistan, the Taliban regime systematically destroyed art and musical instruments for religious ideological reasons, while in Kosovo the Serbian occupation of 1990 banned all Albanian art and culture for political reasons.

Third is the looting of artworks during the chaos of war. Recent examples include the pillaging of Baghdad's museums after the coalition's victory, witnessed worldwide on television screens, as well as the undocumented looting of invaluable art and sculpture from war-torn Democratic Republic of the Congo (DRC) by both petty thieves and organized transnational criminals.

Less well-known is the regeneration of art during violent crisis. "Transcending violence is forged by the capacity to generate, mobilize, and build the moral imagination," John Paul Lederach notes, and "the fundamental belief in and pursuit of the creative act" is one of the four capacities essential to do so.[48] From the perspective of international relations, Alex Danchev corroborates that "art exercises the moral imagination," and he identifies art's multiple functions in war that can "crystallize, define, mobilize, protest, dissent, critique, offend, unsettle, agitate, arouse and haunt."[49] As the Palestinian poet Mahmoud Darwich discovered, the poem can be "a threat to the sword."[50]

Ironically, the blood-washed battlefields of human suffering have proven fertile ground for poignant creativity. Art takes on new forms and meanings and assumes multiple functions under the duress of crisis and mass atrocities. Sometimes these artistic expressions carry direct and simple messages, as the graffiti and street art that appeared on walls in Kenya, Palestine, and East Timor. Sometimes, in repressive climates, the messages are cryptic, oblique, and symbolic. Examples are a Hutu writer's allegorical tale of a greedy rat to allude to the mounting corruption and violence of politicians prior to the genocide,[51] the allegorical poetry of Mahmoud Darwich in Palestine, or epic plays of Milan Krasniqi in Kosovo.

Art in crisis resembles feminist and Southern aesthetics in some ways, as noted earlier. Three key features of the Southern aesthetic are evidenced in artistic responses to crisis. First, the artists are personally engaged. Whether their messages are direct or oblique, they take a clear—and potentially life-threatening—political stand through their work. Their art is not passive, neutral, or contemplative, but passionate and committed.

Second, even when it is an individual expression, the emergent artwork has a democratic or participatory effect that includes wider war-affected populations; it speaks directly to and for them, and expresses collective experiences of suffering and hope. The Kosovo poet Basri Capriqi described the Serbian occupation of the 1990s, when art was forbidden to Kosovar Albanians: "There was a contract—a hidden relationship between writer and readers. They could un-code the code the writer wrote with."[52] There emerges a close contact between artists and communities as beleaguered populations turn to their best-loved artists to express on their behalf. Further, oppression gives birth to new creative voices reflecting ancient aesthetic traditions or new artistic outlets. The Quechua village women of Peru who replaced traditional patterns with vivid depictions of their suffering and hope sewn into their traditional quilts or *arpilleras* are an example.

Third, and as a consequence of the first two, art in crisis particularly during mass atrocities has a regenerative or transformative effect. The re-emergence of art and defiant creative expressiveness symbolizes survival, hope, and potential transformation. Artists may not succeed in transforming the realities on the ground in real time. Nor are artists organized like military campaigns with the deliberate and instrumental intent of political transformation. The transformation is above all internal, communal, and socio-spiritual. Yet, due to the societal glue that art provides in such situations, it may result in external political change as well.

Two additional specific features of artistic responses to crisis in contexts of mass atrocities in the South bear mentioning: they are endogenous and civic, and spontaneous and independent. First, although elicited by political events, such art is inherently an indigenous civic expression, not an exogenous political one. It is endogenous and unleashed from the heart of a specific culture. In Somalia artistic responses to war tended to be oral poetry due to tradition, whereas in South Africa *a capella* music was the predominant form. Second, art in crisis regenerates spontaneously from within the blood-soiled earth of destruction. Art in crisis is autonomous; it is independent and distinct from propaganda art financed by the state, or charity art commissioned by well-intentioned donors. Although external financial and moral support for art in crisis can be crucial for their survival and preservation and should be encouraged, funding must carefully eschew co-opting these home-grown, free-spirited artistic responses to crisis.

This characterization of artistic responses to crisis depicting the emergence of art during mass atrocities was developed specifically for the analysis in this chapter, and aspires to complement the small but growing literature examining the nexus between art and war in different contexts.[53] With the theoretical groundwork now laid, the following section offers concrete examples.

Artistic responses to mass violence across the global South

Across the globe, when war and atrocities strike, both charismatic artists and entire communities have found innumerable ways to live out what Lederach describes as the violence-transcending capacity to believe and engage in the creative act. For instance, Kosovo's author Milazen Krasniqi tells us, "There is no way to forget and pass the pain. Therefore literature is a way of expression in such a situation."[54] Here a brief repertoire of selected examples from Africa, Latin America, and the Middle East helps to illustrate endogenous and spontaneous art expressions.[55]

Africa

Africa's long tradition of expressing opposition to slavery, colonialism, and dictatorship through poetry, music, literature, and other art forms finds new expressions in today's wars and atrocities.[56] South Africa's anti-apartheid music, for instance, mobilized and cemented the anti-apartheid struggle within the country and invigorated the civic alliance of anti-apartheid activists around the world. Creative expressions against apartheid went beyond music and included literature and poetry. Further, a range of dance styles such as *toyi-toyi, isicatamiya, mapuntsula*, and gumboot dancing, and the theatre of the oppressed[57] emerged as distinctive art forms during the mass civic-led anti-apartheid struggle. Each of these has been a resilient form of protest, resistance, and mobilization.[58]

In neighboring Zimbabwe, traditional art was kept alive and new art forms emerged as signs of resilience through repression. Resisting isolation and financial crisis, Zimbabwean artists host the Harare International Festival of Arts, which showcases theatre, music, dance, and other art forms by local, African, and global artists.[59] Poetry has emerged among Zimbabwe's youth as a strong and poignant response to political violence and uncertainty of the Mugabe regime. The House of Hunger Poetry Slam meets monthly in Harare and other cities; Magamba, a cultural activist network, conducts poetry sessions and workshops with youth; and Poets for Human Rights Collective uses street poetry to lobby for their causes.[60] The poet Chirikure states, "We will carry on making art, with our eyes and ears open. I am simply asserting my right to express myself. The basic premise must be that you always have the freedom to think. It's a freedom that no-one can take away from you."[61]

In the DRC over 5 million people died from armed conflict and ethnic cleansing since the late 1990s, but art survived. Ordinary people continued their cherished celebration of life through music and dancing through war, while new artists and art centers emerged. For example, in Goma a group of youth started the Yole Arts Centre, where music, theatre, film, painting, and other arts were performed and shared.[62] Faustin Linyekula, a world-renowned dancer and choreographer who returned to his native Kisangani to reinvigorate arts, says, "with my work I strive to open spaces, to create new windows with other perspectives."[63]

In Rwanda the gradual art revival following the devastating genocide was aided by the return of exiled diaspora artists as well as solidarity with other African artists. Returnees from older generations, such as anthropologist Celestin Kanimba and playwright Jean-Marie Kayishema, have ensured that ancient cultural traditions and myths are revived. Younger artists such as visual artist Collin Sekajugo, dancer Hope Azeda, actress Carole Karemera, and playwright Odile Katese have innovatively addressed genocide, loss, and reconciliation, and mobilized younger artists. Museums have been built to regenerate repressed cultural traditions and memorialize history, largely through the assiduous efforts of Kanimba.[64] Significant among African supporters, Chadian musician/playwright Koulsy Lamko spent a decade in Rwanda from

1995 to 2005 training youth in theatre, and helped establish the University Centre for Arts in Butare and the Festival Arts Azimuts together with Kayishema and Odile Katese. According to the rector of the National University of Rwanda, Emile Rwamasirabo, "If arts and culture had been dynamic in Rwanda, so many people would not have been implicated in the killings perpetrated during the genocide in 1994. People would have learned to say 'No' to the appeal of genocidal politics."[65]

In Côte d'Ivoire musical productions, new forms of dance, and caricature theatre have appeared as regulators of tension and conflict management since 1989. *Zouglou* is the rehabilitation of an ancient dance called the "*woyo*" and was born on university campuses. Spreading across the country, it allowed young musical groups such as Magic System, the Garagists, and Brou Kouadio to channel latent tensions between ethnic groups.[66] *Zouglou* became a "language in which can be read the transformations and social tensions, the aspirations of certain factions of society, as well as the innovativeness and creativity of contemporary Africa."[67] Ticken Dja Fakoly's militant reggae music sought expressly to awaken consciences and address burning issues with his provocative albums *History Lesson* and *Mangecratie.* Exiled to Mali following death threats, this intrepid young "voice of the voiceless" nonetheless established schools for the poor and continues to sing about the crises of Côte d'Ivoire and Africa.[68]

In Algeria poets, writers, visual artists, and art critics were at the forefront of opposing violence and frequent targets for assassination.[69] Poetry emerged as a defiant response to atrocities. In a tradition of opposition starting with the Algerian war of independence from France, a continuous stream of Algerian poets and writers denounced violence throughout the country's decade-long civil war. Some were imprisoned, others deported or exiled, and others simply assassinated for their literary protests: Tahar Djaout, Bakhti Benaouda, Abdelkader Alloula, and Lounes Matoub. Such survivors as Zyani Chérif continued resolutely to perform engaged activist theatre. Writers like Assia Djebar, celebrated author of *Vast is My Prison*, and Malika Mokeddem courageously continued writing novels that denounced state authoritarianism and religious fundamentalism.[70] The well-known poem attributed to Tahar Djaout summarized it well: "If you speak, you die. If you remain silent, you die. So, speak and die." And indeed, Djaout was assassinated by Islamist extremists in May 1993.[71]

Latin America

Art and revolution have always gone hand-in-hand in Latin America.[72] Illustrious novelists and poets were bards of hope and protest during brutal dictatorships, including Gabriel García Márquez, Pablo Neruda, Mario Vargas Llosa, and Eduardo Galleano. García Márquez said in his Nobel acceptance speech that his art is inseparable from the "monstrous reality" of Latin America.[73] Beyond literature, cultural, theatrical and visual expressions, and memorialization have emerged during dictatorships and atrocities.[74]

In Peru the wealth of creative and artistic expressions that emerged during the country's civil war (1980–2000), which claimed 70,000 lives, spans traditional and contemporary forms. *Arpilleras* or quilts woven by indigenous Quechua women survivors depicted scenes of war and atrocities as well as imagined scenes of peace—acts of both mourning and defiance. The explicitly political theatre group Yuyachkani sought to memorialize victims through their theatre and used community theatre, folk dance, and music to work with war-affected populations. Yuyarison was an annual art competition started by a group of local and international nongovernmental organizations (NGOs) that allowed ordinary Peruvians to depict through painting and other means their experiences of war. This artwork was presented to Peru's Truth and Reconciliation Commission as part of its proceedings. In the absence of an official state-sponsored museum to memorialize the dead, the poignant Museum of Memory was established by ANFASEP (The National Association for the Relatives of the Kidnapped, Detained and Disappeared of Peru), an indefatigable group of mothers demanding justice for their disappeared children with the help of local Quechua artists like Wari Zarate.[75]

In war-torn Colombia, poetry has emerged as a major outlet for expressing protest and hope. Nine poets created the international poetry festival in 1991 in Médellin. The festival transformed the world's drug capital into a poetry capital, which has spawned replicas worldwide. The festival was awarded the Right Livelihood Award, known as the Alternative Nobel Peace Prize, for its positive impact.[76]

Middle East

Palestinian and Israeli music, theatre, and visual and performance art have emerged to express protest, defiance, and solidarity against continuing atrocities.[77] The West-Eastern Divan Orchestra, jointly created by Israeli musician Daniel Barenboim and the late Palestinian intellectual Edward Said, is the best-known initiative seeking to bridge Israelis and Palestinians through art.[78] The late Mahmoud Darwich captured in his poetry the mundane realities of despair, the hopes of the Palestinian people, and universal themes of exile and freedom.[79]

Artistic responses have not been limited to such renowned individuals.[80] Spontaneous and popular outbursts of artistic expression are found in street art and graffiti that capture the frustration, fear, and hope of a population caught interminably in a prison-like situation. Irish writer and photographer Erin Murray noted that street art represents "a sort of urban tattoo, acts of rebellion, individuality and celebrations of freedom."[81] The Alrowwad Cultural and Theatre Society seeks to foster artistic imagination, and initiated the Beautiful Non-violent Resistance to cultivate Palestinian creativity and identity, break stereotypes, and counter the ugliness of violence.[82]

"War is, in a way, embedded in the work of artists in Lebanon, even when it is not 'about' the war," observes Christine Tohme, director of Ashkal Alwan, the Lebanese Association for Plastic Arts.[83] Tohme describes how video art took off in Lebanon after the Israeli attacks of 2006. Visual art, too, was deeply impregnated by the war. "Convergence: New Art from Lebanon," an exhibit showcasing the work of numerous contemporary artists, confirms how inescapable the theme of war has been for visual artists. "You are either making art about the war, or you are making irrelevant art."[84] Art can be both political and politicized. In 2007 a site in Dahiyeh devastated during the Israeli attack of 2006 was converted into an open-air art exhibition by Hezbollah.[85]

The two countries most affected by international intervention since 2000, Afghanistan and Iraq, are undergoing gradual artistic revival. In Afghanistan prescient curators of the National Museum and National Art Gallery stealthily hid precious artifacts and artworks in 1998–99, while most cultural monuments and artworks were destroyed in ensuing decades of war. Today, the same dedicated individuals, notably Omar Khan Mossoudi, director of the National Museum, and Fatah Adil, director of the National Art Gallery, are overseeing painstaking renewal with their dedicated staff, despite inadequate budgets and absurdly low salaries. Young architects, designers and artists like Zabi Majidi, Zolaykha Sherzad, and Aman Mojadidi, back from exile in Europe and the United States, are both restoring ancient cultural traditions and infusing contemporary ideas into Afghan arts.[86]

In Iraq the horrors of war and destruction of cultural heritage are themes preoccupying artists. Naseer Shamma, renowned musician of the ancient *oud*, uses his music to both address and build peace. He notes, "We are building peace through music, maintaining our culture despite incredible violence against our people, in Baghdad and also in Gaza, sustaining our culture is also resistance."[87]

Art in the three stages of R2P

The specific impact of art movements or expressions on political outcomes cannot be limited in time and space; they extend well beyond their immediate geography and time of production, for example Picasso's *Guernica* or South Africa's apartheid music. However, artistic manifestations have played an essential role in shaping key moments of violent conflict. This section identifies artistic responses during the three stages of conflict addressed by R2P and develops a typology of their functions. The categories are not exclusive; art can serve several functions or change with time.

Prevention

As is well known in the social sciences, conflict prevention is problematic because success is invisible but failure is not. Nevertheless, four preventive functions served by art are distilled: awakening conscience, civic mobilization, sensitization, and nonviolent resistance.

Art's preventive function of awakening conscience is exemplified in Kenya. When ethnic violence exploded after the flawed Kenyan elections of December 2007, artists were at the forefront of the instantaneous civic reaction that contained ethnic violence and prevented a potential spillover into genocide. Paintings and graffiti spontaneously appeared on walls across Nairobi and the affected countryside, calling for reconciliation and coexistence. Art and artists appealed to the consciences of ordinary Kenyans to resist incitement to violence and recall their fraternity in spite of ethnic differences. Solomon Muyundo lives in the sprawling Kibera slum and became famous for his infectious peace graffiti.[88] Kenya is a possible success story for R2P's preventive logic as a result of the simultaneous international mediation and mobilization of local civil society.[89] Artists were vital in the latter.

Second, art's function of civic mobilization was witnessed in Nepal. Civic action and mass mobilization by the people's movement, known as the Lok Andolan (see Chapter 6 on Nepal in this volume) played a major role in preventing the violence from spiraling out of control in the Nepali war and limiting civilian brutalities. Primarily conflict transformation from below, artists played a major mobilizing role in the Lok Andolan. Ashmina Ranjit informs us that artists initially remained passive when violence began in 1996, as they felt impotent to influence politics. Following the highly mediatized royal massacre in June 2001 and intensification of the war, artists and writers mobilized and played a critical role in preventing escalating violence.[90] The Gurukul theatre group performed at each demonstration, and their rudimentary office became a meeting place for politicians and the civic movement. The child musician Rubin Gandharva traveled the countryside, mobilizing people with his songs. The comedian Manoj's hilarious caricatures of politicians cemented people through humor. Thus artists were entirely integrated in the Lok Andolan and passionately committed to peace. The very presence of artists at demonstrations and deployment of music, theatre, comedy, and performance art showed that nonviolence was a viable response to deter violence.[91]

Third, art's ability to sensitize populations is seen in Colombia. The international poetry festival that transformed Médellin from the world's crime capital into a poetry capital played a crucial and unimagined conflict prevention role. Wide public participation in the festival and its expansion from a single location within Médellin to many areas of the city and subsequently to several cities across Colombia has had the effect of sensitizing and uniting the population through the magic of poetry. Jakob von Uexkull is the founder of the Right Livelihood Award and comments that the poetry festival won in 2004 among many distinguished nominees because of its demonstrable impact on peace: "It is incredible: guerillas, druglords, youthgangs, all join together to recite and listen to poetry for a week. After hearing poetry together, you don't feel like killing each other."[92]

Fourth, nonviolent resistance through art can be seen in Kosovo. The North Atlantic Treaty Organization's (NATO) 1999 intervention in Kosovo attracts enormous analytical attention, but the unprecedentedly creative, meticulously organized nonviolent resistance to Serbian occupation by the Kosovar Albanian population for an entire decade in the 1990s is largely ignored. Artists played a major role during this clandestine period in the parallel system. All Albanian art was effectively banned, and theaters, concert halls, and museums of Albanian culture were closed during Serbian occupation. During this time, artists met clandestinely to create art and the purged art faculty from the University of Pristina continued teaching in a parallel institution. Underground theater performances, poetry readings, and concerts signaled civic defiance and rallied enormous crowds despite severe sanctions upon discovery. "Poets spoke directly to the public and the public looked to artists for political messages—there was a close direct relationship between them," says poet Basri Capriqi.[93] For almost 10 years, art and civic resistance enabled defiance of occupation to remain nonviolent.

Protection

At the peak of mass atrocities, creativity is stifled because survival takes precedence. Yet, some of the most innovative and courageous art can emerge phoenix-like. Six specific functions with distinct examples are highlighted: mobilization and defiance as in South Africa; non-verbal expression of war's impact as in Palestine and East Timor; political protest as in Kosovo; crossing enemy lines and humanizing the enemy as in Bosnia; honoring the dead and reclaiming civic space as in Sri Lanka; and transforming violent conflict as in Nepal.

First, regarding mobilization and defiance, *a capella* music, recited poetry, and dance galvanized mass demonstrations in South Africa against apartheid. Music and film were important as well in shaping global support for disinvestment and pressure on the regime. Poetic songs and dance bound together an entire nation in protest, defiance, and hope. As with Mahatma Gandhi's *satyagraha* against British colonial rule a century earlier, anti-apartheid protesters defied police and army brutality with songs.

Art often expresses defiance subtly and covertly during atrocities. The *arpilleras* of Quechua women in Peru, the celestial *oud* music of Iraqi Naseer Shamma, and the tanks and guns that appeared amidst traditional Islamic designs on Afghan kilims (carpets) are not strident challenges to political power but rather weave threads and strike notes of silent but powerful resistance and defiance.

Second, when repression renders the population mute, art can provide a method of non-vocal expression. Street art has appeared in various conflict zones often during the worst periods of violence to express through images and words what cannot be spoken. It also provides a series of reflections on war's impact on ordinary people. The street art of Palestine referred to earlier does this evocatively. During East Timor's war, stranded youth used the streets for vivid self-expression, as memorialized in Chris Parkinson's *Peace of Wall: Street Art from East Timor*. "In 2006, when divisions in East Timor's armed forces inflamed a larger social rift that was beamed across the world, these streets were both refuge and tormentor. Survival was life. Life was survival. It still is … The street art is the powerful annunciation of emotion in what common space exists for a population restricted by physical and emotional borders."[94] The "media of the marginalized" conveys what no statistical survey could.

Third, regarding art for political protest, after NATO's intervention in Kosovo, VETËVENDOSJE! (Self-determination) burst on the scene using art in deliberately provocative ways through graffiti, banners, and performance art to attract public attention to their protests and demands for Kosovar Albanians to have a greater say in determining their own political future. While accepting the existential need for and protective function of NATO's intervention, the group was very critical of the aftermath: the international transitional administration and ensuing political limbo, which alienated the hitherto engaged citizenry. In addition to open confrontation with the United Nations Mission in Kosovo (UNMIK) and police, VETËVENDOSJE! criticized Kosovo's politicians for corruption and inaction, usually using banners, graffiti, and theatrical demonstrations. As expressed by their spokesperson, it is "not art for art but art for achieving political goals."[95] Referring to the characteristics of Southern art in mass atrocities, VETËVENDOSJE!'s art was a political rather than purely civic expression and thus differs from the others described here. In contrast, contemporary artist Albert Heta established the art gallery/forum *Stacion* to provide a meeting ground. It exhibits provocative, politically symbolic art works and convenes forums to debate controversial social, political, and aesthetic issues and propose alternatives. Heta states unequivocally, "Art has to question. In the context today we cannot afford to have a practice that is irrelevant to the social structure."[96]

From each mass atrocity, however barbaric, emerge examples through which enemies were not demonized but humanized. Art is often able to provide a safe haven for such humanizing experiences. The fourth function of art as a means of crossing enemy lines and humanizing the enemy is seen in Bosnia. In Mostar, during the worst of the fighting, which pitted Bosnian, Croat, and Serb neighbors and friends against one other, enemy soldiers put down their guns at nightfall and met in darkened rooms to play music until dawn. From this experience the now-famous Mostar Sevdah Café group of musicians was born. In Sarajevo, centuries-old café culture survived war; certain cafés became venues of resistance for artists, poets, and writers to meet across sectarian lines.[97] In Sri Lanka, artists also opposed the dehumanization of the enemy and highlighted similarities between Sinhalese and Tamil culture through diverse art forms, including dramatist Dharmasiri Bandaranayake, filmmaker/writer Tissa Abeysekara, and visual artist Chandragupta Thenwara.[98] For Jagath Weerasinghe, seeing a Tamil boy stripped naked during the 1983 riots was the trigger for his relentless, politically engaged art movement.[99]

The fifth function of art in honoring the dead and reclaiming civic space is seen in Sri Lanka, where, despite the devastating war during which innumerable artists and intellectuals were murdered or exiled, art and civil society still survive. Artists insisted on continuing with life as normal to defy the abnormality of war. Sinhalese artists such as Weerasinghe braved stigmatization by denouncing government violence as non-Buddhist, while Tamil artists who remained in Sri Lanka such as writer/playwright Sivamohan Sumathy defied state censure in depicting the trauma of victims. Following the brutal 1999 assassination of moderate Tamil leader and human rights activist Neelan Tiruchelvam, a small group of his supporters sprang into action. In the night they broke curfew and repainted the blood-stained area of the road where the assassination took place, and the normally belligerent security guards stood back. A non-partisan art movement was born. Whether the government security forces, extremist militia, or Tamil Tigers committed a crime, a group of painters appeared and transformed blood into art. And each time the security guards held back, as though in deference to these artistic acts that served to both honor the dead and reclaim civic space stolen by war.[100]

Sixth, while mentioned earlier for its preventive function, the role of Nepali art can best be characterized as transformative. Civic mobilization and the charismatic mobilizing role of musicians, visual and contemporary artists, actors, and comedians not only prevented mass atrocities but also transformed the course of events and precipitated peace by their cohesion, determination, and nonviolence. Ashmina Ranjit describes herself as an "artivist" and recounts that when violence peaked she and other artists and journalists mobilized. Realizing the urgency of action, they embedded themselves in the civic movement. The founder of Gurukul Theatre Group notes that the synergy between political leaders, artists, and the masses was perhaps the magic formula that transformed war into peace. An inspiring example is a young Dalit (untouchable) boy, Rubin Gandharva, a street musician barely 12 years old who was inspired by the Lok Andolan and created songs that became the movement's slogans. He toured the country singing songs to mobilize the rural and urban population and was solicited by top political leaders to advise them on the path to peace![101]

Post-conflict peace building

In the aftermath of atrocities, art slowly re-emerges as civic space opens. Cambodia's Hen Sophal tells us: "Although the genocide ended 30 years ago these images are still within me. And I still want to express them, so I have painted many things from my memory."[102] However, violent repression of artistic expression can reappear without warning. For example, anonymous death threats were issued in 2009 to the former chairman of Peru's Truth and Reconciliation Commission, simply for supporting the proposed establishment of a museum for memory, six years after the commission's report was published and his official mandate ended.[103] Of art's diverse peace building functions, seven are highlighted: preserving memory; deterrence or preventing recurrence; restoring culture and tradition; breaking from tradition and crafting new identities; reconciliation; healing; and reparation.

First, art preserves memory, a fundamentally important function after war. DRC's dancer/choreographer Faustin Linyekula affirms: "The most urgent is learning to see ourselves again and looking back into our collective past. The various regimes in DRC have brought manipulation and amnesia. But how can we ever deal with the future without learning from the past?"

In Cambodia visual artists who experienced the genocide have viewed it as their duty to depict the horrors of the Khmer Rouge. They believe that as time passes, memories of the horror will fade and it is only through the preservation of memory through all means, and in their case through paintings of the scenes of horror, that its recurrence can be deterred. Vann Nath, whose paintings of Pol Pot made him one of the sole survivors of the deadly S21 prison, today exhibits in his former prison, now turned into a museum, the paintings of the scenes of torture he witnessed as a prisoner there.[104] In Peru ANFASEP's modest Museum of Memory was created by the mothers of the disappeared with their own meager resources to honor their unburied dead. Yuyachkani's theater performances not only depict the suffering of ordinary Peruvians but also revive diverse folk and cultural traditions in danger of disappearing through conflict and displacement. Thus, art serves not only to commemorate mass atrocities but also to commit to collective memory the aesthetic and cultural diversity and unity of a nation in the aftermath.

Second, in addition to historical memory, deterrence is a distinct motivation for artists and a separate function of art. When asked why he paints scenes of the Khmer Rouge regime, Vann Nath replied: "So that people know what happened, so that they never forget, so that it never happens again."[105] Faced with the tendency of post-conflict countries to sink frequently back into violence, the deterrent function of art in such situations is particularly relevant for the UN Peacebuilding Commission and peace builders.

The third function is restoring culture and identity. When the Taliban imposed its draconian prohibition of culture and destroyed invaluable works of art and musical instruments, artists, curators, and musicians found ingenious ways to conceal artifacts, artworks, and musical instruments to save them from destruction, and actors organized theater clandestinely.[106] The new plaque at the National Museum in Kabul states unequivocally, "A nation stays alive when its culture stays alive," and this motto galvanizes Massoudi and his intrepid staff in restoring the shards of Afghanistan's shattered millennial past.[107] "The first sign of the identity of a country is through its art, its cultural expressions. Art witnesses and expresses the human feelings of members of its society, so it is essential for life," says Fatah Adil of the National Art Gallery.

In Cambodia, the Khmer Rouge executed numerous artists, and many art forms faced extinction. Immediately after the genocide and a change in government, the new regime encouraged the few surviving artists to become teachers. This effort has intensified through many civic initiatives in recent years. Khi Mom, now aged 86, was the only surviving member of her family of traditional Kee opera singers/performers dating back to the time of the Buddha. Today she teaches young children the nearly lost opera form at Cambodian Living Arts, a civic association created by a prize-winning Cambodian artist specifically to revive Cambodian arts. Khi Mom thoughtfully articulates that it is important to balance tradition with innovation in order to keep art and culture alive and evolving.[108] Zimbabwe's poet Chirikure captures the centrality of preserving ancient culture in modern art: "The age-old Shona tales, the music, the carvings, the language—I draw strength from these to carry on. No one can destroy these manifestations of our culture."[109]

The fourth function, in sharp contrast, is breaking from tradition and reinventing identity. In Kosovo the burgeoning of new and radical forms of contemporary art after 1999 has served both purposes. One, it unleashed a new creative energy that enabled young artists to go beyond the confines of traditional and conventional visual art, which to them was patriarchal and parochial. Several young Kosovar artists have gained worldwide renown through their iconoclastic and radical artistic expressions, which were fostered by the underground art movement that encouraged artists to explore alternative means of expression during the Serbian occupation of the 1990s. Two, this radical re-questioning through art has also played a major role in enabling the newly born Kosovo to imagine and craft a new identity. The art project Missing Identity dedicated five years to this theme, under the direction of Professor Mehmet Behluli.[110]

Healing is the fifth fundamental function. Art therapy for psychosocial healing has deployed dance, theater, music, film, and photography in diverse violent conflicts.[111] Beyond this, endogenous artistic initiatives can have profound healing effects without being designed as art therapy per se, as in Peru. Visual artist Wari Zarate, a Quechua Indian from the Ayacucho region where the Sendero Luminoso originated, used visual arts with orphans and widows and led art therapy workshops for the indigenous women's association Chirapaq. Ana Correa, co-founder of Yuyachkani, describes how art and theater help women victims slowly heal themselves and youth find their lost identity, self-esteem, and confidence. Of her theater work, she muses, "Estamos luchando para una utopia" ("we are fighting to create a utopia").[112]

Sixth, art can foster reconciliation, which is an overused term but an under-analyzed and frequently misunderstood process in post-conflict peace building. At the community level, efforts often solely focus on fostering political reconciliation to avoid upsetting the status quo or provoking economic disinvestment—as in Mozambique, Namibia, and South Africa. Genuine people-to-people reconciliation is harder to co-opt. Mostar symbolized the breakup of former Yugoslavia with the destruction of its historic bridge. Although the bridge was repaired, Mostar's society remains fissured and its people divided, with distinct schools, hospitals, municipalities, and even orphanages serving Bosnian, Serb, and Croat populations. The popular music of the ethnically diverse band Mostar Sevdah Reunion, which emerged during the war, has had a reconciliatory effect in Bosnia and across the Balkans that no formal program could. Of the several music initiatives in Mostar, including Luciano Pavarotti's Music School, the most notable is the World Music Festival started by a young Serbian woman, Alesandra Mitic. She fled her home in Mostar for Kosovo—only to find herself trapped in war there too. Realizing the power of music to unite divided groups, she returned to Mostar and conceived the World Music Festival to bring together musicians across the former Yugoslavia and the world. With minimal resources and despite opposition from local politicians, the old undivided Mostar lives again under the spell of music.[113] "Art knows no language; it brings all people together, whatever their differences. This itself is peace," muses visual artist Faroq Faryab, former dean of the Fine Arts Faculty of Kabul University.[114]

Seventh, the principle of reparations and the rights of victims in international humanitarian law are rarely enforced, but here too art can perhaps fill the gap. Artistic expressions can convey to affected populations that some moral reparations have been paid by society. Shame and collective guilt impelled a young Hutu boy to become a poet and filmmaker. Edouard Bamporiki describes his first poem written after witnessing the murder of Tutsi neighbors, teachers, and schoolmates at the age of 10: "That is when I wrote my first poem—asking my Hutu neighbours, what have you done with our friends, our neighbours? Why did you kill them? I am so ashamed. It is that shame that has driven me so long. I kept writing poems and my poems became quite famous."[115] He subsequently made the film *Long Coat*, which provided a Hutu experience of the genocide. His work has been understandably controversial, infuriating some Hutus and viewed as tokenism by some Tutsis. Nonetheless, it has had a significant reparative effect on both ordinary Tutsi survivors and senior government officials. The work of Sinhalese artists cited above has similar reparative effects on Tamils.

Conclusion

The study of art during mass atrocities in the global South can inform the continued development of R2P conceptually and assist in practical aspects of its implementation. The artistic responses to crisis analyzed above arose spontaneously—before, during, and after mass atrocities. They were embedded, engaged, personal, collective, and transformative. Above all, they were not banal or unimportant civic phenomena to be ignored by peacemakers and peace builders, but merit careful study by them.

Art in crisis provides invaluable information about the state of civil society and its responses to violence. The feedback from art may be positive or negative, approving or disapproving, despairing or hopeful. Such gauges of public opinion may not find other channels of expression in the environment of armed conflict, and we ignore them at our peril. Decoded and heeded, they can help shape the evolution of the R2P norm, including how to gauge the efficacy of and response to various types of outside intervention.

The chapter now outlines specific recommendations for each stage of the R2P norm—prevention, protection, and post-crisis peace building—based on the foregoing analysis. First, two recommendations emerge for the preventive stage, one specific and one generic. The UN secretary-general's report on R2P of January 2009 and the General Assembly debate of July 2009 have stressed capacity building, but it is unclear how this will translate in practice beyond bolstering early-warning mechanisms. Drawing on the lessons of Kosovo in the 1990s and Nepal more recently, the specific recommendation related to R2P prevention is for the UN and regional organizations to pay closer attention to artistic and civic initiatives in countries undergoing duress, decode their messages, and act upon them as additional early warnings. Relying on official, state-run statistics will be as inadequate in the future as in the past. International organizations should also pay close attention to a key lesson from Rwanda—echoed in Algeria, Kosovo, Afghanistan, and elsewhere—namely, cultural ethnocide precedes mass atrocities. When artists are being executed or silenced, aesthetic expressions prohibited or destroyed, alarm bells are already ringing. Cultural repression and the execution of artists are usually not considered threats to international peace and security and are relegated to cultural organizations without political clout. As seen in this chapter, they are portents of impending disaster and thus require decisive, rapid responses from the UN Security Council and NATO.

The generic recommendation emerging from this analysis is that one of the most important human capacities required for preventing mass atrocities is treating "art as life": therefore, art and creativity need to be inculcated in all preventive and educational initiatives.

Scholars made two unforgettable observations during my first consultations in Cambodia and Rwanda in 2009. First, they said that the population's unquestioning submission to authority enabled them to be manipulated easily; hence, the capacity to inquire, critique, and oppose has to be instilled in youth. Second, the erosion of human bonds between and across communities fostered by age-old and now destroyed cultural values and traditions such as sharing, solidarity, compassion, and hospitality had facilitated genocide, and these values and social bonds needed to be regenerated. Art plays a vital role in rebuilding both social values and a spirit of curious inquiry and creativity that are essential to prevent or transform violence. Art is not a remote, dispassionate, intellectual, and elite urban activity but rather a vibrant collective, cultural, and participatory process that maintains, deepens, and constantly re-energizes human values and bonds.

Today in schools in the global South and North, critical inquiry and creative curiosity are discouraged or even punished while conformity and uniformity are emphasized. If it exists at all, art is reduced in the curriculum to a few hours of mimicry and repetition. Art—in the sense of creativity, curiosity, and originality—should be returned to the center of education. Achieving the Millennium Development Goal of education will be pointless if all it produces is uncritical, unreflective, uncreative computer-literate and commercially savvy clones who can staff corporate and government offices capably but could never discern societal divisions and deflect potential violent conflict.

Turning to the protective stage of mass atrocities, a particular responsibility falls upon the UN and regional and nongovernmental organizations to recognize and respond urgently to the messages conveyed through artistic responses in crisis. Communities and artists find avenues for expression during the height of mass atrocities at grave risk. Ignoring these tell-tale signs in the near-closure of civic space can cost valuable lives, but attending to them can avert tragedy.

Peace builders will have to overcome their aversion to criticism and instead treat these creative messages as allies for appropriate decision making in crisis. Second, the targeted assassinations or even the harassment of artists augur impending or ongoing calamity, and require swift response. During the Nazi Holocaust, it was the risky efforts of diaspora Jews and their secular supporters worldwide that provided safe passage to Jewish artists and saved some artworks. Artists should be considered untouchable, as they are crucibles of culture and representatives of repressed civil societies. UN officials and diplomats must provide special protection and safe havens to targeted artists, as they do for political and civic leaders.

Finally, in the post-conflict stage after mass atrocities, the centrality of regenerating art and culture for peace building should be recognized. Support for restoring art and culture is essential for nation building and re-establishing national identity, while memorializing through art amplifies the deterrent effect of transitional justice. The arts should also be supported as a vehicle for reconciliation—not only to overcome hatred and bitterness but also to prevent a return to arms. While financial reparations are crucial for desperate victims, art serves as a vehicle for social reparations. The imperative of instilling art and creativity at the center of the educational curriculum and within social life in post-conflict peace building is as fundamental for preventing relapse into violence as for preventing mass atrocities in the first place.

Notwithstanding these recommendations, governmental, intergovernmental, and nongovernmental organizations should not instrumentalize the arts to serve their political objectives, or co-opt art through well-intentioned but distorting funds. Financial and moral support to art and culture are essential in all three stages of R2P, but should be thoughtfully channeled. The endogenous and spontaneous emergence of art within violence-wracked societies contains the seeds of solidarity, mutual responsibility, and protection. It is this embedded, inclusive, committed, and transformative art that can germinate and nurture the responsibility to protect.

As Anthony Appiah observed, "The rewards of exploring other peoples' arts have, in the end, a humanizing dimension that explorations with the microscope—even when it is turned on our own bodies—never quite achieve."[116] The challenge of implementing the R2P norm, so appealing in concept yet so confounding in practice, is to reawaken in our deeply divided world the sentiment of unity and interdependence. Art knows no language and brings all people together, noted Afghani professor Faryad; art offers an opening to the heart, mused Hafiz in fourteenth-century Persia. Such art in crisis can help us rediscover our innate human solidarity to activate the responsibility to protect.

Notes

Acknowledgements: This chapter benefitted from early collaboration with Professor Koulsy Lamko. Special thanks to Udo Janz, director of the UN High Commissioner for Refugees in New York, for insightful feedback at the final project seminar on 22 October 2010 in New York. Warm appreciation to Laurel Borisenko for feedback on earlier drafts, Cynthia Cohen for her work, and Alex Danchev and Scilla Elworthy particularly for their contributions to a seminar on Culture in Conflict moderated by the author at the University of Oxford, 15 May 2010.

1 Daniel Ladinsky, trans., *The Gift: Poems by Hafiz, the Great Sufi Master* (New York: Compass/Penguin, 1999), 52.
2 Interview with the author, Phnom Penh, July 2009.
3 Michael Robinson, "Foreword," in *Asian Art*, Michael Kerrigan (London: Flame Tree, 2005), 10.
4 See, for example, Abdou Sylla, *Création et imitation dans l'Art africain traditionnel* (Dakar: IFAN-CAD, 1988); Ola Balogun, *Introduction à la culture africaine* (Paris: UNESCO, 1977); Oriana Baddeley and Valerie Fraser, *Drawing the Line: Art and Cultural Identity in Contemporary Latin America* (London: Verso, 1989); Bérénice Geoffroy-Schneiter, *Primal Arts: Africa, Oceania and the Southeast Asian Islands* (London: Thames & Hudson, 2000).
5 Krydz Ikwuemesi and Ayo Adewunmi, *A Discursive Bazaar: Writing on African Art, Culture and Literature* (Enugu, Nigeria: Pan African Circle of Artists, 2001), 5.
6 For information on this project, see www.ceri-sciencespo.com/themes/re-imaginingpeace/vf/ressources/themes.htm
7 A news update on the website's funding crisis is available at: www.powerofculture.nl/en/current/2010/june/power-of-culture-on-hiatus.
8 Fascinating discussions of art's origins are presented in Ellen Dissanayake, *Art and Intimacy: How the Arts Began* (Seattle: University of Washington Press, 2000); and David Lewis-Williams, *The Mind in the Cave: Consciousness and the Origins of Art* (London: Thames & Hudson, 2002).
9 Ellen Dissanayake, *Homo Aestheticus: Where Art Comes From and Why* (New York: Free Press, 1992), 228.
10 Noel Carroll, "Art and Human Nature," *The Journal of Aesthetics and Art Criticism* 62, no. 2 (2004): 102.
11 See Lewis-Williams, *Mind in the Cave*, for these specificities and similarities.
12 Georg Wilhelm Friedrich Hegel, *Aesthetics: Lectures on Fine Art* (Oxford: Clarendon Press, 1975).
13 While citing many sources, I am inspired particularly by Cynthia Cohen's *A Poetics of Reconciliation: The Aesthetic Mediation of Conflict*, unpublished doctoral dissertation, University of Hampshire, 1997.
14 Hegel, *Aesethetics*, 5.
15 Immanuel Kant, *Critique of Judgment*, trans. James Creed Meredith (Oxford: Clarendon Press, 1952).
16 SS 41: "The empirical interest in the beautiful," in Kant's *Critique of Judgement*. See James Creed Meredith's full translation at: philosophy.eserver.org/kant/critique-of-judgment.txt.
17 Hegel, *Aesthetics: Lectures on Fine Art*; Arthur Coleman Danto, *The Abuse of Beauty: Aesthetics and the Concept of Art* (Chicago: Open Court, 2003).

18 Arthur Danto, "Beauty and Morality," in *Embodied Meanings: Critical Essays and Aesthetic Meditations* (New York: Farrar, Straus and Giroux, 1995), 363–75.
19 Kathleen Marie Higgins, "Whatever Happened to Beauty? A Response to Danto," *The Journal of Aesthetics and Art Criticism* 54, no.3, (1996): 281.
20 Higgins, "Whatever Happened to Beauty?," 283.
21 Carroll, "Art and Human Nature," 97.
22 Estella Lauter, "Re-enfranchising Art: Feminist Interventions in the Theory of Art," in *Aesthetics in Feminist Perspective*, ed. Hilde Hein and Carolyn Korsmeyer (Bloomington: Indiana University Press, 1993).
23 Heidi Gottner-Abendroth, "Nine principles of a matriarchal aesthetic," in *Feminist Aesthetics*, ed. Gisella Ecker (Boston: Beacon Press, 1986).
24 Renee Cox, "A Gynecentric Aesthetic," *Hypatia* 5, no. 2 (1990): 43.
25 Developed in Renee Lorraine, "A Gynecentric Aesthetic," in *Aesthetics in Feminist Perspective*, ed. Hilde Hein and Carolyn Korsmeyer (Bloomington: Indiana University Press, 1993), 35–52.
26 See, for example, Michael Kampen-O'Riley, *Art beyond the West* (London: Pearson Prentice Hall, 2006); and Geoffroy-Schneiter, *Primal Arts.*
27 Discussed extensively by Geoffroy-Schneiter, *Primal Arts*, especially in chapter 1.
28 Ananda Coomaraswamy, *On the Traditional Doctrine of Art* (Ipswich, UK: Golgonooza Press, 1977).
29 On African art see also Abdou Sylla, "Le Parallélisme asymétrique dans l'Art africain," *Ethiopiques* 4, no. 46–7 (1987), available at: ethiopiques.refer.sn/spip.php?article160; Jacqueline Delange, *Arts et peuples de l'Afrique noire. Introduction à une analyse des créations plastiques* (Paris: Gallimard, 1967).
30 Dele Jegede, "Art for Life's Sake: African Art as a Reflection of an Afrocentric Cosmology," in *The African Aesthetic: Keeper of the Traditions*, ed. Kariamu Welsh-Asante (Westport, Conn.: Greenwood Press, 1993), 237–48.
31 Jegede, "Art for Life's Sake: African Art as a Reflection of an Afrocentric Cosmology," 237.
32 Cited in his Preface to Mary H. Nooter, ed., *Secrecy: African Art that Conceals and Reveals* (New York: Museum for African Art, 1993), 14. See also Kwame Appiah, "What is African Art?" *New York Review of Books* XLIV, no. 7 (1997): 46–51.
33 Coomaraswamy, *On the Traditional Doctrine of Art*, 5.
34 Ananda Coomaraswamy, *Coomaraswamy, Vol.1: Selected Papers: Traditional Art and Symbolism* (Princeton, NJ: Princeton University Press, 1978).
35 Ananda Coomaraswamy, "The Significance of Oriental Art," *The Art Bulletin* 2, no.1 (1919): 19–22.
36 Leopold Senghor, *Liberte 1: Negritude et Humanisme* (Paris: Seuil, 1964), 207. See also his "L'esthétique négro-africaine," *Diogène* 16 (1956): 50. See also Abdou Sylla, "Senghor et les Arts Plastiques," *Ethiopiques* 69, no. 2 (2002), available at: www.refer.sn/ethiopiques/article.php3.
37 Wole Soyinka, *Art, dialogue and outrage: Essays on literature and culture* (London: Methuen, 1993), 20.
38 Cohen, *A Poetics of Reconciliation*, 202.
39 Kampen-O'Riley discusses this well in "Art without Boundaries," in *Art beyond the West*, 304–20.

40 See www.fespaco.bf; artradarasia.wordpress.com for Art Radar Asia and www.africancontemporary.com; and www.africancolours.com for African Contemporary art. See www.dakart.com for Dakar's Biennale of African Contemporary Art, 2010.

41 Kerrigan, *Asian Art*, 105.

42 See also Sylla, "Le Parallélisme asymétrique"; and Delange, *Arts et peuples de l'Afrique noire.*

43 Babacar Diop, "Approche des Arts Africains: Centième anniversaire de L. S. Senghor. Cent ans de littérature, de pensée africaine et de réflexion sur les arts africains," *Ethiopiques* no. 76 (2006): available at: ethiopiques.refer.sn/spip.php?rubrique522. Translated by the author from French; thanks to Koulsy Lamko for this citation.

44 I thank Alexander Schieffer for developing the notion and relevance of the arc to describe this phenomenon.

45 Interview with the author, Kigali, July 2009.

46 On propaganda art, see: iml.jou.ufl.edu/projects/Fall98/Wolfe/frame.html

47 Comments by Kayishema at project authors' conference, Centre for International Studies of the University of Oxford, 15 January 2010. Also Kayishema's Chapter 4 in this volume.

48 John Paul Lederach, *The Moral Imagination: The Art and Soul of Building Peace* (Oxford: Oxford University Press, 2005), 5.

49 Professor Alex Danchev's comments at a panel discussion entitled "Culture Conflict and the Building of Peace," convened and moderated by the author, at Peacebuilding Conference, St. Johns College, University of Oxford, 15 May 2010. See also Alex Danchev, *On Art and War and Terror* (Edinburgh, UK: Edinburgh University Press, 2009).

50 Cited at www.mahmouddarwish.com/english/introduction.htm.

51 Interview with author (identity of artist is not revealed for security reasons), July 2009.

52 Interview with the author, July 2009, Pristina.

53 See for example, Danchev, *On Art and War and Terror*; Fintan O'Toole, *Cultures, art and conflict* (Dublin: City Arts Centre, 1999); Gordon Hon, ed., *What remains to be seen: Art & political conflict. Views from Britain, Israel, Palestine & Northern Ireland* (London: Multi Exposure, 2004.); Matti Hyvärinen and Lisa Muszynski, eds., *Terror and the arts: Artistic, literary, and political interpretations of violence from Dostoyevksy to Abu Ghraib* (New York: Palgrave Macmillan, 2008); Mariann Liebmann, ed., *Arts Approaches to Conflict* (London: Jessica Kingsley Publishers, 1996); Donald Meltzer and Meg Harris Williams, *The apprehension of beauty: The role of aesthetic conflict in development, art, and violence* (London: Published for the Harris Meltzer Trust by Karnac, 2008); Vaughan Allen, *Warning shots! Contemporary art exploring themes of conflict & violence* (Leeds: Royal Armouries, 2000); Wendy and Jack Richardson, *Conflict: Through the eyes of artists* (Oxford: Heinemann, 1993).

54 Interview with the author, July 2009.

55 In few cases, such as Yuyarison in Peru, there was a small degree of sponsorship by international NGOs as well as local ones, but the cases here are primarily endogenous and spontaneous. The recent rise in funding and sponsorship of art projects during or after conflict signals a recognition of their importance by donors and UN agencies.

56 I am grateful to Professor Koulsy Lamko for his personal experiences and analysis on the African cases, particularly Rwanda, South Africa, Côte d'Ivoire, Algeria, and the DRC, which I have further corroborated from other sources.

57 Theatre of the oppressed, founded by Augusto Boal in Brazil in 1971, is "of, about, by and for the oppressed," the simple aim of which is to "humanize humanity." It has now spread to over 70 countries worldwide with different manifestations: forum theater, as it is popularly known, invisible theater, or legislative theater. See www.theatreoftheoppressed.org.

58 Gail Iris Neke, *[Re]forming the past: South African art bound to apartheid* (Johannesburg: University of the Witwatersrand, 1999); Stephanie Marlin-Curiel, *Truth and consequences: Art in response to the Truth and Reconciliation Commission* (Johannesburg: University of the Witwatersrand, 1999).

59 Hege Aasgaard, "Harare arts festival stands up against isolationism," May 2010, available at: www.powerofculture.org/en/current/2010/may/hifa.

60 Linda Gabriel, "Poetry Keeps Hope Alive in Zimbabwe," April 2009, available at: www.powerofculture.nl/en/current/2009/april/house-of-hunger-poetry-slam.

61 Peter Vlam, "Chirikure: 'I assert my right to express myself,'" August 2005, available at: www.powerofculture.nl/en/current/2005/august/chirikure.html.

62 Arne Doornebal, "Art centre in Goma defies war," February 2009, available at: www.powerofculture.nl/en/current/2009/february/goma.

63 Inge Ruigrok, "Faustin Linyekula and the esthetics of survival," available at: www.powerofculture.nl/en/current/2007/november/faustin.

64 Interviews with all named artists by Rama Mani, Rwanda, July 2009. On Rwanda's museums see www.museum.gov.rw.

65 As reported by Koulsy Lamko to author.

66 Alain Christian Eyoum-Ngangue, "La musique dans le débat politique et identitaire en Côte d'Ivoire, le cas du Zouglou," thesis presented at Ecole des Hautes Etudes en Sciences Sociale, 16 October 2009. This reference and case were provided by Koulsy Lamko.

67 Cited in Elikia M'Bokolo, "Musique et identités: le zouglou ivoirien—Interview with Dr. Eyoum Ngangue," radio program (Radio France Internationale, 1 May 2010), which explains the origins of *zouglou* in the 1990s during Côte d'Ivoire's anti-dictatorship movement and subsequent war, and specifically its role, impact, and messages. Translated from French by author. See: www.rfi.fr/contenu/20100501-musique-identites-le-zouglou-ivoirien.

68 Assane Kone, "Tiken Jah Fakoly: La voix des sans voix," 29 October 2009, available at: www.bamanet.net/index.php/musique/generale/6079-echostar-tiken-jah-fakoly-la-voix-des-sans-voix.html.

69 See, for example, Elie Chalala, "Many Causes Underlie Assassinations of Algerian Journalists and Intellectuals: Why Death of a Nation's Conscience Has Met With Cold Indifference," *El Jadid* 4, no. 24 (1998): available at: www.aljadid.com/essays_and_features/0424chalala.html.

70 Assia Djebar, *Vaste est la prison* (Paris: Albin Michel, 1995); Malika Mokeddem, *Des rêves et des Assassins* (Paris: Grasset, 1995).

71 See Djaout's bibliography and popular citations at: azeffoun.over-blog.net/article-6675253-6.html.

72 See David Craven, *Art and revolution in Latin America, 1910–1990* (New Haven, Conn.: Yale University Press, 2002).

73 Baddeley and Fraser, *Drawing the line*, 2.

74 Macarena Gómez-Barris, *Where memory dwells: Culture and state violence in Chile* (Berkeley: University of California Press, 2009).
75 Author's field trip to Peru, 2–9 December 2009.
76 See: www.festivaldepoesiademedellin.com.
77 For Palestinian and Israeli testimonies, see Gordon Hon, ed., *What remains to be seen: Art & political conflict: Views from Britain, Israel, Palestine & Northern Ireland* (London: Multi Exposure, 2004); and Dana Arieli-Horowitz, "Art in the age of terror: The Israeli case," in *Terror and the arts: Artistic, literary, and political interpretations of violence from Dostoyevksy to Abu Ghraib*, ed. Matti Hyvärinen, and Lisa Muszynski (New York: Palgrave Macmillan, 2008), 41–59.
78 See Daniel Barenboim and Edward Said, *Parallels and Paradoxes: Explorations in Music and Society* (New York: Pantheon, 2002).
79 Drawn from www.mahmouddarwish.com/english/introduction.htm. Although Mahmoud Darwich is Palestine's poet laureate and beloved across the Arabic-speaking world, hardly any of his voluminous works are translated into English.
80 While artists have mobilized both in Israel and Palestine, space constraints do not allow a coverage of art expressions in Israel.
81 Erin Murray, "The Art of War," Electronic Intifada, 13 January 2005, available at: electronicintifada.net/v2/article3524.shtml.
82 See organization's website at: www.alrowwadacts.ps/eindex.php. See also the BBC's coverage of street art in Gaza City in "Artists of Conflict," BBC World Service, 3 October 2001.
83 Christine Tohme, "War and art practice in Lebanon," October 2006, available at: www.powerofculture.nl/en/current/2006/october/tohme.html.
84 Phillip Kennicott, "War is Hell (on Art too): Lebanese Art of Convergence at American University," *Washington Post*, 25 April 2010, available at: www.washingtonpost.com/wp-dyn/content/story/2010/04/23/ST2010042304200.html?sid=ST2010042304200.
85 Nafez Zouk, "Art of war: Open-air exhibition in Dahiyeh takes visitors on a tour of conflict," *The Daily Star*, 27 July 2007, available at: www.inminds.co.uk/article.php?id=10194.
86 Personal interviews with all cited artists in Kabul, 27 November–1 December 2010.
87 Stefan Christoff, "Naseer Shamma and the music of resistance," *The Electronic Intifada*, 4 February 2010, available at: http:/electonicintifada.net/content/naseer-shamma-and-music-resistance/8662.
88 "Fighting with a Brush," interview with the artist at: current.com/news-and-politics/88858589_fighting-with-a-paint-brush.htm.
89 Thomas G. Weiss, "Halting Atrocities in Kenya," in *Great Decisions 2010* (New York: Foreign Policy Association, 2010), 17–30.
90 Manjushree Thapa's *Forget Kathmandu* (Delhi: Penguin India, 2005) begins in June 2001 and exemplifies this creative activism.
91 Author's field visit to Nepal and interviews with artists, August 2009.
92 Author's conversation with von Uexkull, 14 June 2010, Hotonnes, France.
93 Interviews with artists and many members of Pristina's population by author in July 2009.
94 Chris Parkinson, *Peace of Wall* (Melbourne: Affirm Press, 2010). The introduction and select photos are available electronically at: blog.vandalog.com/2010/04/east-timor.

95 Author's interview with Glauk, VETËVENDOSJE!, Pristina, July 2009.
96 Author's interviews, Pristina, July 2009.
97 Author's visit to Sarajevo, Mostar, and Srebrenica and interviews with artists, July 2008.
98 Author's discussions with artists in Sri Lanka during 2007. See Prasanna Ratnayake, "A New Documentary Series from Dharmasiri Bandarnayake," 17 July 2007, available at: www.countercurrents.org/ratnayake170707.htm.
99 Televised interview, "Art, War and Politics in Sri Lanka," 18 June 2009, available at: www.youtube.com/watch?v=6CXi0S8K37A. See also ha-jagat hweerasinghe.blogspot.com and www.artsrilanka.org/today for a repertoire of contemporary artists.
100 Experiences shared with me by initiators of the art movement, first in February 2003, then in January–February 2007 when I served as Executive Director of the International Centre for Ethnic Studies (ICES). The assassination of the ICES's founding Executive Director, Neelan Thiruchelvam, had triggered the spontaneous art movement in 1999. In 2007, as violence worsened, initiators attempted to relaunch the art movement, but failed due to dramatically heightened insecurity.
101 Interview with the artist, Kathmandu, August 2009.
102 Interview with the artist, Cambodia, August 2009.
103 Author's personal interview with Salomón Lerner Febres, past chairman of the Truth and Reconciliation Commission, and professors leading the Memory Museum Project, Lima, 3 and 9 December 2009. See: www.powerofculture.nl/en/current/2007/november/faustin.
104 Personal interviews by author, Cambodia, July 2009.
105 Interview with artist, Cambodia, August 2009.
106 Interviews with actors and curators, Kabul, July 2003, supplemented in November–December 2010.
107 Interview with museum staff, Kabul, 28 November 2010.
108 Personal interview, Cambodia, July 2009.
109 Vlam, "Chirikure."
110 Personal interviews, Kosovo, July 2009.
111 Debra Kalmanowitz and Bobby Lloyd, eds., *The portable studio: Art therapy and political conflict, initiatives in former Yugoslavia and Kwa-Zulu-Natal, South Africa* (London: Health Education Authority, 1997); Rama Mani, *Beyond Retribution: Seeking justice in the shadows of war* (Cambridge: Polity, 2002).
112 Personal interviews with artists in Ayacucho, 8 December 2009, and Lima, 3 and 9 December 2009.
113 Personal interview, Mostar, July 2008.
114 Interview with artist, Kabul, 30 November 2010.
115 Personal interview, Kigali, July 2009.
116 Kwame Appiah, "Preface: Art and Secrecy," in *Secrecy: African Art that Conceals and Reveals*, ed. Mary H. Nooter (New York: Museum for African Art, 1993), 14–16. See also Appiah, "What is African Art?"

Part two

Country cases

4 Rwanda

Culture against machetes

Jean-Marie Kayishema

- **Behind Rwanda's genocide: the traditional Rwandan equilibrium**
- **From traditional equilibrium to colonial destabilization**
- **From national cultural ethnocide to genocide**
- **Restoring equilibrium**
- **A cautionary note**
- **Conclusion**

When examined through the lenses of the emerging norm of the responsibility to protect (R2P), an analysis of the 1994 genocide in Rwanda and its genesis results in two major arguments. First, the genocide was preceded by a long and systematic process of cultural ethnocide—and this destruction and dismantling of traditional culture actually facilitated mass atrocities. Second, the prospects for R2P can best be improved when citizens themselves assume the responsibility for protecting fellow citizens during crises, and in particular draw on their own cultural values and practices to do so rather than expecting external help or blaming outsiders who do not come to the rescue.

Thus, this chapter's main contribution to the elaboration and implementation of the responsibility to protect is to highlight the crucial importance of understanding the role of culture in preventing mass atrocities. This analysis does not presume that culture provides the only or even the most complete explanation for either the perpetration of mass atrocities or for successfully preventing them. Nor does it suggest that other dimensions—economic, political, legal, and military—are unimportant. While numerous studies have been conducted on these other dimensions in the aftermath of the Rwandan genocide and in the context of R2P, the cultural dimension has so far not yet been examined sufficiently. As the foundation for human society, culture defines the social context and the motivations and actions of populations. This chapter is a first attempt to fill these gaps and explore a vast subject that requires considerable additional research to challenge, deepen, and expand the preliminary observations made here.

This chapter has five main sections. The first briefly describes the genocide and the relevance of culture as a prelude to a discussion of the original equilibrium and harmony in Rwandan society, including its organization, founding myths, and religious beliefs. Rwanda's founding myth of Gihanga is especially important as it involves brotherhood among Rwandans through their eponymous ancestors (Gatwa, Gahutu, and Gatutsi).

The second section analyzes the descent from this traditional equilibrium to genocidal disequilibrium and violence during Belgian colonization. The founding myth of Gihanga was set aside and replaced by two new myths, one during colonization and the other after independence. These sowed the seeds of division, which ultimately grew into mass atrocities. The divisive processes started by colonizers and missionaries were exacerbated by Rwandan leaders in successive post-independence governments.

The third section examines in some depth the myth of Hutu supremacy that was propagated with the Social Revolution of 1959, which stoked policies of hate and further degraded traditional cultural values. This continued denigration of values—which happened elsewhere in sub-Saharan Africa but more thoroughly in Rwanda—sapped the socio-cultural, political, and economic bases of ordinary Rwandans and rendered them unable to shape their own destiny and identity. Cultural ethnocide, generated and manipulated by the ruling class since independence, culminated in the 1994 genocide.

The fourth section addresses the challenges of reconstruction after genocidal devastation and the search for a new equilibrium. It begins by holding Rwandans themselves responsible for their own fate and destiny. In the task of rebuilding a society that can guarantee peaceful coexistence for future generations, is it possible to return to the *status quo ante* of cultural values, myths, and traditions and adapt them to the contemporary post-conflict context? Is there any alternative?

The fifth section responds affirmatively to these questions. However, it also puts forward several cautionary notes before concluding.

The aim of this analysis is to foster a greater sense of self-reliance among populations torn by mass atrocities, and to call upon them to assume responsibility for their own collective and individual protection because the history of international efforts to protect victims—starkly illustrated in the case of Rwanda—suggests that they are unreliable and often harmful. Endogenous resources exist in all cultures, although in Rwanda they were weakened by foreign domination and by corruption of local elites. The responsibility to protect is a significant normative innovation that could help foster a greater sense of responsibility both nationally, internationally, and transnationally. For their part, intergovernmental and nongovernmental organizations (NGOs) should recognize and halt cultural ethnocide before it turns into deadly ethnic cleansing and genocide. However, only greater reliance by peoples and societies on their own cultural values can generate the requisite responsibility to protect themselves.

Behind Rwanda's genocide: the traditional Rwandan equilibrium

This section begins with an overview of the 1994 genocide and identifies its cultural dimensions. It subsequently examines the cultural foundations of the equilibrium of traditional Rwandan society.

An overview of the 1994 genocide and its precursors

That Rwanda succumbed to genocide of unprecedented proportions and brutality should perhaps be unsurprising. Populated by a Hutu majority and Tutsi and Twa minorities, Rwanda was distinguished prior to colonization by its sophisticated sociopolitical organization, which led early European colonizers to the conclusion that its Tutsi rulers were Hamites—whites with black skin. The 1959 Social Revolution led by the Hutu majority, and aided by the Belgian colonial administration and Catholic Church, has been analyzed in considerable detail.[1] In the context of R2P, what is essential to recall is that the role of the United Nations during the 1959 revolution was controversial and counterproductive. Rwanda was still officially under UN trusteeship, but the world organization proved incapable of countering the perverse actions of the Belgian administration. Independence in 1962 took place amidst indescribable chaos. The consequences of Rwanda's failed decolonization would provoke, three decades later, the genocide and the country's liberation by the largely Tutsi Rwandan Patriotic Front (RPF) from the genocide orchestrated by the Hutu extremist regime. Meanwhile, Rwanda was considered a model by many donor countries and aid agencies.[2] International actors essentially ignored the country's longstanding ethnic and social tensions, and may have even inadvertently exacerbated them,[3] until the rude awakening of 1990, when the exile-based RPF invaded Rwanda. The UN was able to broker the Arusha Peace Accords ostensibly to end the war in 1993. However, once again the UN proved unable to monitor and safeguard the peace as violence grew, and finally its UN Mission in Rwanda (UNAMIR) withdrew the vast majority of its peacekeepers just as the genocide began in earnest. Notwithstanding the courage and commitment of the 270 peacekeepers led by Roméo Dallaire who remained and unquestionably saved countless Rwandan lives in the ensuing carnage, it was grossly insufficient to deter the *génocidaires*. A lack of trust in the UN understandably persists in Rwanda due to the experiences of both 1959–62 and 1991–94.

The tragic events in 1994 took place between 6 April, when President Juvénal Habyarimana's plane was shot down, and 4 July, when the RPF captured Kigali and Butare, and formally declared an end to the war. Statistics indicate that close to 1 million individuals were massacred within just three months. The overwhelming majority of victims of the attempted ethnic purification were Tutsis, although Hutu moderates were also killed. This contemporary history has been widely examined in Western scholarship and policy circles and will not be repeated here.[4]

The logic of discrimination and racial ostracism that began with the 1959 Social Revolution is generally considered to be the ideological basis of the genocide. From 1959 onward, Tutsis were considered traitors, infiltrators, and second-class citizens. They were treated as foreigners originating in Ethiopia or ancient Abyssinia. Indeed, just before the onset of the genocide, they were warned: "your home is in Ethiopia, and we will make you pass by the River Nyabarongo[5] so that you arrive there rapidly."[6] Tutsis became hostages in their own land and scapegoats during every political crisis; they were persecuted and killed, as anti-Tutsi sentiments were fanned to reinforce the so-called racial unity of Hutus, as noted by French sociologist Claudine Vidal.[7] This happened, for example, during the confrontation between leaders of the north and central-south regions in 1973, shortly before General Habyarimana's coup d'état. Following the RPF's first attack in 1990, pent-up hatred of Tutsis, particularly within the army, proved an inexhaustible driver of violence.[8] Genocidal acts occurred in full view of the UN and diplomatic communities, which the extremist regime justified as reprisals for RPF attacks. Rehearsals for the final showdown of 1994 included the massacres of Kibilira (October 1990), Bagogwe in the north (January 1991), and Bugesera in the east (March 1992).

The perpetration of these criminal acts was facilitated by a psychological background of fear, rumors, and stereotypes that demonized and animalized Tutsis, which eroded insidiously the age-old Rwandan cultural taboo against shedding blood. Tutsis were called "cockroaches" and "serpents"; their attributes included a thirst for blood and power, arrogance, and slyness. During the war, RPF combatants (Tutsi and non-Tutsi alike) were portrayed as having tails like the half-man, half-animal (*impaca, insibika*) monsters in traditional Rwandan legends.

By 1994 there was a widespread tolerance of violence directed at Tutsis among the Hutu population, who succumbed to the political elite's propaganda. All that remained was a pretext to unleash the carefully prepared apocalypse, which included detailed death lists. The trigger was the downed presidential plane on 6 April 1994. The militias of the *Interahamwe* (those who attack together) and *Impuzamugambi* (those who share the same objective) as well as the Rwandan Armed Forces (FAR) mobilized Hutus to hunt down Tutsis.[9] The order was to spare no one, including women, the elderly, the sick, children, and even fetuses. Hutus who dared to resist were either threatened or killed by the militias, the FAR, and the presidential guard, who led the genocide. Some also yielded to the temptation of benefiting from the pillage of Tutsi assets. Impunity, as in previous massacres, encouraged mass participation in the mass murder.

Given that the details of this tragedy are well known, it is sufficient to just note that Rwanda became an immense killing field on a scale and with a rapidity that even the Nazis were unable to attain. The unprecedented savagery indicates the degree of premeditation and planning, especially of proximate murders: neighbors killed neighbors, spouses killed spouses, uncles killed nephews, and grandparents killed grandchildren. No completely satisfactory explanation has been found for the scale of brutality, which leads to the central argument of this chapter that cultural ethnocide preceded and facilitated the genocide. Without the systematic breakdown of traditional cultural harmony and ethnic fraternity, and the demonization of Tutsis, genocide perpetrated by ordinary civilians en masse would not have been achievable.

There are two additional reasons for the focus on culture in this chapter. First, and as noted earlier, culture has been little studied in comparison with economic, social, political, legal, and religious factors, leaving a gap in our comprehensive understanding of the causes of Rwanda's genocide. Second, culture underpins and explains the totality of human conduct and influences, and it thus provides a lever for change; through this lens, we can better understand sociopolitical events and conduct, and comprehend how they might be transformed.

While the notion of culture is contested, Edward Taylor's definition is worth noting: "A complex ensemble which includes knowledge, beliefs, art, morals, law, customs as well as all the other dispositions and habits acquired by man as a member of a society."[10] It has been noted that "the structure of personality is closely dependent on the cultural characteristics of a particular society, taking culture to mean the system of fundamental values of a society … The 'I' is a cultural product."[11]

Thus, culture not only offers us a central explanation of mass atrocities but also provides a major resource to every country that can help prevent mass atrocities. External intervention, including outside military intervention for human protection purposes, could be avoided by understanding and reinforcing the role of culture, and by restoring equilibrium in societies by reinvigorating valid traditional values related to peace, stability, and social harmony. Moreover, the cultural variable enables us to measure the chasm between the alienation of people from their own cultures as a result of colonization, manipulation, imposed ideologies, and exploitation by local elites—and contemplate how this chasm might be bridged to re-ground unstable societies.

Pre-colonial Rwanda

Despite its small size—about the dimensions of the former colonial power Belgium or the US state of Vermont—lack of significant natural resources, and landlocked geography, the so-called country of a thousand hills[12] was one of the rare parts of Africa to have established a well-structured state before European colonization. Rwanda was part of a larger cultural ensemble encompassing the Great Lakes region, which shared the triangular social organization of cultivators, herders, and hunters.[13] Why then did only Rwanda and Burundi experience such grave catastrophes due to the failure of peaceful cohabitation amidst its populations?

Rwanda was a monarchy dominated by the royal clan of the Banyiginya whose origins date back to the eleventh century. Gihanga, the first king, was enthroned in about 959 CE,[14] although some European historians claim that the monarchy only began in the fifteenth century.[15] Through a series of conquests and political reforms, the kingdom was largely centralized by the eighteenth century. The royal court "thus became the pivot of a territorial and administrative unity, in the sense that it was now necessary to pass through the court to succeed socially and benefit from its privileges. Military power also played an important federating role, as it allowed the king the capacity of 'projecting his power over long distances.'"[16] Pre-colonial Rwanda was "neither paradise nor hell," and, like all societies, it experienced wars, conquests, and succession disputes. Furthermore, it was ruled by an aristocratic system with all the usual defects of such a government. Nonetheless, "it had created a whole ensemble of mechanisms to preserve and develop both society and power," which fostered social cohesion and a national identity.[17]

Shared myths of origin, religious beliefs, and social organization ensured harmony and stability. In any society, myths play an indispensable role, as "they express, reinforce and codify beliefs; they safeguard and impose moral principles; they guarantee the efficacy of ritual ceremonies and offer practical rules to humans."[18] Origin myths are particularly important because they "prolong and complete the cosmogenic myth." When a myth is renewed, "the entire community is renewed; it finds anew its 'sources,' it lives again 'its origins.'"[19] Creation myths are a source of pride and social cohesion among most peoples, especially in traditional societies in Africa, Asia, and Latin America. Myths cement societies and nations by creating a community of shared memory, values, and aspirations. Origin myths establish order and harmony among the inhabitants of a culturally and geographically delimited territory.

In Rwanda there are two founding myths, Kigwa and Gihanga. Kigwa, the ancestor of the Banyiginya-Basindi, the reigning clan, is believed to be a hero who descended from the sky. Kigwa is the symbol of renaissance and prosperity, who represents the Rwandan people before God.

Gihanga was a descendant of the celestial Kigwa and son of the blacksmith Kazi. He himself is a blacksmith, endowed with great skills, especially woodwork and tannery. He was also a great hunter and adventurer with all the qualities of a hero and creator of an empire, as is appropriate for the purported founder of the Rwandan monarchy.

According to myth, Gihanga established the Rwandan community by fathering three sons—Gatwa, Gahutu, and Gatutsi, who became the ancestors and eponyms of the three human groups living in Rwanda: Batwa, Bahutu, and Batutsi. Gatutsi's succession to the throne reflected his success in fulfilling the tests imposed on all three sons by their father to determine who was most fit to rule.[20] As with most myths, there are multiple interpretations, both benign and malign. Some criticize this as an unjust creation myth—for example, Maniragaba Balibutsa denounces it as a "story of an eternally failed fraternity."[21] Certainly, in Belgian times and again before the genocide, divisive interpretations of the unfairness of the myth were highlighted, rather than its main message underlining fraternity and thus equality. What is often overlooked in such criticism, however, is that the king ritually renounces his membership in any particular social group; the king had to rise above any ethnic or group belonging in order to rule justly over all his citizens.[22] The myths of all civilizations, whether European or American, Asian or African, echo the trials and initiations that the heir-apparent must undergo to prove himself worthy and shed his egocentric personal identity in order to assume a cosmic identity and universal responsibility to protect all citizens.[23]

Turning to religious beliefs, Rwanda was traditionally monotheistic, with a single God named Imana, another rarity in Africa. Though he loved all humankind, Imana favored Rwandans: *Yirirwa ahandi igataha i Rwanda* (God spends the day elsewhere but comes home to stay in Rwanda).[24] Imana was also worshipped in Burundi, Bugufi, Bufumbira, and Rutshuru. Although he was considered omnipotent, he was not demanding. For instance, he did not require sacrifices or even a cult as did the gods of other monotheistic religions. Rwandans believe that Imana knows everything and understands and fulfills all needs according to His will. Nevertheless, Imana is invoked in moments of distress, and several legends recount Imana's many interventions to save those who call upon his aid and to punish ruthlessly those who merit it. While eternal happiness in the company of Imana is unthinkable, the just are compensated with a happy sojourn in the snow-covered, pearl-bedecked volcano of Karisimbi, and the evil are thrown into the flames of the eternally erupting volcano Nyiragongo.

Several intermediaries existed between Imana and ordinary Rwandans. The first were the souls of ancestors, who mediated between God and the living.[25] The second was the king, who was Imana's representative on earth. Making the monarchy a right of divine law created social stability by limiting rival claims to the throne. As in other royal myths around the world, the Rwandan king manifested three great attributes: royalty, holiness, and heroism. He had political and divine powers that enabled him to conquer enemies; he was the great priest who commanded the cosmic forces—he stopped torrential rain, ended drought, and ensured the prosperity and power of the country. The royal symbol was the *Karinga* or sacred drum, which was considered even superior to the king, who swore to die for this symbol if necessary.[26] The king was situated between Imana and men; he was thus considered a divinity and celebrated in poems.[27] The monarchy was sacred, represented above by thunder and on earth by the sacred drum and the king, who co-reigned with the queen mother.

The third intermediary of Imana was Lyangombe. According to legend, he was a prince and the younger brother of the last king of the prestigious kingdom Cwezi of Gitara,[28] who arrived in Rwanda in the sixteenth century during the reign of Ruganzu II Ndoli. He incarnates the myth of Cwezi, which is said to have survived the submersion of the entire population in a lake. As a similar catastrophe attributed to the Cwezi kingdom befell Rwanda at this time, a cult called Kubandwa emerged with Lyangombe as its great priest to mollify the spirits. Soon

Lyangombe became equated with a Rwandan Christ figure and was considered the intermediary to Imana.[29] The cult continued and was appealed to particularly in times of crisis or for special protection.[30] Even the king paid special respect to Lyangombe and, for example, never attacked Gitara, Lyangombe's homeland.[31]

A final and crucial part of Banyarwanda religiosity was the belief in numerous taboos, "the most ancient unwritten code of humanity."[32] According to Jean Maisonneuve, a taboo "designates everything that is taken away from common usage, thus prohibited and inviolable; this could concern objects, places, actions, animals or humans. Ethnographic enquiries reveal that such interdictions exist in all religious systems."[33] Taboos are wide-ranging: they may protect property, arms, tools, and farmland from robbery; or protect people from natural forces such as thunder and lightning. They also determine the inviolability of certain social unions like blood pacts. Thus taboos are at once sacred and consecrated, commanding adherence, and yet menacing, dangerous, and impure if violated.[34]

In traditional Rwandan culture, taboos served to regulate social relations, especially the submission of children to parents and elders, respect for supreme authority, sexual relationships, and sacred unions. Their power emanated from their magical force.[35] This force is formidable, as it is unleashed automatically whenever a taboo is violated. With rare exceptions, the fear of breaking taboos was sufficient to maintain social order. Breaking a taboo necessitated the performance of purification rituals (*kunywa amasubyo*) to exorcize the impurity of the perpetrator and reintegrate him or her within society without contaminating it.

It is particularly significant to note that two of the strongest taboos were routinely violated during the genocide. The first was the sanctity of women's bodies and the prohibition against rape. The second was the crime of spilling blood, which constituted a particularly strong taboo because murderers, especially outside the context of war, were considered contaminated until they were purified ritually. Even warriors returning from military expeditions had to perform certain rituals in order to be reincorporated into normal society, since contact with human blood was so dreaded. The organization of a mass ritual cleansing ceremony, *kunywa amasubyo*, abolished by Christian churches as pagan, could well be considered as part of transitional justice and reconciliation.

Rwanda's traditional social organization and political institutions rested on a shared belief in the fraternity of all Rwandans through the myth of Gihanga. The individual was not isolated but part of a Rwandan family. An individual's identity was not based on personal characteristics but rather on community belonging. This community and family-based vision reflected the Rwandan philosophical conception of *kuba, kubaho, kubana* (to be, to be in the world [or to exist], and to be with others [or to socialize]).[36] Thus all three roles—individual, interactive or social, and cosmic or spiritual—had to be fulfilled to be considered fully human, echoing Mutombo Nkulu-N'Sengha's observation in Chapter 1 on spirituality. The *urugo* (nuclear family) played multiple roles in the individual's life: affective, social, political, economic, legal, religious, and ethical. It is within the nuclear family that *kubana* (being with others) began.

Rwandan culture had cultivated strong values and basic solidarity to generate mutual help and confidence among people. Hutu, Tutsi, and Twa lived side by side as neighbors and worked together, especially during the demanding periods of sowing and harvesting. They jointly participated in such community events as vigils, chants, dances, and war elegies, which solidified collective unity.

Further, an entire system existed for education and the protection of vulnerable groups. Each adult had the duty to educate all children. Adults had the responsibility to discipline or punish children committing errors in the absence of their parents. Values and morals were transmitted by elders to youngsters through stories that taught how good is rewarded while evil is punished; how intelligence is indispensable for survival; and how the greedy and arrogant fail while the virtuous and impoverished receive eternal justice.

Travelers caught at night received hospitality wherever they stopped. Mothers who did not possess cows were obliged to be provided with milk by those who had cattle.[37] Women and girls were respected and sheltered—indeed girls were called *nyampinga*, or persons to be assisted in desperate situations. It was a social obligation for men to accompany women safely home. Rape was taboo, as noted above, and severely repressed, and could elicit a vendetta against the miscreant's family. During wars, women and children were not harmed.

A system of customary law operated to prevent or minimize crime. Punishment was severe for robbery, especially of cattle, the nation's main wealth. Murder, considered taboo, was submitted to the ancient *loi du talion* (law of retaliation, or an eye for an eye and a tooth for a tooth). A single person was to be killed as reprisal, and the king then declared an end to the never-ending cycle of vendetta. Some customary laws were, unsurprisingly, excessive and unjustifiable—for example, girls found pregnant outside wedlock were killed or exiled.[38]

Rwandans worked together either to defend their country from invasion or to invade other countries. The services and favors that people routinely rendered to one another cemented friendships without consideration of group or ethnicity. After war, for instance, combatants would make blood pacts, a ritual that tied the descendants by *igihango* (a magic taboo), which ensured that no member of either lineage could harm the other for fear of unleashing the harm of the taboo. Belief in taboos was intertwined with religious faith, myths, and cultural values.

Thus, Rwanda traditionally possessed an unshakeable cultural foundation to safeguard peace, harmony, energy, and strength. That this multifaceted and invulnerable cultural edifice could collapse so completely to neither protect the vulnerable nor inhibit the violation of taboos indicates the thoroughness of the process of cultural ethnocide resulting from colonization and continuing through independence.

The monarchy's decline and colonization

There has been a tendency among Rwandan scholars to unilaterally blame Belgian colonizers and missionaries for the divisive inequalities that shredded the social fabric. While they certainly shoulder much of the responsibility, as examined below, there were already signs of division with the decline of the Rwandan monarchy, which had been able to ensure its role as arbiter and broker until the nineteenth century. Under King Kigeli IV Rwabugiri, the first cleavages appeared with the installation of a quasi-absolute monarchy and the creation of *ibikingi* (vast pastoral domains). Deep inequalities arose between landlords and the commoners, mainly Hutu, who tilled the soil. The earlier co-existence and relative harmony between Hutus and Tutsis was replaced with an ethnic hierarchy based on economic distinctions between Hutus and Tutsis.[39] Nevertheless, Tutsi smallholders were as disadvantaged by the system as Hutus, and provincial chiefs also lost income.[40] Similar exploitation existed in the north in a system called *ubukonde*, where Hutus dominated other Hutus.

The introduction of *uburetwa* (forced social or communal works) in about 1870 further aggravated social inequalities and affected especially those who were not part of the system of *ubuhake* (pastoral clientelism), in which they were protected by their patrons. *Uburetwa* "was accomplished for the chief two days out of five of the traditional week, and was generally done by Hutus" as well as by some Tutsis.[41] "The imposition of *uburetwa* on agriculturalists and not on herders was the proverbial straw that broke the camel's back. It created very rapidly a social cleavage that would tear society from top to bottom into two hierarchical categories, henceforth called Tutsi and Hutu."[42]

In 1896 the coup d'état at Rucunshu rang the death knell for the monarchy and unleashed an internecine war of succession, which only ended with German colonization in 1911. The arrival of European explorers, missionaries, and colonizers meant that Germany governed Rwanda indirectly: "Musinga [the king] avoided all occasions for confrontation; in exchange the Germans left him a certain liberty."[43]

After World War I Rwanda was placed under a League of Nations mandate administered by Belgium, which then became a UN trusteeship after 1945. Belgium administered the country more as a colony than a trusteeship until the violence of 1959 and independence in 1962.

From traditional equilibrium to colonial destabilization

We noted earlier that myths provide the cement that seals societies and that the founding myth of Rwanda relied upon fraternity and solidarity among all Rwandans. The destruction of traditional harmony can be attributed to two divisive counter-myths that were erected to replace the common ancestor Gihanga. The first was the Hamite myth propagated by early European scholars that Tutsis were descendants of white ancestors, presumably from Abyssinia, thus predestined to rule and dominate the "inferior" Hutu majority. This theory served to justify Tutsi domination during 50 years of Belgian rule. The second counter-myth, the Bantou-Hutu myth, was ironically a mirror image that reversed the traditional hierarchy. As foreigners who had unjustly usurped power and dominated and oppressed Hutus, Tutsis deserved to be driven out and sent back "home" to Abyssinia. This counter-myth provided the mobilizing call for the Social Revolution of 1959 and the discriminatory policies of successive Rwandan governments after independence. The result of both counter-myths was the disappearance of fraternity and solidarity among all Rwandans, along with shared values and customs of mutual help.

It is worth revisiting the arrival of European explorers and missionaries in Rwanda in the nineteenth century and their incredulity at finding a hierarchical and ordered society that, they believed, could not possibly be indigenous to Africa. Racism against blacks or Negroes appeared in Europe in the eighteenth century, especially in the philosophy of Voltaire, Hume, and Hegel. Hegel's oft-cited remark bears repeating: "the negro lives in a natural immediateness and individuality without any idea of an absolute God or the spiritual … beyond good and evil."[44]

Given the rampant pseudo-scientific racism at the time, European explorers insisted that Rwandan civilization had to have Caucasian antecedents.[45] The origin of the Hamite myth can be traced to Joseph Arthur de Gobineau's *l'Essai sur l'inégalité des races* in 1853. The biblical story of Cham or Ham—one of Noah's three sons, who was condemned by his father to become "a servant of servants … unto his brethren"[46]—was often used to justify the enslavement of Africans, especially in Rwanda. Cham and his descendants are claimed to be the noble conquerors of Asia Minor and East Africa, and their success was attributed to "the treasure of the power specific to 'white nature.'"[47]

European colonizers concluded that the tall Tutsis were Abyssinian conquerors who arrived in Rwanda in the fifteenth century with their long-horned cows. All aspects of society were viewed through the lens of Jacques J. Maquet's "premise of inequality," which posits "the existence of innate and fundamental differences between members of different castes."[48] For Maquet and such other pseudo-scientists as Marcel d'Hertefelt and Jan Vansina, Tutsis were not only conquerors but also members of a superior caste who were to be served by Hutus, "a difference springing from nature."[49]

Although numerous researchers disproved these hypotheses, they remained entrenched in colonial ideology and devastated Rwandan society.[50] For five decades, colonizers and missionaries used this Hamite myth as the ideological basis for restructuring Rwandan society. In the process, they destroyed the traditional foundations of Rwandan culture in eight ways.

First, the myth of Gihanga common ancestry of all Rwandans was discarded as a romantic fabrication and replaced with the notion of entirely distinct ethnic origins.[51] Furthermore, the king, who traditionally transcended his particular group identity on assuming the throne, was now declared to be a Tutsi. The colonial administration made identity cards with an ethnic affiliation obligatory. Thus, earlier social mutations and fluidity disappeared. Earlier, a Hutu who owned cows could become a Tutsi, while a Tutsi who lost his cattle could become an agriculturalist and thus a Hutu. On occasion Batwas, who were normally looked down upon by other groups, might be made nobility as recompense for a service to the king and thus become Tutsi. Once ethnicity was deemed irreversibly patrilineal, social mobility ended.

Second, the longstanding triple chieftainship of Rwanda that brought together all three major populations was suppressed, and a single chief of Tutsi origin was established through the Mortehan Law of 1926.[52] This mechanism also guaranteed Tutsis privileged access to the best schools and top administrative posts. As Filip Reyntjens explains: "The abolition of the system of three chiefs had a profound impact on social relations and on the situation of dependence of Hutus in particular … Social relations between ethnic groups were fundamentally affected in the sense of a rapid evolution towards a more authoritarian system, centered around a single provincial authority."[53]

Third, the god of Rwanda, Imana, was replaced by Mungu, the Swahili name for the universal Christian god. Mungu was a foreigner who lacked the closeness of Imana to Rwandans. Conversions were numerous, but they may not have been as meaningful as many observers thought. For instance, despite the fact that over 70 percent of Rwandans practiced Christianity in 1994, the faith neither prevented genocide nor provided safe haven in churches.[54]

Fourth, Christianity, with its notion of sin, hitherto unknown to Rwandans, and focus on individual salvation, demolished the traditional communitarian alliances of Rwandas. *Kubandwa* and the practice of ancestor worship were abolished and prohibited as "pagan." To be baptized one had to renounce all the rituals, sociocultural ceremonies, and taboos that maintained social cohesion. *Kiliziya yakuye kirazira* (the Church has abolished taboos) was an expression that implied that everything and anything was permitted. Converts also repudiated wives in a society where polygamy had functioned to weave multidimensional alliances across groups and regions. Thus enforced monogamy unwittingly marginalized women and fragmented society.

Fifth, the colonial administration connived with missionaries to desacralize the royal function and encourage civil disobedience, particularly when King Musinga refused to convert. To insult him, missionaries undermined his authority in the eyes of converts while administrators eventually dethroned him for his refusal to submit. The king's function as grand priest was transferred to Christian clergy, who became the sole intermediaries between God and the people. The sages, the keepers of the esoteric royal code, were accused of sorcery and banished, and traditional chiefs were publicly humiliated by priests. The successor king put in place by the Belgians, Mutara III Rudahigwa, accepted baptism, which signaled to the population at large that they too should be baptized, starting with nobles, if they wished to keep their posts.

Sixth, the cultural education system of *itorero* that inculcated values of humanity and solidarity was replaced by modern missionary education. Baptism and conversion were prerequisites for education and health services. The social and communal method of educating children and the sense of shared responsibility for all children thus also ended. The philosophical conception of Rwandans, their worldview and communitarian lifestyle were thus shattered, particularly their principles of being (*kuba*), being in the world (*kubaho*), and being with others (*kubana*), and their cherished relations with ancestors.

Seventh, even the juridical domain was not spared. The king was stripped of his juridical authority, whereas earlier he alone decided to grant life or death sentences to his subjects. Historically, any citizen could directly arrive at the king's doorstep at any hour of day or night to seek justice; the Rwandan kings were considered benign and impartial arbiters of justice of last resort, and they resolved many disputes without recourse to violence and pardoned convicts who genuinely expressed contrition. European tribunals adjudicated justice according to European law. Only the traditional tribunals of *gacaca* were able to continue largely unchanged; however, they could operate only at the level of basic collectivities and determine minor punishments or fines. Thus the reconciliatory manner of adjudicating justice based on mercy, social reparation, and reintegration was replaced by an alienating adversarial legal system of retribution.

Eighth, in economic terms traditional chiefs were obliged to collaborate with colonial agents who implemented a monetary economy and the organization of forced labor, which had not existed in traditional society. This made the chiefs hated by their own people and sowed further division. Further, to maintain subordination, administrators would regularly humiliate traditional sub-chiefs in front of their subjects, purportedly for not fulfilling their duties.

The depth and thoroughness of this cultural decimation was only possible with the acquiescence of large segments of the Rwandan population. National elites and ordinary people renounced their own ancestral cultural heritage. Collaborating with colonial and ecclesiastic authorities was the only source of economic or educational opportunity, public services, or career advancement. Tutsi elites willingly adopted the Hamite myth and its accompanying benefits, and they began to believe in their own superiority. Abbe Kagame, the most renowned scholar of the time, glorified the Hamite myth in his *Inganji Karinga* (Karinga the victorious),[55] which Hutu extremists later invoked to justify the annihilation of Tutsis. A document signed by the royal corps, titled *Abagaragu bakuru b'i bwami* (the great servants of the court),[56] was circulated in 1958 and asserted Tutsi superiority and their consequent right to govern the country conquered by their ancestors. Tutsi elites also tolerated the increasing inequality and destitution of ordinary Rwandans, Hutu in the majority, but also impoverished Tutsis and Twas. It was within this context that the tables turned with the Social Revolution of 1959, which was underpinned by a new myth.

From national cultural ethnocide to genocide

Barely 50 years after the Hamite myth had annihilated the original Gihanga myth of Rwandan brotherhood, a new myth—that of Hutu supremacy—was fabricated on the eve of independence. With support from the Soviet bloc, Tutsi elites demanded independence, wooed by the ideas of nationalism and self-determination that swept across much of the colonized Third World. In swift response, Belgium switched allegiance from the privileged Tutsis to the underprivileged Hutu majority. Colonial administrators and missionaries elaborated a new countermyth: the earlier deprecated Bantu (Hutu) were glorified as the worthy indigenous people of the land: honest, hardworking, and unjustly victimized by the feudal Tutsi minority. The positive qualities attributed earlier to Hamites were reversed, and Tutsis were described as cunning, feudal, dominating, and lazy. Cold War paranoia, on one hand, and Christian ideology, on the other hand, frightened colonial powers that newly independent states could fall prey to godless communists or Islamists. These concerns weighed heavily in the strategic choice of political alliances at independence because "separating from Europe signified falling automatically into Communism, Islam, nationalism."[57]

In Belgium, moreover, the newly formed Jeunesse Ouvrière Catholique (JOC), a social movement formed in 1925 to fight the rise of communism, and Christian Democratic leaders identified Hutus as the working class and championed their cause.[58] Furthermore, "Flemish missionaries, particularly active in Rwanda, reproduced in Rwanda the 'racial' schema that they had in Belgium. In the same way that they branded all francophones in their country as the bourgeoisie, they labeled all Tutsis as the dominant minority."[59] Colonial policies now inflamed anti-Tutsi sentiments. The majority of chiefs and sub-chiefs appointed and recognized by the colonial administration were Tutsis. Hutus readily turned against local officials who had imposed forced labor, collected colonial taxes, and punished recalcitrants.[60]

In the late 1950s, buoyed by the support of the Belgian clergy and administration, Hutu supremacy rose. The infamous *Manifesto of the Bahutu*[61] of 1957 sounded the clarion call for the Social Revolution of 1959. It was written by Hutu leaders Grégoire Kayibanda, Maximilien Niyonzima, and Aloys Munyangaju, members of the Parmehutu party (Parti du Mouvement d'Émancipation des Hutu), although it is claimed that Belgian priests played a key role in its production.[62] Kayibanda, who would later become the first elected president of the Republic of Rwanda, was the editor-in-chief of the Catholic journal *Kinyamateka*, and Munyangaju was a member of the redaction team of *Les Temps Nouveaux*, the most important journal in Rwanda and Burundi written in French.

The second mobilizing document that captured the new myth of Hutu supremacy was the *Ten Commandments*, originally circulated in 1960 at a political meeting by Joseph Habyarimana Gitera. Fuelling anti-Tutsi hatred, he condemned all social, commercial, or romantic relations between Hutus and Tutsis. He stopped short of condemning interracial marriage, perhaps because he himself had a Tutsi wife. The preamble states: "The relation between a Tutsi and a Hutu is an incurable wound in the leg, a leech in the body, a pneumonia in the ribs." Three decades later this document would serve to mobilize the final frenzy of hatred in the lead up to genocide, when Hassan Ngeze reprinted *Ten Commandments* in his infamous journal *Kangura*.[63]

Among the Hutus leading the 1959 revolt were former Hutu seminarians frustrated by their inability to attain senior indigenous administrative posts reserved for Tutsis by colonial decree. The revolution awoke the conscience of Hutus as being the original inhabitants of the land, long-dominated by usurping Tutsi "foreigners," and revolutionary songs such as *Ibigwi by'abaparmehutu* (Exploits of the Parmehutu members) and *Turatsinze* (We triumph) proclaimed: "Gahutu, wherever you are, Rwanda is yours!". Belgian help was at hand. Both the resident military attaché, Col. Guy Logiest, and vice-governor-general of Rwanda-Urundi, Jean-Paul Harroy, documented the aid that Belgium provided to Hutu insurgents.[64]

It should be underlined that Hutus were not unanimously in favor of the revolt. Some were ardent supporters of the multiethnic nationalist party, supported the monarchy and Tutsi elite, and even joined Tutsis in exile and remained faithful to the cause until their return after the genocide. Some of them were caught and killed or burnt alive for their treachery by the First Republic, including Michel Rwagasana, cousin of President Grégoire Kayibanda.

Colonization deepened the inequalities created during the monarchy, and independence required political change and social justice for a variety of reasons: the flagrant injustice done to Hutus (without mentioning the eternally forgotten Twas); the arrogance of the Tutsi elite; and the decadence of the royalty left without a direct descendent after Mutara III. However, the revolutionaries of 1959 missed the opportunity for genuine social change based on inclusion and equality; instead they substituted domination by the Western-influenced Tutsi elite with extreme Hutu supremacy. The victims of the so-called revolution were often impoverished Tutsis living as miserably as their Hutu neighbors.

This chapter is not the place to summarize the policies of successive Rwandan governments between 1962 and 1994 and accompanying events including the war of 1990–93 (led by mainly Tutsi rebels exiled since 1959 primarily in Uganda and with President Museveni's support), which paved the way for the genocide. Rather, the focus is on how post-independence political leadership not only continued cultural ethnocide but also intensified it and contributed to the further dismantling of the value base that fostered social cohesion among Rwandans. The greatest harm was caused by the continued and amplified destruction of cultural values that presumed all things cultural to be uniquely Tutsi and thus worthy of desecration, which resulted in a culture of anti-values instead of common values.

Independence in 1962 marked the formal introduction of Hutu supremacy. President Kayibanda and his Parmehutu Party installed what was effectively an apartheid system, especially after 1964 when Parmehutu became the single political party. Tutsis were demonized in political rhetoric, the media, and popular songs, excluded from all sectors of national life, and denied diplomatic, political, military, and administrative posts. They were considered at best second-class citizens and at worst foreigners with no citizenship rights. In 1963 Kayibanda had already alluded to genocide in response to the first attack by Tutsi rebels: "Imagine if despite its impossibility you managed to take Kigali, how would you measure the chaos of which you would be the first victims ... it would be the final and precipitated end of the entire Tutsi race."[65] Toward the end of his rule, threatened by political opposition from the north, Kayibanda tried to defuse the political crisis by making Tutsis scapegoats and preparing another pogrom with help from Catholic clergy, particularly Belgian Abbe Naveau and the Swiss Msr. Perraudin.

The Second Republic of President Juvenal Habyarimana, who seized power from Kayibanda through his Mouvement Revolutionnaire National pour le Developpement (MRND), used subtler means to alienate Tutsis, in order to appease human rights concerns about regular pogroms and massacres. Tutsis were allowed to participate in the economy, and some quickly became prosperous. Nevertheless, what was given with one hand was taken away with the other. Habyarimana's policy of so-called ethnic and regional equilibrium reinforced exclusionary practices and even extended them to certain Hutus. In the powerful military, for instance, segregation was particularly strict and intermarriage was strictly forbidden.

Throughout this period, the parallel processes of physical and cultural violence against Tutsis were striking. Physical violence was prevalent starting in 1959, prompting the first mass exodus of Tutsis. Regular massacres of Tutsis, notably in 1963 in Bugesera and Gikongoro and again in 1966 in Bugesera, were justified as reprisals against Tutsi rebel invaders. However, the parallel process of cultural violence also was flagrant, as described by Gérard Prunier: "One concrete, political and violent process is physical elimination (approximately 10,000 deaths in just over one year). And then there was the other process, intellectual and cultural, more calm, but eventually bearing even further violence. This process consists of delegitimizing first the Tutsis' earlier socially dominant role, and then, the negation of their right to Rwandan citizenship."[66]

No dimension was spared. In education, for instance, Tutsi professors were boycotted and insulted while students were molested or threatened.[67] With rising violence from September 1972, Tutsi students in university and secondary schools, both public and private, were sent home between February and March 1973. Psychological violence was further perfected after July 1973. While physical violence was somewhat reduced, Habyarimana enforced methodically the system of ethnic and regional equilibrium. Secondary school places were at a premium, but the quota for Tutsis was only 9 percent and often manipulated by Hutu politicians to get their own children in. Hutu parents also bribed officials to modify their ethnic affiliation to obtain places for their children.

Even in the aesthetic domain, the psychology of perversion was evident. All elements of Rwandan culture deemed to be Tutsi—such as certain ways of dressing, singing, dancing, or behaving—were denigrated and destroyed. The ruling Hutu ideology even rejected any display of elegance in manners or conduct that characterized *imfura*, the Rwandan ideal of virtuous character. As in other popular revolutions, the rejection of previous ideals of beauty was institutionalized to such an extent that statues of the Virgin Mary were decapitated in 1994, because they apparently had a "fine nose" like the Tutsis.[68] With the same perverse logic, some Hutus were massacred during the genocide because they supposedly had the fine features of Tutsis, while some Tutsis were spared because of their "ugliness." It is common knowledge that these stereotypical, ethnically defined traits are entirely misleading due to generations of intermarriage and ethnic mobility. This veritable "culture of ugliness" promoted by Hutu extremists to efface so-called Tutsi notions of beauty was not merely unfounded, but aesthetically crippling and morally bankrupt. Such a mindset restrained artistic creativity and cultural rejuvenation. The use of popular songs by leading musicians and the use of the media, such as Radio Milles Collines and journals like *Kangura*, to demonize Tutsis is well documented.

The consequences of these multiple attacks on all aspects of traditional culture at the societal level were appalling. The young were unmoored. Seeing their elders commit physical and psychological violence as well as engage in crimes of all sorts, they lost respect for elders and for traditional values and customs. Robbery and murder were tolerated and even encouraged by the authorities with the myopic belief that they were only targeting Tutsis. A maxim introduced by the government led to total permissiveness: *kwishyira ukizana* (do everything you wish). Both longstanding taboos prohibiting rape and murder,[69] and age-old values of mutual help, protection, and solidarity were violated in the ethnic chaos post-1959. Formerly, staunch feminine solidarity prevented or limited the violation of women, but during the genocide many women were known to encourage the rape of their own sisters or family members. The publicized case of Pauline Nyiramasuhuko, on trial in Arusha by the International Criminal Tribunal for Rwanda, is a case in point.

This cultural vacuum has now spanned three generations. The rebels of 1959, infected by colonization's ethnic and cultural erosion, passed the virus to their children who committed the crimes of 1973, and their grandchildren perpetrated the genocide of 1994. In 1959 massacres were widespread, but the task of dismantling culture and values had not yet reached a degree where genocide was possible. By 1994, however, the entire edifice of culture had been so thoroughly destroyed that large numbers of the population succumbed to fratricidal violence, convinced that they were annihilating dangerous monsters and not their own kin.

Several studies have analyzed meticulously the preparations for the genocide, the external military assistance provided to the regime and the *Interahamwe*, and the UN's collective incapacity to respond robustly to UNAMIR's early warnings of genocide. We need not repeat them here nor analyze the political factors that rendered UNAMIR and the UN Security Council incapable of halting the genocide, let alone acting earlier to prevent it. Rather the fundamental point is that without the systematic cultural ethnocide initiated by the Belgian colonizers and missionaries and completed by the post-independence Rwandan political leadership, the genocide would not have been possible. Without dismantling traditional culture, the masses could not have been mobilized or encouraged to perpetrate such brutal crimes. The challenge now is how to undo the monumental harm done not just to the bodies, but the souls of Rwandans.

Restoring equilibrium

The genocide raises the grave and inevitable question of individual and collective responsibility, as well as the urgent need for cultural renewal. Both are discussed in this section.

Assuming responsibility

Since 1994 many attempts have been made both internationally and within Rwanda to establish a chain of responsibility for the mass atrocities.

The responsibility of the Belgian colonial state and of Christian missionaries cannot be denied, nor can that of European countries that armed an increasingly ethnocentric regime after independence. Of particular relevance is France's murky role before, during, and after the genocide, including its controversial Opération Turquoise. The failure of the UN and UNAMIR is also questionable, even if most of the nations engaged in UN peacekeeping in Rwanda chose to withdraw their troops at that crucial moment, weakening by this action the role of the UN. However, the world organization remains also partly responsible through the deliberate miscommunication between the secretary-general's office and the Security Council, as noted by Colin Keating, president of the Security Council during the genocide in Rwanda. Furthermore, the UN authorized the permanent representative of Rwanda to continue sitting on the Security Council while it knew that his government was perpetrating mass atrocities on its own people.[70] Finally, the Organization of African Unity can also be held responsible for its inability to fill the vacuum left by the UN and its failure to intervene to stop the bloodshed. More indirectly, bilateral and international development, humanitarian, and human rights agencies are also partly to blame, as they failed to either recognize or prevent the descent into genocide.

Nevertheless, the genocide occurred three decades after Rwanda's independence. Alibis and scapegoats are easier to find than assuming responsibility for one's own destiny. Rwandan leaders, preceding and during the colonial period and since independence, are squarely responsible for the discriminatory policies they adopted and their dire consequences. So, too, are the people of Rwanda who accepted and followed or executed these policies without critical reflection, despite their amorality. All adults and independent organizations must accept responsibility for their acts. It is Rwandans themselves who must assume responsibility for their fate. But how?

In this author's considered opinion, two essential ingredients are required: responsible citizens who act based on national solidarity and rise above narrow ethnic calculations; and a return to traditional cultural values and practices.

Generating the momentum to assume responsibility

Where can responsible Rwandan citizens be found today who can assume responsibility to undo the damage done? The depressing picture of cultural and political genocide may hint that no fertile ground exists for beginning and sustaining the momentum within Rwanda for individuals and communities to take charge of their own destinies.

However, not all Rwandans were victimized or complicit in mass atrocities. Many Rwandans, young and old, acted during and since the genocide with solidarity and courage, and they could provide the foundation to protect Rwandans from future violence. There remains in the country a kernel of human capital, the existence of which is demonstrated by four examples.

First, basic solidarity was not dead or moribund even during the genocide, as evidenced by numerous acts of courage by a far larger number of Hutus than was earlier thought to be the case. To save Tutsis during the genocide, they often risked their own lives. "To Honour the Just" is currently a research effort attempting to document these forgotten but courageous individuals. Coordinated by the author of this chapter and supported by François Masabo, this project is compiling extensive interviews with both victims and "just" Hutus, and aims to identify the motivations of the "just" and their backgrounds. One preliminary finding indicates that over 80 percent of the "just" were over 45 years old and lacked secondary school education. One implication is that the "just" were often people from modest backgrounds and still in touch with traditional values. In contrast, youth and the highly educated with sociopolitical ambitions joined the militias in large numbers and engaged in genocide. Numerous acts of courage, even during the darkest hours of mass murder, suggest that humanity remained intact among the "suns in the night" (a common synonym for the "just"). Although we do not yet have accurate data, these individuals could serve as role models for the kind of responsibility that is required to rebuild Rwanda. The Kigali Genocide Memorial Centre honors them.[71]

Second, while many youth were in the killing fields, others were not. An inspiring example of heroic resistance took place in March 1997 during an incursion by rebel Hutu refugees into the Democratic Republic of the Congo (DRC, then Zaire). A group of secondary school students in Nyange provided a remarkable lesson in courage and solidarity. Attacked by the rebels and given the order to separate into ethnic groups, the students refused and unanimously proclaimed, "We're all Rwandans." Infuriated by the obstinacy, the rebels shot indiscriminately and killed several students. This event has been memorialized in a feature film directed by Jean-Claude Uwiringiyimana, entitled *One Night at Nyange.*[72]

Third, in the aftermath of genocide, countless numbers of Rwandan exiles, largely Tutsi but also many Hutus and people of mixed parentage, have courageously returned to Rwanda, taken responsibility for what transpired, and contributed to creating a safer and more inclusive future.

Finally, innumerable Rwandans of all backgrounds have undertaken initiatives in virtually all domains to manifest both their sense of shame and responsibility. Intellectuals have analyzed the genocide and explored alternative outcomes; secondary schools and universities have organized clubs and activities to root out genocidal ideologies and foster reconciliation; playwrights have staged plays to sensitize populations; and poets, writers, and musicians have used their art to express their opposition to divisive violence and the need, especially out of respect for victims, to honor life and create a more peaceful society.

These citizens represent the emergence of a new class of Rwandan citizens who feel immutably responsible for shaping their own destiny and ensuring the protection of the most vulnerable, regardless of political regime or ideology. However, these individuals and their actions will not sustain change without deeper cultural, communal, and psychic transformations. After the cultural ethnocide of the last century, an equally comprehensive and lengthy process of cultural renewal is required for peace to endure.

Cultural renewal

Despite cleavages, traditional Rwandan society had cultural mechanisms to manage conflicts and ensure peace within the kingdom. Shared values and customs generated pride in being Rwandan rather than Hutu, Tutsi, or Twa. These values and the traditional cultural practices that underpinned them should be revisited, adapted, and re-adopted. Culture is dynamic and must change with the times, needs, and mentalities.

Realizing their potential for restoring harmony and co-existence, the Rwandan government, as well as independent agencies, has gradually revisited various cultural practices and adapted them to meet current needs, particularly the central national goal of reconciliation and unity. The Commission of National Unity and Reconciliation (NURC), originally envisaged in the Arusha Peace Agreement of 1993 and established in 1997, is now a permanent body to sensitize and educate the population and mediate conflicts. NURC has taken the lead in innovating and implementing certain traditional practices, and many government ministries have done likewise in their respective domains. We briefly overview some of these renewed cultural practices and their initial contribution to Rwanda's reconstruction. Government ministries and agencies have pioneered these practices, often with outside donor support, but they have not yet been subjected to detailed analysis to measure their impact. While it thus may be premature to draw conclusions, or even suggest that their impact is unambiguously positive, it is worth enumerating six intriguing types of experiment.

Gacaca (traditional courts): The first and most widely studied traditional cultural practice is the *gacaca* court. Traditionally, the *gacaca* were customary law courts that covered both civil and criminal cases; their purpose was not punishment but socialization, not humiliation but conciliation, as all disorderly acts were considered to impact society as a whole.[73] *Gacaca* literally means "little grass," which signified that this gathering took place in the open air, sitting on grass. Faced with the impossibility of subjecting all the accused *génocidaires* individually in modern courts, *gacaca* were adapted and enacted across the country to enable communities to participate in the process of rendering justice. Those who cooperate are given more lenient sentences—frequently community service for those who abetted but did not commit crimes—while those who do not cooperate but committed serious crimes may be severely punished, including life imprisonment. As the *gacaca* process closes, 16 years after the genocide, the jury is out on its impact. While criticized for not following strictly universal principles of fair trial, its dual social impact of both reversing the impunity installed since 1959, and allowing the community as a whole to participate in trials and reconcile with and even forgive and reintegrate miscreants, is of great significance in the Rwandan context.[74]

Ingando (solidarity camps): The word *ingando* has two sources. One comes from the verb *kugandika* and refers to halting normal activities to reflect on and find solutions to national challenges.[75] Second, the armed forces traditionally developed *ingando*, which referred to a "military encampment or assembly area where the troops traditionally received their final briefing while readying for a military expedition abroad."[76] Contemporary *ingando* began as solidarity camps to re-educate demobilized rebels who returned to Rwanda, especially from the Democratic Forces for the Liberation of Rwanda (FDLR). They subsequently expanded into solidarity training camps in which secondary school children learned about reconciliation and national and cultural values. By 2002 *ingando* addressed such diverse social groups as victims, prisoners, women, youth, and traders. These tough schools inculcate the virtues of patriotism, ethics, and political socialization in order to create citizens who are brave, capable, honest, competitive, and well educated. Youth at the National University of Rwanda who attended *ingando* reported that they had found it deeply inspiring. Many commented on how they learned to appreciate and cooperate with fellow Rwandans with no concern for their ethnic or social origins.[77] Some regretted that members of older generations in remote areas, who still nursed divisive ideologies, had not had the opportunity to overcome their past.[78]

Itorero (traditional education): A more recent NURC innovation is an adapted version of the *itorero* to impart traditional values.[79] The *itorero* trained youth in various disciplines and also inculcated values and skills to become *intore*, or noble gentlemen. While the traditional *itorero* was only for boys and nobles and included military training, the contemporary version is open to both sexes and all social categories.[80] While they discuss a host of specific themes, their most essential aim is to inculcate a culture of peace, harmony, flexibility, reconciliation, impartiality, and justice. Additionally, they attempt to instill a respect for the national Kinyarwanda language as well as for courage, honesty, truth, mutual help, humanity, and citizenship. The *itorero* also seek to reinvent respect for traditional taboos and prohibitions on violent behavior. The *itorero* is also an arena for fostering national unity and patriotism, and includes physical and military training, which has attracted criticism in Rwanda and for the recent attempt to introduce it among the diaspora in Belgium.

Imihigo (performance contracts): Traditionally, *imihigo* signified promises of exceptional bravery during the armed vigil preceding military expeditions. Each individual who wished to make such a promise would rise, pronounce his warrior elegy, and promise the king to surpass all others on the battlefield. He would then drink specially prepared beer to seal his promise, the breaking of which would bring dishonor to the individual and the community.[81] This practice has been reinstituted to stimulate good governance practices in achieving development goals, in the form of performance contracts between district mayors and the president. Each mayor presents his detailed annual plan and promises to fulfill it dutifully. An annual evaluation and prizes for performance have apparently stimulated high performance and achieved desired outcomes by eliciting the same desire to fulfill a public promise as in ancient times.

Ubudehe (community work): *Ubudehe* is similar to seasonal collective labor, particularly during sowing and harvesting. The Ministry of the Territorial Administration and the Ministry of Social Affairs note that the practice draws on the Rwandan cultural value of working together to solve problems. They have re-introduced this practice in various fields, like trade, animal husbandry, handicrafts, and agriculture. Today, *ubudehe* is inclusive; the groups form cooperatives with their elected representatives, who are trained to manage the plans to overcome jointly identified problems.[82]

Girinka (the gift of the cow): In Rwanda cows traditionally were the ultimate socioeconomic asset and also the most valuable unit of exchange.

They cemented matrimonial unions, as the bride price was paid in cattle. Cows were sacred and used in the royal court and in divination rituals, and thus had economic, social, religious, political, and nutritional value: "The indigenous in Rwanda didn't hesitate to defend his cow to the peril of his life, against lions and leopards, justifying the saying, '*ntakilut'inka*'—nothing is superior to the cow."[83] Traditionally, the gift of a cow was the highest form of appreciation and distinction, which cemented bonds of friendship. In an attempt to fight poverty and provide livelihoods to the poor, the Ministry of Agriculture has instituted a version of *girinka*, whereby poor families are provided with a healthy cow. The ministry both gives direct gifts of a cow and indirect gifts by which a family distributes calves to neighbors, who continue the practice, thereby sharing the original gift with the community.[84] Consequently, in addition to the direct socioeconomic and health benefits to the poor, *girinka* serves to reinforce community solidarity and sharing.

These innovations by government ministries and agencies to adapt and introduce traditional cultural practices and foster communal values to achieve social and developmental goals is certainly interesting and might provide a major boost to the task of restoring a cultural foundation in post-genocide Rwanda.

A cautionary note

It is too early to say how widespread, deep, or durable the impact of these initiatives will be, and indeed whether the results will be on balance positive or negative. Certainly, the return to cultural values and traditions in a rapidly modernizing country faces obstacles.

Seven cautionary thoughts come to mind. First, it is questionable whether the government-sponsored attempts to restore cultural values and practices will suffice without an equal autonomous embrace and emphasis of culture by individuals and communities beyond government-mandated practices.

Second, in a culture that cultivates secrets, and where much remains unsaid, it is essential to conduct field research as well as anthropological and psychological observation. This task would help determine the extent to which government-led attempts to restore cultural values and practices have had their intended impact and how they are appreciated by different groups.

Third, some unrepentant *génocidaires* and other Rwandans continue to harbor resentment, hold genocidal ideologies, and have not benefitted from experiences like the solidarity camps to revisit and abandon their ideas. They possibly interpret these practices as attempts by a "Tutsi-led" government to again impose "Tutsi" values, and thus deny that they are authentically "Rwandan."

Fourth, there has been a dramatic increase in new religions and sects, particularly evangelical groups, in Rwanda as elsewhere in the global South. These sects strongly resist a return to communal and cultural values and, like their colonial predecessors, condemn them as pagan.

Fifth, technology and modernization can make traditional values appear outdated, with limited traction for some youth who crave all things Western. Higher education in Rwanda, as in much of the global South, has radically moved away from social sciences and humanities and embraced technology and business. This trend is accompanied by an emphasis on English-speaking education—even efforts to make English the only language of higher education. While the effort to train youth to be competitive in the global marketplace is understandable, Kinyarwanda as a single common language that binds Rwandan communities is being lost. Moreover, technological and business studies typically leave little room for investigating and debating values and norms and for the critical inquiry essential to express dissent.

Sixth, many Rwandans remain apprehensive about the so-called international community, not only donor governments and the UN but also other actors with vested interests. They fear that even if a genuine return to traditional values were desirable, international actors may again find ways to undermine or manipulate them. Would a return to cultural and communal values not constitute a threat to dominant countries' economic interests in the global market?

Finally, even if these attempts to restore cultural values and practices were to succeed, there is no guarantee that cultural values in themselves will suffice to provide a bulwark against violence and mass atrocities. If economic, social, political, and other conditions are adverse, the edifice of cultural values and norms may be swept aside, as was the case in Cambodia and the Balkans, not just in Rwanda. It should be emphasized that the Rwandan government has encouraged a return to traditional culture. However, it is not governments that create cultures but rather societies themselves. We do not yet know how the Rwandan people will respond to attempts to return to the past. If support arises spontaneously from the grassroots, then the government will have succeeded in this endeavor.

Conclusion

Rwandan history since 1994 has attracted criticism and praise, both internally and internationally. The controversial involvement of government troops in the DRC—including the leaked 2010 UN report that pointed to abuse[85]—and the 2010 presidential elections have elicited considerable criticism. At the same time, Rwanda's strong economic performance, order, and political stability have won widespread praise. Despite these inevitable polarities at the political level, closer to the ground, a new Rwanda, less divided and more inclusive, nonetheless appears to be emerging. Despite the persistence of genocidal ideologies in parts of Rwanda and among the diaspora, most Rwandans cherish a heartfelt desire to never again experience the nightmare of mass atrocities.

In the course of research for this chapter, a consultation was organized in August 2010 at the National University of Rwanda in Butare with the members of the Students' Club for Unity and Reconciliation. Participants were asked, "Do you believe genocide is still possible today in Rwanda?" The unanimous reply was "No!" The explanation they offered was that today Rwandans have become so deeply conscious of the devastating consequences, and thus would never allow such mass atrocities to unfold. Those attempting to galvanize a repeat performance would be unable to mobilize people, especially youth, to perpetrate violence as they had in 1994. Ethnic segregation and even feelings of ethnic differentiation have been attenuated if not entirely eradicated. The students identified themselves quite simply as "Rwandan" and also noted that the strategies of prevention, early warning, and reconciliation championed by the government had played an important role in effecting this shift in identity. Many of the students had attended the solidarity camps and found them inspiring and motivating.

Nevertheless, such optimism is not shared by everyone. NURC professors of different ages were more circumspect in an academic seminar held on the same day, on the same campus. While ruling out genocide on the scale of 1994, they called for continual vigilance.

Clearly, a society fractured by war and mass atrocities should be rebuilt from within. Traditional societies in the global South such as Rwanda were weakened, even dismantled, and made dependent for much of their recent history by a conjuncture of historical factors: colonization, Christianization, neocolonialism, Cold War rivalries, and more recently the war on terrorism. New equilibria will require not merely the mobilization of financial resources but more importantly the human resources to be found within the cultural genius of peoples and societies.

This chapter points to the possibility of stimulating a sense of responsibility within populations torn by mass atrocities along with a parallel quest to re-establish social harmony based on their own cultures and values. The analysis of Rwandan culture, myths, and beliefs demonstrates the foundations of social cohesion that exist within all societies, even one in which cultural ethnocide had facilitated genocide.

One main lesson emerges for the UN and human rights organizations seeking to forestall genocide, and one for UN member states that agreed to the R2P norm at the 2005 World Summit. If the piecemeal breakdown of culture does not attract early and urgent attention and immediate responses by human rights defenders, the path to genocide is predictable. Societies bereft of values, customs, and myths lack the internal capacity to protect themselves from internecine violence and fratricide. A society like Rwanda's, which believed so long in unity and fraternity and considered murder a taboo even in wartime, does not become genocidal overnight. The UN and human rights organizations should be vigilant for precursors of cultural ethnocide and respond swiftly when crucial indicators suggest a threshold is about to be crossed.

As part of the agreement on the responsibility to protect, UN member states have committed themselves to protecting their own populations from mass atrocities and building capacities to do so. There are no panaceas, but the Rwanda case suggests the value of each citizen assuming the responsibility for the protection of his or her own society and its inhabitants, rather than waiting for external help or seeking scapegoats. To develop this capacity, the most promising indigenous resource is culture, with its panoply of values, norms, myths, beliefs, and practices that give meaning, grounding, and cohesion to society. Infusing R2P with a genuine cultural dimension could dismantle or at least mollify the influence of denigrating ideologies. Inputs from philosophy, religion, spirituality, anthropology, arts and aesthetics, gender, development, law, and international relations are equally relevant to the construction of inclusive visions of a society based on deeply held values.

Culture is not a rigid monolith that remains fixed, but rather a dynamic firmament that constantly adapts to the changing needs and demands of its constituents and location. Citizens in Rwanda and elsewhere in the global South should constantly revisit, challenge, and adapt their cultural foundations to be resilient in our turbulent and violent times.

Notes

1 See Jean-Paul Harroy, *Rwanda: Souvenirs d'un compagnon de la marche Rwanda vers la démocratie et l'indépendance* (Hayez, Belgium: Académie des Sciences d'Outre-Mer, 1984); Guy Logiest, *Mission au Rwanda. Un blanc dans la bagarre Tutsi-Hutu* (Paris: Didier Hatier, 1988); André Perraudin, *Un évêque au Rwanda* (St. Maurice, Belgium: Éditions St. Augustin, 2003).

2 See, for example, Peter Uvin, *Aiding Violence: The Development Enterprise in Rwanda* (West Hartford, Conn.: Kumarian Press, 1998).

3 Uvin, in particular, argues that international aid agencies in Rwanda facilitated the violence, as his title *Aiding Violence* suggests.

4 A host of well-respected secondary sources are available to interested readers, including Michael Barnett, *Eyewitness to a Genocide: The United Nations and Rwanda* (Ithaca, NY: Cornell University Press, 2002); Samantha Power, *A Problem from Hell: America in the Age of Genocide* (New York: Basic Books, 2002); Gérard Prunier, *The Rwandan Crisis: History of a Genocide* (New York: Columbia University Press, 1995); and Roméo Dallaire, *Shake Hands with the Devil: The Failure of Humanity in Rwanda* (New York: Avalon Publishing, 2003). For an evaluation at the time involving over 50 outside experts, see John Eriksson *et al.*, *The International Response to Conflict and Genocide: Lessons from the Rwandan Experience: Synthesis Report* (Copenhagen: Steering Committee of the Joint Evaluation of Emergency Assistance to Rwanda, 1996), and four other volumes. For an evaluation of the evaluation's impact, see John Borton and John Eriksson, *Lessons from Rwanda for Today: Assessment of the Impact and Influence of Joint Evaluation of Emergency Assistance to Rwanda* (Copenhagen: Ministry of Foreign Affairs, 2004).

5 During the genocide, many Tutsi corpses were thrown into this river, which flows into the Nile, supposedly leading to Ethiopia.

6 This quote is drawn from a speech given by Professor Leon Mugesera on 22 November 1992. Quoted by Human Rights Watch, *Aucun témoin ne doit survivre. Le génocide au Rwanda* (Paris: Éditions Karthala, 1999), 105. Lengthy quotations like this one in French have been translated by the editors; the original text does not appear, only the indication of "trans." In many places, Kinyarwanda terms are used with the author's translation in parentheses.

7 Claudine Vidal, "Situations ethniques au Rwanda," in *Au Coeur de l'ethnie: ethnies, tribalismes et état en Afrique*, ed. Jean-Loup Amselle and Elikia Mbokolo (Paris: Éditions La Découverte, 1985), 169.

8 See the secret memorandum of 21 September 1992 by Col. Déogratias Nsabimana, the Army's chief of staff. See Human Rights Watch, *Aucun témoin ne doit survivre*, 77.

9 The MRND (Mouvement Révolutionnaire National pour le Développement), the single party in power founded by Habyarimana, created the *Interahamwe*; the CDR (Coalition pour la Défense de la République), the extremist party responsible for initiating Hutu Power, allied with the MRND, created the *Impuzamugambi*.

10 Edward Burnett Taylor, *Primitive Culture* (New York: J.P. Putnam's Sons, 1871), 1.

11 Raymond Boudon and François Bourricaud, *Dictionnaire critique de la sociologie* (Paris: Presses Universitaires de France, 1982), 142.

12 Jean Damascène Nduwayezu, *Les fondements physiques, humains et économiques du développement du Rwanda* (Ruhengeri: Éditions universitaires du Rwanda, 1990), 24.

13 Jean-Pierre Chrétien, "Mythes et stratégies autour des origines du Rwanda (XIXe–XXe Siècles). Kigwa et Gihanga, entre le ciel, les collines et l'Ethiopie," in *Histoire d'Afrique. Les enjeux de mémoire*, ed. Jean-Pierre Chrétien and J.L. Triaud (Paris: Karthala, 1999), 297.

14 Alexis Kagame, *Inganji Karinga*, 2nd edn. (Kabgayi, Rwanda: Imprimerie de Kabgayi, 1959), 106.

15 Jan Vansina, *Le Rwanda ancien* (Paris: Karthala, 2001), 61.

16 Françoise Digneffe and Jacques Fierens, eds., *Justice et gacaca. L'expérience rwandaise et le genocide* (Namur, Belgium: Presses universitaires de Namur, 2003), 10.
17 Gamliel Mbonimana, "Les institutions traditionnelles constitutive de l'identité nationale," in *Ruptures socioculturelles et conflit au Rwanda*, ed. National University of Rwanda (Butare: Éditions de l'Université Nationale du Rwanda, 2001), Cahiers du Centre de Gestion des Conflits no. 2, 6–7.
18 Mircea Éliade, *Aspects du mythe* (Paris: Gallimard, 1963), 32. Trans.
19 Éliade, *Aspects du mythe*, 34, 50. Trans. Gamliel.
20 The two tests set by Gihanga were: first to carry milk to Imana, and second to go to Kibariro the Calculator and ask the cultural or cultivating seasons. Gatutsi succeeded due to three qualities: patience, ruse, and sobriety.
21 Balibutsa Maniragaba, "Le mythe des fils de Gihanga ou l'histoire d'une fraternité toujours manquée," in *Les relations interethniques au Rwanda à la lumière de l'agression d'octobre 1990*, ed. François Xavier Bangamwabo (Ruhengeri: Éditions Universitaires du Rwanda, 1992), 61.
22 Servilien Sebasoni, *Les origins du Rwanda* (Paris: L'Harmattan, 2000), 32.
23 Thomas Campbell, *The Hero with a Thousand Faces* (Princeton, NJ: Princeton University Press, 1949), 126–71.
24 During the genocide, a common explanation, ironically, was: "Because Imana only comes to Rwanda at night to sleep when he is exhausted, he wasn't able to intervene to stop the genocide."
25 Bernardin Muzungu, *Le Dieu de nos pères*, vol. 3 (Bujumbura, Burundi: Presses Lavigerie, 1981), 63.
26 Mbonimana, "Les institutions traditionnelles," 10.
27 See poems of the eighteenth century, during rule of Mibambwe III Sentabyo, by Semidogoro, *Umwami si umuntu ni Imana* (The King is not a man, he is god), and by Muganza, son of Nyungura, *Ntawe urenga icyo azira* (One cannot escape the evil to which one surrenders oneself).
28 Bunyoro-Kitara was a very vast kingdom that stretched across present-day western Kenya, northern Tanzania, and eastern Democratic Republic of the Congo. See John Middleton and Joseph C. Miller, eds., *New Encyclopedia of Africa* (New York: Scribner, 2007), 125. Ryangombe was a prince at the Court of Wamara, the last emperor.
29 See Aloys Bigirumwami, who described the rituals of Kubandwa and the cult of Lyangombe in *Imihango n'imigenzo n'imiziririzo mu Rwanda* (Nyundo, Rwanda: Diocèse de Nyundo, 1974), 229–53; Alexis Kagame, *Un abrégé de l'ethnohistoire du Rwanda* (Butare: Éditions de l'Université Nationale du Rwanda, 1972).
30 Mulago gwa Cikala, "Initiation africaine et initiation chrétienne," in *Actes du Deuxième colloque du CERUKI* (Bukavu: Éditions du CERUKI, 1979), 33.
31 Cikala, "Initiation africaine et initiation chrétienne," 26–7.
32 Cikala, "Initiation africaine et initiation chrétienne," 30.
33 Jean Maisonneuve, *Les rituels* (Paris: P.U.F, 1988), 28. Trans.
34 Maisonneuve, *Les rituels*, 29.
35 Ibid., 32.
36 Bernardin Muzungu, *Histoire du Rwanda pré-colonial* (Paris: L'Harmattan, 2003), 54–59.
37 Anyone contravening this custom was deprived of all his cattle by the king, who was the true proprietor of all cattle in the kingdom.

38 Such women were thrown into ravines, lakes, or banished—preferably to the Island Idjwi. This abnormal severity maintained strict morals in society, which considered bastard children as taboo. Sadly girls bore the brunt of punishment though sometimes a vendetta might be taken against the male perpetrator.

39 Faustin Rutembesa *et al.*, *Rwanda: Identité et citoyenneté* (Butare: Editions de l'université Nationale du Rwanda, 2003), 38.

40 Rutembesa *et al.*, *Rwanda: Identité et citoyenneté.*

41 While many scholars contend that *uburetwa* was introduced by colonizers, this study draws on Rutembesa's work which provides proof that it predated colonization. Rutembesa *et al.*, *Rwanda: Identité et citoyenneté*, 40–1. Trans.

42 Joseph Rwabukumba and Vincent Mudandagizi, "Les formes historiques de la dépendance personnelle dans l'État rwandais," *Cahiers d'Études africaines* XIV, no. 53 (1974): 6–25, 40–1.

43 Jean Rumiya, *Le Rwanda sous le régime du mandat belge (1916–1931)* (Paris: L'Harmattan, 1992), 19. Trans.

44 Cited in Maniragaba Balibutsa, *Une archéologie de la violence en Afrique des Grands Lacs* (Libreville, Gabon: CICIBA, 2000), 190–1.

45 Jean-Pierre Chrétien, "Hutu et Tutsi au Rwanda et au Burundi," in *Au cœur de l'ethnie*, ed. Jean-Loup Amselle and Elikia Mbokolo (Paris: Éditions La Découverte, 1999), 130. Trans.; Luc de Heusch, *Une république devenue folle: Rwanda 1894–1994*, film, 1995; Vidal, "Situations ethniques au Rwanda," 167–84.

46 Genesis 9: 18–27; 10: 1. King James version.

47 Balibutsa, *Une archéologie de la violence*, 202.

48 Jean-Jacques Maquet, *Le Système des Relations sociales dans le Ruanda ancien* (Tervuren, Belgium: Annales du Musée Royal du Congo Belge, 1954), 195. Trans.

49 Maquet, *Le Système des Relations sociales dans le Ruanda ancien*, 189. Trans. For different analyses, see Balibutsa, *Une archéologie de la violence*; Louis de Lacger, *Ruanda* (Kabgayi, Rwanda: Diocèse de Kabgayi, 1939), 189; and André Pagès, *Un royaume hamite au Centre de l'Afrique* (Brussels: Institut Royal Colonial Belge, 1933).

50 See Chrétien, "Hutu et Tutsi au Rwanda et au Burundi"; Vidal, "Situations ethniques au Rwanda," 183.

51 Aloys Bigirumwami, *Ibitekerezo. Indilimbo. Imbyino. Ibihozo. Inanga. Ibyivugo. Ibigwi. Imyato. Amahamba n'Amazina y'inka. Ibiganiro* (Nyundo, Rwanda: Diocèse de Nyundo, 1971), 11–2.

52 See, for example, Josias Semujana, *Origins of Rwandan Genocide* (New York: Humanity Books, 2003).

53 Filip Reyntjens, *Pouvoir et droit au Rwanda. Droit public et évolution politique, 1916–1973* (Tervuren, Belgium: Musée Royal de l'Afrique Centrale, 1985), 113–5. Trans.

54 After the Second Vatican Council, God could be called "Imana," but the damage was done.

55 Alexis Kagame, *Inganji Karinga* (Kabgayi, Rwanda: Imprimerie de Kabgayi, 1959).

56 See Fidèle Nkundabagenzi, *Rwanda politique 1958–1960* (Brussels: CRISP, 1962), 35–6.

57 Rutembesa *et al.*, *Rwanda: Identité et citoyenneté*, 46. Trans.

58 Paul Rutayisire, "Politique et Religion en Afrique Subsaharienne: le cas du Rwanda," in *Les religions au Rwanda: défis, convergences et competitions*, ed. P. Rutayisire *et al.* (Butare: Éditions de l'Université du Rwanda, 2009), 158.

59 Rutayisire, "Politique et Religion en Afrique Subsaharienne: le cas du Rwanda," 56. Trans.

60 In the 1950s, apparently at the request of King Mutara III, some Hutu subchiefs were included, notably Dominique Mbonyumutwa in Gitarama and Balthasar Bicamumpaka in Ruhengeli. The 1959 events were triggered when young nationalists of the Union Nacionale Rwandaise molested Mbonyumutwa after mass in Byiman. In reprisal, Hutus from the chieftaincies of Marangara and Ndiza attacked Tutsis, killing, pillaging, and unleashing the revolution.

61 The full title was "*Note sur l'aspect social du problème racial indigène au Rwanda. Le Manifeste des Bahutu.*" It is reproduced in Nkundabagenzi, *Rwanda Politique*, 20–9.

62 The article tellingly was titled: "Mon Père, revenez demain, nous en aurons tué d'autres" (My Father, come back tomorrow, we will have killed others). The principal promoters of violence were the white fathers Bellomi, Duchamp, Noti, de Vincke, Paul Klepp, Jules Guyssens, Aelvoet, Dejemeppe, Endriatis, Ernotte, and Perraudin. The last was the principal animator (6). Jean-Paul Gouteux, "Mon Père, revenez demain, nous en aurons tué d'autres", *Golias*, no. 101 (March/April 2003): 4.

63 See Anonyme, "Appel à la conscience des Bahutu," *Kangura* no. 6 (December 1990): 8.

64 Guy Logiest, *Mission au Rwanda. Un Blanc dans la bagarre Tutsi-Hutu* (Paris: Didier Hatier, 1988); and Jean-Paul Harroy, *Rwanda: souvenirs d'un compagnon de la marche Rwanda vers la démocratie et l'indépendance* (Hayez, Belgium: Académie des Sciences d'Outre-Mer, 1984).

65 Laurent Nkusi, "Crispation identitaire sous les deux républiques," in *Rwanda. Identité et citoyenneté* (Butare: Éditions de l'Université Nationale du Rwanda, 2003), 138. Trans.

66 Gérard Prunier, *Rwanda 1959–1996: Histoire d'un génocide* (Milan: Dagorno, 1997), 273–74.

67 Vidal, "Situations ethniques au Rwanda," 168.

68 Ironically, in canons of traditional Rwandan beauty the eyes are never mentioned, while many other traits are. The reference to fine noses was introduced by colonizers to determine racial belonging. Few Tutsis have fine noses.

69 Males not present on the battlefield were spared, generally old men, sick people, women, and children.

70 See Colin Keating, "Rwanda: An Insider's Account," in *The UN Security Council from the Cold War to the 21st Century*, ed. David M. Malone (Boulder, Colo.: Lynne Rienner), 500–11.

71 See www.kigalimemorialcentre.org.

72 See www.youtube.com/watch?v=7yiSIfR52Es.

73 Digneffe and Fierens, *Justice et gacaca.*

74 Of numerous analyses, see Phil Clark, *The Gacaca Courts, Post-Genocide Justice and Reconciliation in Rwanda: Justice without Lawyers* (Cambridge: Cambridge Studies in Law and Society, 2010).

75 Information drawn from the NURC website: www.nurc.gov.rw/index.php?option=com_content&view=article&id=50&Itemid=12.

76 Commission Nationale pour l'Unité et la Réconciliation/National Unity and Reconciliation Unity, *Itorero ry'Igihugu* (Traditional Education of the Country) (Kigali, Rwanda: NEC Press, 2010), 7.

77 Project consultation, held at the National University of Rwanda, Butare, 23 August 2010.

78 Member of University Dance Troupe *Inyamibwa*, project consultation, held at the National University of Rwanda, Butare, 23 August 2010.

79 Ignace Beraho, *Ingando. Impact Assesment on Unity and Reconciliation of Rwandans* (Kigali, Rwanda: National Unity and Reconciliation: 2007), 7.

80 Beraho, *Ingando. Impact Assesment on Unity and Reconciliation of Rwandans*, 11–4. See the NURC website, at: www.nurc.gov.rw/index.php?option=com_content&view=article&id=74&Itemid=11.

81 See www.unifem.org/progress/2008/whoF5_box1b.html.

82 See National Poverty Reduction Programme and the Ministry of Local Government and Social Affairs, "Ubudehe to Fight Poverty," available at: www.cdf.gov.rw/ubudehe/UBUDEHEDOCS/aboutubu/rwanda-nprp.pdf.

83 Léon Delmas, "La vache au Ruanda," *Anthropos* XXV (1930): 950.

84 For information on the Girinka Program, see the website of the Ministry of Agriculture and Animal Resources at: www.minagri.gov.rw/index.php?option=com_content&viez=qrticle&id=207%3Agirinkaprogram&cqtid=66%3Agirinka& Itemid=43&lang=en.

85 Haut Commissariat des Nations Unies aux Droits de l'homme, *République Démocratique du Congo, 1993–2003*, Mapping Report 02062010 (UN: New York, 2010).

5 Interventions in Kosova

Un/welcomed guests?

Nita Luci

Recently I was invited to appear on a television show in Pristina and asked to comment on current issues in Kosova[1] and the apparent indiscriminate hospitality of Albanians. The producers of the show had collected archival images of key historical moments from Albania and Kosova, which illustrated that foreign rulers and armies, dignitaries, and presidents were welcomed in the city streets of Tirana, Durrës, Prizren, and Pristina. The visitors included ranged from Prince William of Wied (who was placed on the throne of Albania in 1914) to Mussolini's army entering Albania in 1939, Tito during his visit to Kosova in 1975, North Atlantic Treaty Organization (NATO) forces entering Kosova in 1999, and Bill Clinton during his most recent visit in 2009. The collage of sepia-toned and HD-quality images depicted a seemingly timeless narrative, about which the host asked: "Can you as an anthropologist explain, culturally, if there is a reason why we always seem to welcome others with open arms?"

The question made me pause because clearly these images were not made up. Events, however, are constructed through memories and social practices. Culture plays a role in shaping them, but it is not a system of unchanging values and power relations. For example, people in Kosova rejoiced when NATO bombs were dropped in order to stop Serbian ethnic cleansing in 1999, but in time Kosovars grew tired from the lack of political solutions provided by outside interveners. Who were these "others" in question? Were they all guests of the same kind? What might anthropology have to say?

I assume that the welcomed response would have been that Albanians are a hospitable people, their traditions provide for honoring guests, and they share a common belief in peace and in the victory of the just. Indeed, most ethnographic research on and from Kosova would confirm such a conclusion.[2] Another observation, frequently offered in public discussions and collective renderings of history, would be that Albanians have become accustomed to occupation, have allowed others to rule them, and thus offer hospitality to the more powerful. When one of my students asked Blerim Hadri, a high-school teacher from Gjakova, whether the welcome given to NATO troops in Kosova can be seen as a matter of perceived inferiority, love for the West, or an understanding that guests must always be honored, Hadri insisted that these are inseparable. Many Albanians will also state that once one has a guest in one's home, the obligation to provide protection and respect becomes a matter of honor for the host.[3] In 1999 following NATO's intervention in Kosova and afterwards by the United Nations and the European Union (EU), all outsiders were welcomed as guests. The mutual obligations of guests and hosts were complex and shaped by the circumstances—political, legal, and cultural—upon which they were built. Such is clear in Hadri's correction to the student's question: " … but NATO soldiers in Kosova are more than 'guests' as you might say. For us they are no longer that. They are a part of us, because together we managed to overturn that which is bad and open the way for a new history."[4]

My answer, which may have appeared evasive to the audience, rested on the argument that these different explanations are telling of a tension present in Kosova's social memory and history, a tension that is also produced by the necessity of understanding and claiming agency in the social, political, and cultural realities of Kosova. Any present reading of such events is also a discussion conducted through experiences of Serbian-Albanian relations, the conflict and NATO's intervention in Kosova, and the international postwar peace building and state-building interventions. Therefore, a reading of the projected images could be scrutinized by historical methods, but they also become a reference of present concerns. For me, they summon attention to the power dynamics that shape cultural realities and memories, political responses, and everyday experiences of the past. They are also about definitions of self and cultural belonging shaped by constantly shifting social and global political landscapes.

This chapter attempts to shed light on the responsibility to protect (R2P) through a contextualization of the circumstances surrounding the outsiders who came to the rescue. It aims to elaborate the basic tenets of R2P through the prism of Kosovar Albanian culture, as it was shaped historically and changed with the events of the 1990s and 2000s. A shortcoming in this chapter's analysis is inadequate probing of the social and political cultural context of Serbia and Serbs in Kosova, and the politics of identity practiced among Serbs. Future research should elaborate on the ways in which Serbs in Kosova and Serbia negotiated and enacted the cultural and political realities, particularly as diverse protests in support of and against Slobodan Milosevic's regime have deeply informed analyses of interventions from local and international perspectives.[5]

Drawing on the experience recounted at the outset of this chapter, I demonstrate how the Albanian cultural traditions of hospitality, *besa* (vow), and honor played a key role in shaping the political events of the 1990s and Kosovar Albanian responses to them. I argue that dignity was turned into a political and social responsibility, creating new practices for enacting cultural particularity and strategies for action and, as Hadri's points make clear, served to take people in and out of emotional and political commonality.

The breadth of research and writing on the undoing of the former Yugoslavia warrants caution in pursuing an inquiry into a field and a literature that not only is copious but also debilitating at least for this anthropologist. A growing number of texts published on related topics, including most specifically those about NATO's intervention in Kosova, have produced and promulgated sets of glossary terms ranging from the descriptive to the more poetic. They suggest such apocalyptic ends as "the death of Yugoslavia," "Balkan battlegrounds," or "Balkan Babel." Most are book titles about which Sabrina Ramet has offered an extensive and compelling analysis, among some 130 different books published in English alone about scholarly debates on the varied social and political formations of Yugoslavia's implosion.[6] While historians, philosophers, political scientists, journalists, and even army generals and casual travelers have provided their analyses, surprisingly anthropologists have been rather timid.[7]

This chapter takes advantage of relevant research in anthropology in order to respond to the challenge of this volume to highlight the potential contribution of anthropology and comparative cultural analysis to explore how R2P might find more resonance in local social practices and contexts. My approach thus employs cultural translation[8]—that is, I consider the R2P norm as a particular cultural and political framework. More specifically, the chapter traces the ways in which R2P finds cultural translation and recognition in the particular cultural and political practices in Kosova. The argument made here is that requests for protection and intervention that came from *within* Kosova—that is, by Kosovar Albanians—along with demands for global acknowledgment of principles of the responsibility to protect should be seen as mutually constituted systems of values and morals. In order to analyze the relationships between them, I contextualize the discussion around two key social formations: the 1990s civil-disobedience movement in Kosova, and the armed response of the Kosova Liberation Army (KLA) and the armed conflict as it involved both NATO and Serbia. This approach allows for an exploration of two of R2P's three pillars, prevention and reaction to mass atrocities. This chronological contextualization enables us to identify the emergence of cultural values and traditions as they were fashioned with the power to mobilize social and political action, which are also relevant to the challenges of post-conflict peace building.

On culture and translation: anthropology and understanding R2P

Michael Herzfeld has noted that "for most ethnographers translating local terms as though they had stable meanings is intellectually indigestible, yet we cannot dispense with it any more than we could survive without reifying the categories of ordinary social life."[9] For the most part, anthropologists have been involved in making the cultural meanings and practices of "others" understandable to "Western" audiences. At the same time, a more accurate explanation would unmask the assumed homogeneity of such an audience, the assumption that anthropologists study cultures foreign to them, and that their interlocutors are fluent in English, French, German, or other European languages. The unease with the dominant language of anthropological production is not only about translating words from say Albanian into English,[10] but also of anthropological conceptual categories, the historical and cultural legacies of which may be taken for granted. From comparative studies of kinship to emotions, anthropologists have engaged the historical relations of the terms of anthropological inquiry and more specifically colonial power by showing their mutual constitution.[11] Understandings of structural relations of power and their use in anthropology is relevant, as is attention to the relations between markers of cultural identity—such as nation, race, class, and gender—through the inclusion of shifting sites of resistance and oppression.

Nevertheless, meanings of lived experience are carried in diverse ways and hold potential for transforming the terms of our analysis. Feminist anthropology has been most insistent on grounding research in political realities and historical and material relations of power.[12] The cultural translation attempted here is rooted in personal experiences, and, perhaps with immodesty, through a reflexive responsibility that aims to suggest research questions and social action. Lila Abu-Lughod has commented about ethnographic responsibility, linking this to the responsibility to address injustice that moves beyond cultural relativism—that is, a passive understanding of cultural differences. According to her, justifications of the intervention in Afghanistan, based on the moral imperative to save Afghan women, resonate with colonial and missionary rhetoric from the past. Therefore, she asks:

> … why knowing about the "culture" of the region, and particularly its religious beliefs and treatment of women, was more urgent than exploring the history of the development of repressive regimes … [and why] instead of political and historical explanations, experts were being asked to give religio-cultural ones. Instead of questions that might lead to the exploration of global interconnections, we were offered ones that worked to artificially divide the world into separate spheres—recreating an imaginative geography of West versus East.[13]

Similarly, according to Vjollca Krasniqi, the politics of peacekeeping in Kosova is entrenched in a web of signification, a representational system that not only embodies "the 'death' of heterogeneity and the 'victory' of universalism over particularities, but also the normalization of hierarchical restructurings of gender."[14] The result is an assumed mimicry of the West, whereby peace building becomes part of a larger system that places democratic governance in opposition to local cultural practices.

This chapter attempts to follow Abu-Lughod's approach and focuses on the historical developments of repression in Kosova. It also seeks to find interlocutors while moving across various disciplinary and geopolitical boundaries, and particularly the hierarchies within institutions of knowledge.[15] This is where cultural translation becomes possible, at the intermediary spaces where one takes hold of seemingly self-evident categories of cultural expression and points to the ways in which "people confront power," as Frederick Cooper suggests.[16] Culture, then, is not a timeless tradition, a mode of behavior, or a tool that aids in explaining why interveners are welcomed. Culture, in Eric Wolf's terms, is that which can "bring together that what might otherwise may be kept apart … If we want to understand how humans seek stability or organize themselves to manage change, we need a concept that allows us to capture patterned social flow in its multiple interdependent dimensions and to assess how interdependent power steers these flows over time. 'Culture' is such a concept."[17]

NATO's military campaign in Kosova has without doubt generated some of the most compelling debates on issues of international law and the relevance of international organizations, particularly the UN. Genocidal and ethnic-cleansing campaigns of the 1990s inflicted death and suffering on millions, and events appeared as turning points not only in imagining the "international order" but in rethinking the value of human life. Debates among international lawyers and political scientists have focused on the legality, legitimacy, and forms of wars waged within the international society of states in which sovereignty and nonintervention are the traditional governing principles,[18] but have been rethought.[19] The research I conducted on the topic, together with students at the University of Pristina, confirms that the people in Kosova are not ready to dispense with such a possibility. "The intervention in Kosova happened because it was impossible to remain disinterested, to stay away, and not act," Linda Krasniqi argues. She concludes, however, that although "Kosova had become a massive prison for Albanians, the aim of the intervention had not been to create freedom in Kosova, [but] rather to force an agreement with Milosevic."[20]

These observations find analogies in recent analyses of relations between violence, governance, and impunity, influenced by Walter Benjamin's notion of "state of exception." According to Aida Hozic, states of exception, or the suspended constitutional order, also can be conceptualized in space as "zones of exception." According to her, the cultural economy of the location of zones of violence rests upon their "decontextualization from other, global, political and economic trends … Construction of boundaries between zones of safety and zones of violence is, therefore, more than performance of security—it is the way to affirm global order in face of its absence."[21] In this regard, what occurred in Kosova, Rwanda, Somalia, Sudan, Bosnia, Chechnya, Angola, Sierra Leone, and Liberia become exceptions to the normal workings of world politics. More poignantly, they appear to tell "the way in which (cultural) violence is governed and contained; the practice that obfuscates the increasing frequency with which sovereign power encounters—and obliterates—bare life with impunity."[22]

The interest is how an imagined and homogeneous "Western" audience and a global order produce and remake a world of "others." Craig Calhoun calls for attention to "the underlying social and cultural dynamics that shape both the production of emergencies and the production of response,"[23] while reminding us of one of the central concerns of social theory and action. He states: "[t]hinking in terms of emergencies draws on the sense of agency in promoting intervention to minimize suffering. But it denies agency precisely to those who suffer."[24] When asked, many Kosovar Albanians do not argue that the intervention in Kosova is an exceptional case, but one that creates possibility for "humane responsibility."[25] Kosovar imaginings of and participation in these events has engaged a historiography that brings Kosova into the picture and illustrates the ways in which individuals intervene in events and redefine the spaces of violence. The central question remains how to elicit responses—in this case, to halt mass atrocities—without denying the agency of those who are suffering from crimes.

Lila Abu-Lughod has suggested that we can "use a more egalitarian language of alliances, coalitions, and solidarity, instead of salvation," when responding to social injustice and oppression.[26] Such language would have to be accompanied by practices that account for the power dynamics that cause such injustices and fail to see culture as no more than an obstacle to "the implementation of political solutions." As Noam Chomsky stated, "it is understandable that the powerful should prefer to declare that we should forget history and look forward. For the weak, it is not a wise choice." He expressed this view in July 2009 to the UN General Assembly Thematic Dialogue on the Responsibility to Protect by stating that R2P is "regularly disturbed by the rattling of a skeleton in the closet: history."[27] However, a student at the University of Pristina dissented in a paper for a course on the anthropology of violence: "NATO's intervention is an example of a raised awareness at a global level for regional responsibilities and a new moment in international law."[28] His respondent, Sadik Bicaj, a journalist, affirmed by qualifying the internal request as a sign "that we not allow ourselves to be degraded to the level of an observer."[29] Chomsky fails to see that before NATO bombed Serbia, Serbia bombed Kosova. This is not an argument along the lines of who initiated the bombing campaign but rather, as any anthropologist would say, about analyzing cultures in their own terms and not in the intellectual and political terms of Western theories.

Challenges abound. For instance, a key term throughout this volume is "mass atrocity," which does not have an Albanian translation. "Atrocity," carrying the meaning of "atrocious," would best be translated as "horrific" in Albanian. During fieldwork and interviews people spoke of massacres, killings, crimes, brutality, and expulsion; horror was always accompanied with a clear adjectival reference to "Serbian horror." As one respondent stated, "during the [NATO] bombing I was afraid, but I do not remember it as a suffering, pain, or sacrifice."[30]

According to him, horror is something that leaves one physically untouched, that is observed from afar and conducted from a distance, and resembles conscience-shocking images seen on television. He continued: "I clearly understand why there was intervention in Kosova and not in Rwanda. We think of the things that happened there as horrible, but we do not feel their pain and suffering. Once you feel the pain yourself, you begin to understand."[31] Here we see that horror and response to violence had to be contextualized without becoming a gloss for political expressions emerging out of moments of particularity and socially heterogeneous practice and meanings.[32] The moment at which something is no longer perceived as just horrible or atrocious—which allows for distancing or containment[33]—produces discomfort with remaining detached.

I now move to a focus on Kosova from 1990 to 2010 in order to see how Kosovar Albanians construed, imagined, and perceived not only their own suffering but also the responses of international "others." I remain concerned about how R2P relates to Kosova's historical and cultural particularities without turning them into exceptions or oddities. Certainly, anthropology can provide a valuable lens for understanding the R2P norm and contextualizing and adapting it to different cultural, social, and historical situations. Anthropology also can illuminate the various social meanings given by various peoples to R2P, and how to interpret and adapt in order to better prevent and react to mass atrocities as well as mend societies after the end of crimes and war.

Prevention and reaction

Civil resistance in Kosova in the 1990s reflects "reinventing traditions"—social, cultural, and political. The decade was a time of solidarity, dignified response, and endurance; it was a space to express social identities as manifestations of particular and universal cultural values. In particular, practices of Albanian customary law were revived. Empowering notions of *besa* (vow) and *ndera* (honor) were placed within a "civilizing mission" of Albanian intellectual and political elites to denote congruity with a universal discourse of human rights. In particular, they served to legitimate discursive practices in the maintenance of moral structures that sustained family and community, while linking national solidarity to dignity of political action.

Many have argued that the 10-year civil resistance, which sought to mobilize international interests and action, failed because it did not manage to produce that action. Nonetheless, the resistance sustained political, economic, and cultural survival in Kosova. It provided an opportunity for the world to take notice and act, perhaps an acknowledgment of the moral burden of responsibility by the powerful. Apart from such early symbolic gestures as peace awards, Kosovar Albanians would have to wait their turn, so it seemed, until the body counts mounted sufficiently. As Susan Woodward has observed, "the unwillingness to intervene at the interests of prevention, acting only when violence occurred, sent a signal that one had to go to war to get attention."[34] Recounting this conclusion, Lindita Hajdari and Fitore Çunaku write, "due to the injustices and the degrading actions against the Albanian population,"[35] they "first *had* to organize a peaceful movement and when that seemed to fail they *had* to organize militarily."[36]

The public emergence of the KLA in 1997 was, therefore, not only a confirmation that nonviolent prevention of conflict had come to an end, but also marked the empowerment of a new national construction.[37] As Jusuf Zejnullahu concludes in his interview, "Kosovar society feels differently after the war. It feels respected, able to decide for itself. This is because people can now make decisions for themselves."[38] Kosovars found justice and moral responsibility embedded in both the KLA and the NATO intervention for a number of reasons. First, the systematic discrimination exercised over Albanians by the Serbian state had oppressed the majority and stripped them of all rights.[39] Second, Belgrade had brazenly breached international conventions and laws. Not only did Serbia not protect many of its citizens, but it also systematically marginalized and brutalized them. Although Albanians did not consider Serbia as a sovereign in Kosova, local values of justice resonated with international customary law and those built into the Universal Declaration of Human Rights. The KLA's fight for liberation and NATO's campaign to stop the ethnic cleansing were mutually reinforcing.

Although formed by different histories, and significantly different in form and intentions, the KLA struggle and NATO's military intervention were seen as a reaffirmation of Kosova's belonging to Europe and of the values of a political and judicial tradition of the West. Cultural and political elites have referenced and constructed relations of such belonging as already existing narratives of cultural reality. A debate between writers Ismail Kadare and Rexhep Qosja developed during 2006, at the moment when Albania was preparing to enter an EU Stabilization and Association Agreement that centered on elaborations of the occidental and oriental character of Albanian culture. Subsequently, many joined the debate, including prime ministers and ministers. Kadare argued that Albanian culture was in its foundations and history European.[40] Qosja, on the other hand, pointed to the relevance of historical influences from the Ottoman Empire, arguing against Kadare's essentialism, but added that Ottoman "leftovers" are "examples of non-Europe" that do not belong in Albanian culture.[41] Enis Sulstarova, an historian, has treated these seemingly opposing arguments as an expression of "an Albanian derivation from European Occidentalism," specifically of its intellectuals.[42]

While in the late 1980s and early 1990s Albanians argued for their right to self-determination as an expression of colonized peoples for freedom, Kosova's statehood has recently been articulated as the will of the people to enter the European "family of nations." Many European governments had claimed the conflict in the former Yugoslavia to be a "European issue," but they had on countless occasions failed to mobilize sufficient political will to act. Eventually, the UN Interim Administration Mission in Kosova's (UNMIK) diminishing role, following the end of negotiations on Kosova's final status and the implementation of the comprehensive proposal on the settlement of Kosova's status drawn up by UN special envoy Martti Ahtisari,[43] led to the establishment of the EU's European Rule of Law Mission (EULEX), which was met with greater enthusiasm.[44]

At first empowered by traditional hospitality, Kosovars welcomed one of the largest-ever international military and peace building missions. Soon thereafter, however, Kosovars began to assess the post-conflict and peace building processes as a situation in which Kosova's people felt like guests in their own homes. This was true for both Serbs and Albanians, albeit with very distinct perspectives. Such sentiments were most explicitly articulated by VETËVENDOSJE!, a self-determination protest movement turned political party that entered the 2010 national elections following a vote of no confidence in government. The main voice of opposition to the UN- and EU-led missions came from this movement and its leader Albin Kurti, a former student leader and prisoner of Milosevic's regime. Although it remains to be seen whether their political platform can mobilize as many voters as protesters, VETËVENDOSJE! is not alone in the claim that the political, economic, and cultural relations of postwar Kosova have maintained a terrain of inequality. The Kosova government, present and past, has also been increasingly assessed, not only by EU progress reports but also by Kosova's citizens, as corrupt and incompetent, and hence a contributor to the current inequality.

It is worthwhile to examine two of these three phases in greater depth, guided by the dominant conceptual calendar in Kosova of before and during the war, as a means of informing two of the three founding components of R2P.

The 1990s

In February 1989, the Milosevic regime imposed martial law on Kosova.[45] The "state of emergency" that lasted for the next nine years consisted of de facto apartheid based upon ethnic segregation and state-sponsored violence against the Albanian majority. On 23 March 1990 the Assembly of Kosova was surrounded by tanks, the military, and police; without a quorum it amended the constitution, which resulted in the revocation of Kosova's status as an autonomous province. The decision also imposed restrictions, the aim of which, as Howard Clark has observed, was "nothing less but to change the ethnic structure of Kosovo permanently."[46]

The 1990s in Kosova, and perhaps the region as a whole, could be characterized as a period of re-inventing traditions.[47] While the West enthusiastically greeted the end of state socialism in the former Soviet bloc, the resulting transformations toward building democratic states and open-market economies did not always reflect common understandings of the past or visions for the future.[48] From the former Yugoslavia emerged nationalist politics and the creation of new states that appeared antithetical to the strengthening of liberal and global political and economic relations. While war broke out in Slovenia (although short-lived), Croatia, and Bosnia and Herzegovina, from Kosova emerged one of the longest lasting nonviolent movements against an authoritarian state.[49]

For Albanians in Kosova this time of change came to signify an opportunity to govern by themselves their political, economic, and cultural resources. For them, this opportunity could not exist as long as they remained part of a rump Yugoslavia or Serbia.[50] On the part of the amorphous so-called international community, there was a desire to recognize the promise of strengthening civil societies throughout the region and such was given support, both in monies and other capacities.[51] As Michael Kennedy has argued, however, "civil society was not just a social formation, but, significantly, a cultural formation."[52] As Belgrade sanctioned the revocation of Kosova's autonomy in March 1989 and legitimated segregation and martial law, Kosovars aimed to articulate pluralism by developing transformative politics integrated by traditions based on articulations of national cultural identity, modern state-building, and belonging to the West. In this context, Stephen Zunes comments that "starting in 1990, Albanian Kosovars challenged Serbian rule through one of the most impressive large-scale nonviolent campaigns in history, including the creation of a parallel government and educational system. Yet during eight years of struggle, the United States and most of the world ignored them."[53]

The cultural practices of the 1990s thus sustained an emerging resistance to violence and ethnic segregation, which involved constant renegotiations between modernity and tradition. The reconciliation of blood feuds among Albanians between 1990 and 1992 made for one of the most powerful enactments of political identities remade within novel framings of human rights, set as a modern political practice based on revived but adapted national traditions.[54] In a series of public gatherings over two years, the reconciliation movement came to constitute—according to Muhamet Pirraku, an historian at the Albanian Studies Institute in Pristina and activists of the movement—"a legal and civilizing confrontation" with Serbian politics in Kosova.[55] Reconciling blood feuds was defined by the student youth that initiated it and the intellectual elite that supported and gave it legitimacy as an expression of Albanian customary law that already reflected the universal discourse of human rights. Following the Kanun of Lekë Dukagjini—an oral tradition since the fifteenth century and codified in 1933 by Franciscan monk Shtjefan Gjeqovi—intellectual elites and student initiatives increasingly referred to this better-known version of customary law to build social cohesion in an uncertain time.[56] Over the two-year period, some 2,500 feuds were resolved in this way. Notions of forgiveness (*besa*) and dignity became the language of protest.[57] *Besa*, which translates into given oath or vow, was used in reconciliation while emitting the binding ties of morality, family, and, in this instance, nation. Anton Çetta, the retired folklorist who emerged as the leader of the movement, as well as other intellectual and political leaders, seemed to be echoing a cohesive assertion: paradoxically traditional values could shed backwardness and initiate Kosova's cultural return to Europe.[58]

The public declarations of "forgiving blood" created possibilities of asserting pride in cultural belonging that had been governed through subjugation and oppression during most years of state socialism.[59] The purported solution to "nations and nationalities" in socialism amounted to repressing cultural distinctions as aberrations, at least those that threatened the regime. Aims to educate and modernize Kosova came from Kosovar elites, particularly through the University of Pristina (established in 1969), the first and only university in Kosova until 2002. Albanians continued to be marked as racially inferior within Yugoslavia. Albanian inferiority in Kosova became marked through categories of cultural differentiation supposedly visible in the physical aspects of citizens. Not only were dominant representations of Albanians based on the dialectic of an infantilized savage, particularly of Albanian men, so were institutional responses to the threat perceived in the high birth rates in Kosova.[60] Many civil society activists of the time remarked that it was no surprise that the gynecology clinic and its staff at Pristina Hospital were the first targets of the special measures imposed by Belgrade. Albanian women became the site on which wanton violence was used, not only during protests of the 1990s but also during the war. Human Rights Watch documented 96 cases of rape in 1999, through testimonies given by victims and witnesses.[61] Most were cases of gang rape, occurring in homes, while fleeing, or in detention. Women's groups, international researchers and observers, and particularly the Center for the Protection of Women and Children in Kosova have argued that the number is in the thousands, but a troubling silence persists, and victims never received adequate support.[62]

In Raymond Williams's terms, the dominant structures of feeling were grounded in references to Albanian "otherness" and cultural particularity within Yugoslavia, but they relied on the discourse of universal human rights. Eric Wolf's use of the concept of "descriptive integration" is helpful here, particularly in thinking of the relationships between cultural practices, enactments of tradition, and political-legal systems.[63] Placed in the contexts of social and cultural life, through selective descriptions of particular and general phenomena, descriptive integration aims to "preserve the 'quality' of phenomena and their relation to each other in time and space," without leading to abstract generalizations. This approach resonates well in the writings of Gani Bobi, philosopher and professor at the University of Pristina who was also a regular columnist in the local press. In his 1982 *Sprovimet e Modernitetit* (Trials of Modernity), specifically in a dialogue with Jean-Paul Sartre's existentialism and Frantz Fanon's critique of colonialism, Bobi places Serbian-Albanian relations in Kosova within the dialectics of power and culture:

> Culture, and thus the universality of the cultural act is created based on principles of uniqueness, which means that the more particular we become the more universal we are, of course if we understand universality as a community of diversity not as their fusion. That is, not as a monocentric culture that suppresses cultural universality (diversity) in the name of an abstract universalism, thus masking its more concrete identity as a dominant culture.[64]

In early 1990 there was still a dominant appeal that "Democracy in Kosovo means Democracy in Yugoslavia." Blerim Reka and Rramush Tahiri, journalists at the daily *Rilindja*, made this statement, which resonated with statements made by Veton Surroi and also by the emerging activist of a group called the "Kosova Alternative."[65] Surroi stated: "we cannot discuss [Kosova's status] through narrow national perspectives … but we have to make attempts at denationalizing the problem, which is a key issue when human rights are at stake."[66] This came one year after the revocation of Kosova's autonomous status, protests that ended in the death, beating, and jailing of hundreds, the strike of more than 7,000 miners, and the apparent poisoning of children following ethnic segregation in schools.[67] In a session of the Provincial Assembly on 6 June 1990, Albanian delegates issued a recommendation to draft a new constitution of Kosova. The chair of the assembly refused to enter the proposal into the meeting schedule, arguing that other competent bodies would have to decide. One frustrated delegate bellowed: "We are not children."[68] In July of the same year, members of the Kosova Assembly gathered on the steps of the building to declare Kosova's sovereignty, and on 7 July proclaimed its constitution. This declaration came after the Serbian Parliament had approved the *Political Action Platform of the Central Committee of Yugoslavia in the Political Circumstances of the Province of Kosovo* and the plan of the Republic of Serbia for *Peace, Freedom, Equality, Democracy and Prosperity in the Socialist Autonomous Province of Kosovo*, which was made official in March 1990.[69] Following the proclamation, the police took over Pristina's radio and television station, RTP. Albanian journalists were expelled, and the expulsion of all government employees from all other state institutions followed, which dramatically affected the services for health care, media, education, and other cultural, economic, and political institutions. During 1990 alone, an estimated 45 percent of Kosovar Albanians were fired, and soon almost 90 percent were unemployed; the Milosevic regime centralized control in Belgrade and annexed the previously autonomous provinces of Vojvodina and Kosova.

Already the poorest unit of the former federation, Kosova saw the emigration of tens of thousands—with the number in exile reaching 350,000. Young men sought political asylum in Europe as they faced mandatory conscription into the Yugoslav People's Army (JNA), which by 1991 already was engaged in the wars in Croatia and Bosnia and Herzegovina. In the same numbers they began to seek asylum in Western European states. As police harassment intensified and made violence routine, ethnic segregation permeated every aspect of social and economic activity. Albanians also lost the right to purchase or sell property without special permission; once expelled from their jobs, they also lost occupancy rights to lodgings formerly attached to their employment. Survival required a parallel economy, which relied on remittances from abroad and even more on the so-called Three-Percent Fund, a voluntary taxation system established in 1993 to which Kosovar Albanians contributed. A state that systematically dismantled rights but enjoyed international impunity also encountered fierce local resistance. This mobilization of economic, political, and cultural labor cannot be understood through the lens of "transition," a process that sought to quickly remedy and rescue socialist economies and societies, or even mark a return to normality.[70] Contributing almost one-quarter of her monthly salary of $30, middle-school teacher Kimete Dida remembers:

> We would divide the salaries among ourselves. There were no more salaries from the state. We created an independent union and would split the money among the teachers. Also, I almost forgot to mention, that our school "Ismail Qemajli," was separated. The Serbs separated it. There were 2,400 pupils. There were 300 Serbian pupils and they took 12 classrooms. We had 2,100 pupils and we worked in five shifts. Children in the 3rd and 4th grades had to come to school at 5:30 in the afternoon, which was the fourth shift.[71]

This recollection makes clear that the 1990s in Kosova are collectively remembered as a time of solidarity in the face of structural inequities and segregation imposed by Belgrade's nationalist politics. Endurance became the real agent of survival. Cultural values were inserted into historical narratives and animated the Democratic League of Kosova (LDK). Led by Ibrahim Rugova, the LDK became the main vector for civil resistance, a new cultural "phenomenon" in Wolf's terms, which created space and possibilities for normality in abnormal circumstances. Kosovars created a parallel government, including a parliament, an education system, and alternative health and other services.

In what Bobi called the "universality of the cultural act," both in its distinctiveness and universalism, dignity came to constitute the forms and contents of protest. As the philosopher and cultural critic Shkëlzen Maliqi noted at the time, "we are not as you choose to present us … but only 'with dignity' [we] express our political will which is different from yours."[72] Dignity also constituted the discursive terrain for marking a new political identity. Discussing the shift from shame to dignity, sociologist Anton K. Berishaj observes how:

> the posing for photography went on with such theatrical ceremony that it was almost as if the beating had not degraded us at all, but had somehow made us proud … The presence of journalists was seen as a gesture of sympathy and curiosity … Kosovo Albanians no longer hesitated to go naked, bearing raw marks of violence in front of witnesses, neighbors and family members, ready to show that they had been wronged.[73]

Calling for an acknowledgment of abuse to motivate "the world to know and take action,"[74] by the end of the 1990s every Albanian family had at least one family member expelled from work, detailed by police, beaten, or jailed. The UN-imposed embargo on Serbia was breached continually, diplomatic negotiations were never supported adequately, and Security Council resolutions were flouted.[75] The civil resistance of the 1990s postponed violent confrontation, but Serbian occupation legitimized new cultural expressions inspired by universal human rights. With feeble international criticism and a lack of democratic alternatives within Serbia, it became clear that no degree of internal, dignified resistance could quickly change an authoritarian regime without the resort to violence. The case of South African apartheid, which took over 40 years of resistance to collapse, is telling.

International intervention, 1999

As sociologist Anton Berishaj notes, Albanians "experienced [the state] as a source of violence and brutality."[76] The long history of state repression and the failure of the LDK's nonviolent strategy to secure a political solution on Kosova's status paved the way for the emergence of the KLA, which had its roots in the Popular Movement for Kosova (LPK), a small underground Marxist organization formed in the early 1980s. After more than a decade of civil resistance against a brutally repressive regime, an armed response in Kosova became a new means of survival.[77] Legitimating new kinds of social and political confrontations with the state on the part of the KLA was inspired by cultural and historical understandings of justice, their marginality in the former Yugoslavia, and the constant state violence strategically exercised against populations in what later became KLA strongholds.[78]

Personal and collective experiences of persecution are crucial to understanding support for the KLA's insurgency and NATO's intervention. In discussing her decision to join the KLA as a medic, Parliamentarian Gjylnaze Syla, for example, asserted: "I knew from my parents that our house was burned and that they [had to] rebuild it. Their experience in that system was very bad … and I had to do something. I was not very certain what I was supposed to do, but I had great will to do something to change the situation."[79]

My own experience of the war has been shaped by an event told to me by my mother. Once NATO's campaign began and my sisters and I were safely outside of Kosova, my parents decided to do their part by staying in Pristina. Indeed, their apartment served as a meeting place for those still living in the city, housing as many as 60 people waiting to speak to relatives who had either fled to neighboring Macedonia or Albania or farther afield. Having escaped execution, two of their closest friends, together with their four children, also came to live with my parents and others also sought refuge. Once the neighborhood had been "cleansed" of most Albanian residents, only a few families remained; my parents' apartment was regularly visited by the police and the army. In an act of what she now calls stupidity, my mother even made the soldiers take off their shoes when entering the apartment: "I said this is still a home. I kept remembering being purged from the clinic and the university [she is a pathologist and professor at the Medical Faculty], and all I had seen working with the [Council for the Defense of Human Rights and Freedoms] ... I cannot remember being happier than the day NATO troops entered."

The statement that her house "was still a home" meant requiring even unwanted visitors to act according to acknowledged rules of conduct. Although the outside world was so messy, the home had to be kept clean. It was also a means of maintaining a routine of normalcy and protecting an intimate inner space from which to draw strength. It is akin to Bahloul's ethnography of the house where the practice of everyday life becomes "the social space for resistance to the dehumanizing effects of war." Most assessments claim that more than 450 villages were destroyed during the armed conflict, leaving approximately 50,000 destroyed or uninhabitable houses, as well as many entire cities in ruins. The fact that sexual violence occurred in people's homes also speaks of the devastation inflicted upon spaces that had served to maintain sociability and normalcy. The critique offered by women's groups in Kosova and Serbia of women's exclusion from postwar negotiations has been framed precisely in terms of neglecting these excruciating experiences. Quite often they were the ones placed at the front lines of the war, protesting as did the Women in Black in Serbia, or being the first to open doors when paramilitaries came searching for the men in Kosova.[80]

Writing about hospitality in the Albanian tradition, ethnographer Mark Krasniqi argues:

> [t]he tradition of hospitality is closely tied to the Albanian character. In his psychology, the main element is honor, face, which are tied to other components that make for the honor of men, such as *besa*, hospitality, bravery, truth, justice, tolerance, love for the fatherland, etc., which are principles of life, and the main national characteristics of Albanian people.[81]

One of the better-known commentators about Albanian culture, Edith Durham, adds:

> A man is answerable, too, for his guest … The sacredness of the guest is far-reaching. A man who brought me water from his house, that I might drink by the way, said that I now ranked as his guest, and that he should be bound by his honour to avenge me should anything happen to me before I had received hospitality from another.[82]

It would be possible to argue that this venerated cultural tradition also underpinned the welcome shown to most international guests in Kosova. Durham's *noble savage* seems to be not only a foreign perspective on customs observed in Kosova, but also a subject of internal critique on the position in which Kosovar citizens found themselves.[83]

Underlying these observations is also a reference to the salience of gender in producing cultural and political boundaries as well as seeking empowerment through local idioms of cultural particularity. Claims to the latter have been built upon shifting identification, bodily and emotional bonds, to experiences of dignity and resistance, as enduring motifs of national tradition. The governing political body based its legitimacy on a moral superiority over its enemy, particularly the values assigned to certain gendered cultural practices. The attainment and enactment of womanly and manly character was made possible, in contexts of extreme impossibility, by suffering the domination over the nation and resistance toward empowerment. Ultimately, different forms of suffering and resistance would be culturally and morally acceptable for men and women, as the national project continued to construct the universal (neutral) political subject as male. The male subject has been reproduced in international mechanisms that enable and disable cultural and political agency. The responsibilities of hosts and guests have relied on a gendered division of labor in peace building, often explaining and justifying "masculine domination"[84] by superficial readings of local cultural, political, and economic arrangements.[85]

Conclusion

The most common assertion in Kosova over the recent past is that the bombing happened in 1999, but the war started earlier. "It is, of course, one of the most significant lessons of the postcolonial experience that no nation is simply young or old, new or ancient, despite the date of its independence," Homi K. Bhaba observes. "'New' national, international, or global emergences create an unsettling sense of transition, as if history is at a turning point; and it is at such *incubational* moments … that we experience the palimpsestical imprints of past, present, and future in peculiarly contemporary figures of time and meaning."[86]

Bhaba references Frantz Fanon's critique of colonialism, and a particular—perhaps universal—historical and intellectual endeavor. What this chapter aims to have shown is that historical turning points are negotiated through diverse social experiences. As people strive to give meaning to such moments, within global emergences of various kinds, they take part in defining their strategies for action. Formed through politics of culture that recreated traditions for social solidarity, Kosovars formed opportunities to ultimately practice and define survival. We must learn to take note of such energies, without remaining helpless to act against injustice.

The means and networks of solidarity created during the 1990s in Kosova, along with the appeal of moving toward and eventually joining Europe, characterized the calls for international military protection. Hospitality shaped the initial response to the presence of NATO soldiers. The emotional politics captured by the oft-used expression of "happiness when the intervention began" constitutes the collective expression of belief and reflected the conviction that the intervention would abide by a common understanding of justice. Resonant in most interviews conducted on the topic is the belief that the "intervention was a humanitarian intervention ... due to continual violations of human rights in Kosovo, individual and collective, by Milosevic's regime ... [T]he extermination and vanishing of an entire people was prevented."[87] In this regard, what the International Commission on Intervention and State Sovereignty (ICISS) described as the use of "military intervention for human protection purposes"[88] signaled to many Kosovars a "new era in international law" with a "global responsibility" that would "not permit the repeat of Srebrenica."[89] Again, the terms of such interventions must be resonant with practices that draw meanings from various histories and trajectories, particularly as people come to feel as guests in their own homes.

According to ICISS, prevention remains "the single most important dimension of the responsibility to protect."[90] The commission's report also noted that "developed countries [should] be aware of the cultural barriers that may inhibit the interpretation of information."[91] The communication and interpretation of culture certainly must inform the application of R2P, at times creating barriers and sometimes creating opportunities for understanding. Yet the assumption is doubtful that only "developed countries" bear this responsibility, or should decipher culture in order to prevent or halt mass atrocities. For instance, the package of post-independence measures for Kosova, assembled by former Finnish president Martii Ahtisaari, consists of key recommendations for the protection of cultural heritage. Accordingly, Kosova's peace and state building has come to revolve around a central discursive and representational axis of ethnicity and cultural rights, mainly built upon UN and EU resolutions and policies. It is nonetheless troubling that definitions of political rights and representation have turned cultural heritage into sites of ethnically defined historicity. The result has been the omission of cultural value from practices of everyday life and the varied creative forms through which history and culture are continuously rethought and remade. In the least, those provide a powerful resource for thinking about the future.

The past 10 years in Kosova have been characterized by unusually large responsibilities assumed by outsiders—from NATO, the UN, the EU, international nongovernmental organizations, and other international actors.[92] Most common have been critiques of the unequal power relations built into decision making, the most evident being the right reserved for the special representative of the UN secretary-general to veto any decision of the Provisional Institutions of Self Governance established by UNMIK.[93] This criticism also applies to local political elites benefiting from the international presence. However, despite the rhetoric of local ownership of peace building processes, little is known about the local cultural underpinnings of workable processes of reconciliation and measures required to improve prevention or reaction to mass atrocities.

Practitioners may doubt the relevance of anthropology to the implementation of the responsibility to protect, but this chapter illustrates why a better and even basic understanding of the culture of Kosova provides insights about alternative policies and approaches to prevention, reaction, and peace building. Globally there appears to be a lack of commitment to the same type of responsibility and sensitivity. A shift of attention to social and cultural relations of power could, in turn, also make unequal economic, political, and security arrangements more visible. Such remains our responsibility.

Notes

1 While the decision to use Kosova over Kosovo continues to require explanation, I will briefly state that I use Kosova as does its majority Albanian-speaking population. I say more about cultural translation below, but here I begin with the observation that choosing one form over the other signals a reflexive examination of power relations in naming practices, for to use Kosovo and say this does not reflect a position on a politics of language would be inadequate.

2 Mark Krasniqi, *Mikpritja në Traditën Shqiptare* (Pristina: Akademia e Shkencave dhe e Arteve e Kosovës, 2005).

3 I would like to thank Shemsi Krasniqi, sociologist at the University of Pristina, who drew my attention to this during the second consultation by the research team in Pristina, 25 May 2010.

4 Lirika Komoni, *Intervenimi i NATO-së në Kosovë*, unpublished paper submitted in partial fulfillment of coursework, University of Pristina, Department of Sociology, January 2010, 9.

5 See Thomas Cushman, "Anthropology and Genocide in the Balkans: An Analysis of Conceptual Practices of Power," *Anthropological Theory* 4, no. 1 (2004): 5–28; Stef Jansen, "The Streets of Beograd: Urban Space and Protest Identities in Serbia," *Political Geography* 20, no. 1 (2001): 35–55.

6 Sabrina Ramet, *Thinking About Yugoslavia: Scholarly Debates about the Yugoslav Breakup and the Wars in Bosnia and Kosovo* (Cambridge: Cambridge University Press, 2005).

7 A number of relevant texts include Pamela Ballinger, *History in Exile: Memory and Identity at the Borders of the Balkans* (Princeton, NJ: Princeton University Press, 2003); Tone Bringa, *Being Muslim in a Bosnian Way: Identity and Community in a Central Bosnian Town* (Princeton, NJ: Princeton University Press, 1995); Anna DiLellio and Stephanie Schwandner-Sievers, "The Legendary Commander: The Construction of an Albanian Master-Narrative in Post-War Kosovo," *Nations & Nationalism* 12, no. 3 (2006): 513–29. Bette Denich, "Dismembering Yugoslavia: Nationalist Ideologies and the Symbolic Revival of Genocide," *American Ethnologist* 21, no. 2 (1994): 367–90; Victoria A. Goddard, Joseph R. Llobera, and Chris Shore, eds., *The Anthropology of Europe: Identities and Boundaries in Conflict* (Oxford: Berg, 1994); Robert Hayden, "Rape and Rape Avoidance in Ethno-National Conflicts: Sexual Violence in Liminalized States," *American Anthropologist* 102, no. 1 (2000): 27–41; Eva V. Huseby-Darvas, "Voices of Plight, Voices of Paradox: Narratives of Women Refugees from the Balkans and the Hungarian Host Population," *Anthropology of East Europe Review* 13, no. 1 (1995): 15–22; Renata Jambresic Kirin and Maja Povrzanovic, *War, Exile, Everyday Life: Cultural Perspectives* (Zagreb: Institute of Ethnology and Folklore Research, 1996); Mirjana Marokvasic, "Nationalism, Sexism and the Yugoslav War," in *Gender, Ethnicity and Political Ideologies*, ed. Nickie Charles and Helen Hintjes (Princeton, NJ: Princeton University Press, 1998); Maja Povrzanovic, "The Imposed and the Imagined as Encountered by Croatian War Ethnographers," *Current Anthropology* 1, no. 2 (2000): 151–61; Janet Reineck, "Seizing the Past Forging the Present: Changing Visions of Self and Nation Among the Kosova Albanians," *Anthropology of East Europe Review* 11, no. 1–2 (1993): 98–106.

8 I would like to thank David Rodin of the Oxford Institute for Ethics, Law and Armed Conflict who pointed to the need for comparative philosophical inquiry and mapping R2P through a "cultural translation" of legal traditions, at a consultation by the project in January 2010 at the University of Oxford.

9 Michael Herzfeld, "The Unspeakable in Pursuit of the Ineffable: Representations of Untranslatability in Ethnographic Discourse," in *Translating Cultures: Perspectives on Translation and Anthropology*, ed. Paula G. Rubel and Abraham Rosman (Oxford and New York: Berg, 2003), 109.

10 See Paul Chilton, *Analyzing Political Discourse: Theory and Practice* (London: Routledge, 2004).

11 See James Clifford and George E. Marcus, eds., *Writing Culture: The Poetics and Politics of Ethnography* (Berkeley: University of California Press, 1986); Frederick Cooper and Ann Laura Stoler, eds., *Tension of Empire: Colonial Cultures in a Bourgeois World* (Berkeley: University of California Press, 1997); Sarah Franklin and Susan McKinnon, eds., *Relative Values: Reconfiguring Kinship Studies* (Durham: Duke University Press, 2001); Ania Loomba, Suvir Kaul, Matti Bunzl, Antoinette Burton, and Jed Esty, eds., *Postcolonial Studies and Beyond* (Durham: Duke University Press, 2005); Catherine Lutz and Lila Abu-Lughod, *Language and the Politics of Emotion* (Cambridge: Cambridge University Press, 1990); Anne McClintock, *Imperial Leather: Race, Gender, and Sexuality in the Colonial Contest* (New York: Routledge, 1995).

12 See Micaela di Leonardo, ed., *Gender at the Crossroads of Knowledge: Feminist Anthropology in the Postmodern Era* (Berkeley: University of California Press, 1991); Frances E. Mascia-Lees, *Gender and Difference in a Globalizing World: 21st Century Anthropology* (Long Grove, Ill.: Waveland Press, Inc., 2009).

13 Lila Abu-Lughod, "Do Muslim Women Really Need Saving? Anthropological reflections on Cultural Relativism and Its Others," *American Anthropologist* 104, no. 3 (2002): 784.

14 Vjollca Krasniqi, "Gender and the Politics of Peacekeeping in Kosovo," in *Gender and Identity: Theories from and/or on Southeast Europe*, ed. Jelisaveta Blagojevic, Katerina Kolozova, and Svetlana Slapsak (Belgrade: Athena, 2006), 368.

15 The research conducted for the writing of this chapter has also been devised as an exploratory intellectual exercise into Kosova's local knowledge production on the topic, a genealogy that is currently absent. The research has also involved the development of an educational tool for students of social and anthropological theory on violence and the state. The research is based on analysis of secondary sources, including memoirs and diaries of local opinion makers, researchers, politicians, and military figures. Here some of the more dominant understandings and symbolic frameworks of the intervention are spelled out. The research based on primary sources consists of a total of 100 interviews. I have personally conducted 20 interviews, 15 of which were semi-structured and five in-depth. The interviews were conducted with important opinion makers in Kosova, particularly those who have defined the dominant meanings of NATO's intervention in Kosova, for its pre-independence and post-independence trajectories. The other 80 in-depth interviews were conducted by students at the University of Pristina as part of a special topics seminar in cultural anthropology.

16 Frederick Cooper, "Postcolonial Studies and the Study of History," in *Postcolonial Studies and Beyond*, ed., Loomba, Kaul, Bunzl, Burton, and Esty, 401–22.

17 Eric Wolf, *Envisioning Power: Ideologies of Dominance and Crisis* (Berkeley: University of California Press, 1999), 289.

18 See Nicholas J. Wheeler, *Saving Strangers: Humanitarian Intervention in International Society* (Oxford: Oxford University Press, 2000); and Mary Kaldor, *New and Old Wars: Organized Violence in a Global Era* (Palo Alto, Calif.: Stanford University Press, 1999).

19 See Gareth Evans, *The Responsibility to Protect: Stopping Mass Atrocity Crimes Once and for All* (Washington, DC: Brookings Institution, 2008);

and Kurt Mills "The Sovereignty Eclipsed? The Legitimacy of Humanitarian Access and Intervention," 4 July 1997, available at: www.jha.ac/articles/a019.htm.

20 Linda Krasniqi, *Intervenimi i NATO-së në Kosovë*, unpublished paper submitted in partial fulfillment of coursework, University of Pristina, Department of Sociology, January 2010, 7.

21 Aida Hozic, "Zoning, or, How to Govern (Cultural) Violence," *Cultural Values* 6, no. 1 & 2 (2002): 185.

22 Krasniqi, *Intervenimi i NATO-së në Kosovë*, 185.

23 Craig Calhoun, "A World of Emergencies: Fear, Intervention, and the Limits of Cosmopolitan Order," *The Canadian Review of Sociology and Anthropology* 41, no. 4. (2004): 373.

24 Ibid., 392.

25 Appearing in 63 of 100 interviews in research conducted (see note 15 above).

26 Abu-Lughod, "Do Muslim Women Really Need Saving?" 789.

27 "Statement by Professor Noam Chomsky to the United Nations General Assembly Thematic Dialogue on the Responsibility to Protect," United Nations, New York, 23 July 2009, available at www.un.org/ga/president/63/interactive/protect/noam.pdf.

28 Fatmir Shala, *Intervenimi në Kosovë*, unpublished paper submitted in partial fulfillment of coursework, University of Pristina, Department of Sociology, January 2010, 1.

29 Shala, *Intervenimi në Kosovë*, 5.

30 Student interview with Rrustem Krasniqi, 12 January 2010, Pristina.

31 Interviews conducted by the author, November 2009–January 2010.

32 See Venuti Lawrence, ed., *The Translation Studies Reader* (London: Routledge, 2000).

33 See Susan Woodward, "Violence-Prone Area or International Transition? Adding the Role of Outsiders in Balkan Violence," in *Violence and Subjectivity*, ed. Veena Das, Arthur Kleinman, Mamphela Ramphelle, and Pamela Reynolds (Berkeley: University of California Press, 1997), 19–45.

34 Woodward, "Violence-Prone Area or International Transition?" 41.

35 Fitore Çunaku, *Intervenimi i NATO-së në Kosovë*, unpublished paper submitted in partial fulfillment of coursework, University of Pristina, Department of Sociology, January 2010, 4.

36 Lindita Hajdari, *Intervenimi I NATO-së*, unpublished paper submitted in partial fulfillment of coursework, University of Pristina, Department of Sociology, January 2010, 3.

37 See Nusret Pllana, *Ushtari Prishtina, Verë '98: Ditar Lufte* (Pristina: GME/Dituria, 1999).

38 Lumni Tërshana, *Intervenimi në Kosovë*, unpublished paper submitted in partial fulfillment of coursework, University of Pristina, Department of Sociology, January 2010, 5.

39 Here I borrow from Saidiya Hartman's usage on "the state of subjection" in *Scenes of Subjection: Terror, Slavery and Self-Making in Nineteenth Century America* (New York: Oxford University Press, 1997).

40 Ismail Kadare, *Identiteti Evropian I Shqiptarëve* (Tirana: Onufri, 2006).

41 Rexhep Qosja, "Kadare, Evropa dhe Jeta Jonë," *Shqip* (Tirana), 7 May 2006.

42 Enis Sulstarova, "The Orientalist Identity of Intellectuals," in *European Identity of Kosova*, ed., *FORUM 2015* (Pristina: Kosovo Foundation for an

Open Society, 2007) 75–80. See also Enis Sulstarova, *Arratisje nga Lindja: Orientalizmi Shqiptar nga Frshëri deri te Kadareja* (Tirana: Botimet Dudaj, 2006).

43 For more information, see the UN Office of the Special Envoy for Kosovo (UNOSEK) website: www.unosek.org/unosek/en/statusproposal.html.

44 The aim of EULEX, the largest mission undertaken under the Common Security and Defense Policy, is to "assist and support the Kosovo authorities in the rule of law area, specifically in the police, judiciary and customs areas. The mission is not in Kosovo to govern or rule. It is a technical mission which will monitor, mentor and advise whilst retaining a number of limited executive powers. EULEX works under the general framework of United Nations Security Resolution 1244 and has a unified chain of command to Brussels." See: www.eulex-kosovo.eu/en/info/whatisEulex.php

45 For a discussion of some of the key events that led to martial law, as well as a discussion of cultural politics behind shifting national identifications in Kosova, see Nita Luci and Markovic Predrag, "Events and Sites of Difference: Marking Self and Other in Kosovo," in *Media Discourse and the Yugoslav Conflicts: Representations of Self and Other*, ed. Pål Kolstø (London: Ashgate, 2008), 83–104. Also see Florian Bieber and Zidas Daskalovski, eds., *Understanding the War in Kosovo* (London: Frank Cass, 2003).

46 Howard Clark, *Civil Resistance in Kosovo* (London: Pluto Press, 2000), 72.

47 See Andrew Lass, "Romantic Documents and Political Monuments: The Meaning Fulfillment of History in 19th Century Czech Nationalism," *American Ethnologist* 15, no. 3 (1988): 456–71; and Katherine Verdery, *What Was Socialism and What Comes Next?* (Princeton, NJ: Princeton University Press, 1996).

48 See Michael Kennedy, *Cultural Formations of Postcommunism: Emancipation, Transition, Nation, and War* (Minneapolis: University of Minnesota Press, 2002); Daphne Berdahl, Matti Bunzl, and Martha Lampland, eds., *Altering States: Ethnographies of Transition in Eastern Europe and the Former Soviet Union* (Ann Arbor: University of Michigan Press, 2000).

49 For a discussion of media construction of identities and the war in Slovenia, see Sabina Mihelj, Veronika Bajt, and Miloš Pankov, "Reorganizing the Identification Matrix: Televisual Construction of Collective Identities in the Early Phase of Yugoslav Disintegration," in *Media Discourse and the Yugoslav Conflicts: Representations of Self and Other*, ed. Pål Kolstø (London: Ashgate, 2008), 39–60.

50 By 1993 Slovenia, Croatia, and Bosnia and Herzegovina had declared independence from Yugoslavia, with Montenegro becoming independent from Serbia in 2006. Kosova also declared its independence in 1990, but was not recognized by any government. As of 2011, 75 UN member states recognized Kosova as independent, but additional acknowledgment was required in order to become a member of the UN.

51 Since 1991 George Soros alone, through the Open Society Institute and national foundations, has provided tens of millions of dollars to civil society programs throughout the region.

52 Kennedy, *Cultural Formations*, 56.

53 Stephen Zunes, "Humanitarian Intervention: A Forum," *The Nation*, 14 July 2003, available at: www.thenation.com/article/humanitarian-interventio n-forum-0.

54 See Nita Luci, "Transitions and Tradition: Constructions of Gender, Nation and Family in Kosova," *Anthropological Yearbook of European Cultures*, vol.14 (*Gender and Nation in South Eastern Europe*), ed. Karl Kaser and Elizabeth Katschnig-Fasch (Wien: Lit Verlag, 2005), 143–70; Muhamet Pirraku, *Lëvizja Gjithëpopullore Shqiptare për Faljen e Gjaqeve: 1990–1992 Koronikë* (Pristina: Instituti Albanologjik i Prishtinës, 1998); Stephanie Schwandner-Sievers, "Humiliation and Reconciliation in Northern Albania: The Logics of Feuding in Symbolic and Diachronic Perspective," in *Dynamics of Violence: Processes of Escalation and De-escalation in Violent Group Conflicts*, ed. George Elewert, Stephan Feuchtwang, and Dieter Neubert (Berlin: Duncker and Humbolt, 1999), 133–52; Drita Statovci, "Femra Shqiptare ne Faljen e Gjaqeve," *Gjurmime Albanologjike* 20 (1990): 97–107.

55 Muhamet Pirraku, *Lëvizja Gjithëpopullore Shqiptare për Faljen e Gjaqeve: 1990–1992 Koronikë* (Pristina: Instituti Albanologjik i Prishtinës, 1998), 12.

56 To forgive blood meant that the parties, specifically families, would reconcile and not seek to avenge any wrongdoing committed against them.

57 Derived etymologically from *be, beja*, "the oath," *besa* is usually translated as the honor of the house, hospitality, the given word, protection guarantee, reconciliation, alliance, etc.

58 See Adem Demaçi's *Gjarpijt e Gjakut* (The Snakes of Blood) (Pristina: Jeta e re, [1958] reprint 1991); and Ismail Kadare's *Broken April* (Lanham, Md.: New Amsterdam Books, [1978] 1990) for literary treatments and their condemnation of this practice. *Broken April* was also adapted in 2001 into a film by Brazilian director Walter Salles, with the title *Abril Despedaçado* (Behind the Sun). For the Albanian context, see Ismet Elezi, *E Drejta zakonore Penale e Shqipëtareve dhe Lufta për Zhdukjen e Mbeturinave të saj në Shqipëri* (Tirana: 8 November 1983).

59 Elsewhere I have argued that the definitions of tradition explicated by the socialist state had also placed the "observance" of "traditional" kin networks as belonging to the past, as objects and material to be collected by folklorists. The past also signified the country and backward rural traditions, which the state's modernist projects had to eliminate, although with little success. For a larger regional perspective on relations between ethnology and the socialist state, see Mark Slobin, ed., *Retuning Culture: Musical Changes in Central and Eastern Europe* (Durham, NC: Duke University Press, 1996).

60 For a discussion of Albanian and Serbian manhood as constructed in Serbian public discourse, see: Renata Salecl, *The Spoils of Freedom: Psychoanalysis and Feminism after the Fall of Socialism* (London: Routledge, 1994); and Wendy Bracewell, "Rape in Kosovo," *Nations and Nationalism* 6, no. 4 (2000): 563–90.

61 Human Rights Watch, *Under Orders: War Crimes in Kosovo* (New York: Human Rights Watch, 2001).

62 See Anne-Marie L.M. de Brouwer, *Supranational Criminal Prosecution of Sexual Violence: The ICC and the Practice of the ICTY and the ICTR* (Antwerpen and Oxford: Intersentia: 2005).

63 Wolf, *Envisioning Power*, 18. This term was introduced by anthropologist Alfred Kroeber, who argued for attention to historical processes and contextualization, rather than sequence of events. For more discussion, see Tim Ingold, "Anthropology is *Not* Ethnography," *Proceedings of the British Academy* 154 (2008): 69–92.

64 Gani Bobi, *Kontektsti i Vetkultures* (Pejë: Dukagjini, 1997), 15–16. See also his *Pradoks Kulturor* (Pejë: Dukagjini, 1997).

65 By the end of 1989 and during the following year, numerous associations and political parties emerged in Kosova, as in other spaces of former Yugoslavia, enabled by new laws permitting new political and other associations. The Kosova Alternative included associations of sociologists and philosophers, women's groups, and the newly established Council for the Defense of Human Rights and Freedoms. New political parties were also established, including Liberal and Social Democrats, the Green Party, Christian Democrats, and the Democratic League of Kosova, which became the dominant force.

66 Blerim Reka, Kelmend Hapçiu, "Demokraci në Kosovë Demokraci në Jugosllavi," *Rilindja*, 1 April 1990.

67 Amnesty International, "Yugoslavia: Police Violence in Kosovo Province—The Victims," September 1994, document EUR 70/16/94, 4. The "poisoning affair"—as it is still referred to—is also discussed by Clark, *Civil Resistance in Kosovo*. See also Evlianë Bajqinovci, "Outbreak of a 'Mysterious Epidemic' in Some Municipalities in Kosovo. Doctors Say: There Are Symptoms of Poisoning," *Rilindja*, 23 March 1990, 1.

68 A recently produced documentary film (*2 korrik 1990*, by Blendi Fevziu, 2010) presents recordings from assembly sessions and material from television archives. These archives provide a rich source for future research.

69 See Clark, *Civil Resistance in Kosovo*, 58.

70 For a discussion on the relations between cultural formations of transition and nationalism, see Kennedy, *Cultural Formations*, 149–90.

71 Also in Nita Luci and Vjollca Krasniqi, *The Politics of Remembrance and Belonging: Life Histories of Albanian Women in Kosova* (Pristina: Center for Research and Gender Policy, 2006). For an analysis of the parallel education system in Kosova, see Denisa Kostovicova, *Kosovo: The Politics of Identity and Space* (London: Routledge, 2005).

72 Shkëlzen Maliqi, "Self-Understanding of the Albanians in Nonviolence," in *Conflict or Dialogue: Serbian-Albanian Relations and Integration of the Balkans*, ed. Dušan Janjić and Shkëlzen Maliqi (Pristina: Open University, 1994). Also see Shkëlzen Maliqi, *Nyja e Kosovës* (The Kosovo Knot) (Pristina: MM, [1990] 2010) for an analysis of 1980 cultural, historical, and political debates; and *Kosova: Separate Worlds—Reflections and Analyses* (Pristina: MM, 1998).

73 Anton K. Berishaj, "Violence Following Violence," in *Archives of Memory: Supporting Traumatized Communities Through Narration and Remembrance*, ed. Natale Lose, Luisa Passerini, and Silvia Salvatici (Geneva: International Migration Organization, 2001), 79–81.

74 Quoted from an interview conducted by the author, Pristina, 14 December 2009.

75 See Alex J. Bellamy, "Human Wrongs in Kosovo: 1974–99," *The International Journal of Human Rights* 4, no. 3 and 4 (2000): 105–26.

76 Berishaj, "Violence Following Violence," 79.

77 Although socialist Yugoslavia's persecution of enemies of the state was by no means reserved for Albanians, "ethnic considerations" had created a political economy based on the ethnic division of labor in Kosova. The political visions of those placed differentially within former Yugoslavia's

economic and political distribution of rights had also created constant social and cultural confrontations. Simultaneously, significant segments of the population who were influenced by Marxism-Leninism and sympathetic to anticolonial struggles were marginalized, but they began to articulate their cause. In Kosova, members of illegal underground movements—including the Popular Movement for Kosova, which later came to constitute the ranks of the KLA—came from backgrounds in which narratives and experiences of resistance since the 1950s had marked their political aspirations, especially in the Drenica region. The fall of Aleksander Ranković in 1966, who headed the State Security Administration (UDBA), was clearly such a moment. The Constitution of 1974 and the student demonstrations of 1981 also signaled that power relations in Kosova were being challenged. See Branka Magas, *The Destruction of Yugoslavia: Tracing the Breakup 1980–1992* (London: Verso, 1993); and Andrew Baruch Wachtel, *Making a Nation, Breaking a Nation: Literature and Cultural Politics in Yugoslavia* (Palo Alto, Calif.: Stanford University Press, 1998).

78 See Isabel Ströhle, "Pristina's 'Martyrs' Cemetry'—Conflicting Commemorations," *Südosteuropa* 54 (2006): 404–26.

79 Interview by the author, Pristina, 23 January 1999.

80 Joëlle Bahloul, *The Architecture of Memory: A Jewish-Muslim Household in Colonial Algeria, 1937–1962* (Cambridge: Cambridge University Press, 1996). See Zarana Papic, "Women in Serbia: Post-communism War and Nationalist Mutations," in *Gender and Identity: Theories From and/or on Southeast Europe*, ed., Blagojevic, Kolozova, and Slapsak.

81 Mark Krasniqi, *Mikpritja në Traditën Shqiptare* (Pristina: Akdemia e Arteve dhe e Shkencave e Kosovës, 2005), 25. See Shtjefën Gjeçovi, ed., *Kanuni i Lekë Dukagjinit/The Code of Lekë Dukagjini*, trans. Leonard Fox (New York: Gjonlekaj Publishing, [1933] 1992), 132: "The house of the Albanian belongs to God and to the mik [friend emanating from various alliances]."

82 Edith Durham, *High Albania: A Victorian Traveler's Balkan Odessey* (London: Edward Arnold, 1909).

83 See Agon Hamza, "The Specter of Ideological Apparatuses," *Reartikulacija* 8 (2009), available at: www.reartikulacija.org/?p=689.

84 Robert Connell, *Masculinities* (Sydney: Allen & Unwin, 1995).

85 Vjollca Krasniqi, "Imagery, Gender and Power: The Politics of Representation in Post-War Kosova," *Feminist Review* 86 (2007): 1–23.

86 Homi K. Bhaba, "Foreword," in *The Wretched of the Earth*, Franz Fanon (New York: Grove Press, 2004), xvi.

87 Interviews conducted by the author, Pristina, December 2009–January 2010.

88 International Commission on Intervention and State Sovereignty, *The Responsibility to Protect* (Ottawa: International Development Research Centre, 2001), xii.

89 Interview by the author, Pristina, 5 December 2009.

90 ICISS, *The Responsibility to Protect*, xi.

91 Ibid., 23.

92 See Blerim Reka, *UNMIK as International Governance in Post-war Kosova: NATO's Intervention, UN Administration and Kosovar Aspirations* (Skopje: Logos A, 2003).

93 Here I have not discussed in any detail the complex relations of governance and administration that emerged in Kosova after the intervention that led

to the independence of the last breakaway republic to emerge from the ashes of the former Yugoslavia. International inputs were essential to achieving Kosova's independence, but they also required diverse interlocutors. The declaration of independence in February 2008 was followed a year later by actual independence in February 2009. The most recent international input came from the complex July 2010 decision rendered by the International Court of Justice (ICJ) that Kosova's declaration of independence was legal, although it avoided declaring that the state of Kosova was legal under international law. The ICJ's decision meant that the legitimacy of the state itself would be legitimized by "others," namely by the countries that recognize it. To date, it has been recognized by 75 of the 192 UN member states—including the United States and the vast majority of EU members.

6 Atrocities prevented in Nepal?

The impact of civic and cultural institutions

Arjun Karki and Jyoti Upadhyay

- **Political transitions, transformations, and civil conflict**
- **Social and cultural institutions in Nepal**
- **Indigenous communities and cultural protection mechanisms: two cases**
- **The disintegration of social safety nets? living within a "culture of terror"**
- **Conclusion: end of atrocities or new divisions? lessons for R2P**

This chapter examines the emerging norm of the responsibility to protect (R2P) populations from mass atrocities through the lens of the armed conflict in Nepal from 1996 to 2006.[1] Despite the presence of several national, bilateral, regional, and international actors, it was local actors who were decisive in preventing atrocities. Nepali civic actors, especially cultural institutions and traditional leaders, were most responsible at critical junctures. The UN secretary-general's 2009 report, *Implementing the Responsibility to Protect*, underscored the primary responsibility of states and placed emphasis on the need for capacity building to prevent mass atrocities. This chapter delves below the national level and looks at the sub-national level to examine how such national capacity could practically be built. It highlights the role of civic actors and cultural institutions in implementing R2P in the preventive and protective stages of violent conflict.[2]

Several actors played a role in preventing the escalation of violence and protecting victims between 1996 and 2006, including: the United Nations in many forms, initially through the UN Office of the High Commissioner for Human Rights (OHCHR) and later through the UN Mission in Nepal (UNMIN); diplomatic missions of regional organizations, especially the European Union (EU); and foreign governments, particularly India and member countries of the EU. However, it was Nepali actors who shaped the path away from violence and toward peace. National human rights defenders and civil society organizations (CSOs) were key during the anti-monarchy movement that resulted in the democracy movement called Jana Andolan II (People's Movement II), and the negotiations that led to the Comprehensive Peace Agreement (CPA) signed on 21 November 2006. However, both national civil society and international actors were predominantly in Kathmandu, while the conflict mainly transpired and affected populations in rural areas beyond the reach of state institutions and international protection. Consequently, we emphasize the contributions of civic and cultural institutions operating within indigenous communities in the countryside, as it was these practices, customs, and actors that filled the gap and served a protective and preventive function in the worst-affected areas.

This chapter also helps fill an existing gap in research. Carolyn Nordstrom notes that "[t]raditional Western approaches to violent conflict do not often recognize the creative strategies people on the front lines employ to survive the war."[3] We are reminded of Stathis N. Kalyvas's contention that despite the fact that most violence takes place in rural areas, studies of civil war violence are generally biased in their focus on urban areas.[4] In this vein Colin Millard observed that literature about resistance in Nepal generally focuses on the Kathmandu valley, with very little information on events and changes in rural areas with the majority of the population.[5] Moreover, given the vast developmental chasm between the Kathmandu valley and the rest of the country, this research bias obscures our understanding of the conflict.[6] Further, with limited exceptions such as work by Judith Pettigrew, the contribution of anthropology and sociology to analyses of the violence in Nepal has thus far been minimal.[7] Less still has been written on how various social or cultural mechanisms might protect communities from the types of mass violence that have characterized civil wars—understandings that would be crucial for implementing R2P.

Ordinary people engaged in creative strategies to survive the conflict, protected themselves and one another from harm, resisted incursions from both sides, and prevented further violence. This chapter shifts the focus not only from urban centers to the rural hinterland, but also from the political elite to the masses. More specifically, by focusing on local cultural practices, institutions and behaviors, our analysis reveals some of the ways in which individuals caught up in webs of violence and fear acted as agents rather than merely as anonymous victims.[8]

The social sciences have always struggled to achieve consensus on "culture." Our examples from indigenous or ethnic groups in Nepal do not suggest that culture is their exclusive domain; rather, we define culture as institutionalized or more informal practices of daily life.

Cultures are not static; they are constantly evolving and adapting to changed circumstances. The generic term "cultural institutions" encompasses customs, practices, and norms as well as formal institutions.

This chapter begins with a brief background of the armed conflict and the role of international and national actors, which is followed by an overview of the cultural diversity of Nepal. The next section contains case studies of two indigenous communities to illustrate how civic and cultural institutions played a decisive role in protection and prevention. Although cultural factors were not solely responsible for protection or prevention in Nepal's armed conflict—nor was their contribution unambiguously positive—nevertheless it is essential to understand the hitherto neglected cultural dimension. The fourth section highlights the impact of the armed conflict on cultural practices and shows how the dynamics of fear eroded and transformed traditional practices and institutions. Finally, the conclusion looks ahead to Nepal's future prospects and puts forward some lessons for R2P.

Political transitions, transformations, and civil conflict

Over the past two decades, Nepal's political process has been defined by transformations. In 1990 the Jana Andolan I (People's Movement I) restored multiparty democracy and overthrew a 30-year party-less *Panchayat* system that was established in December 1960 by King Mahendra with a royal coup against an infant democracy that had been established in 1959. After three decades, the ban on political parties was lifted, a multiparty interim government formed, and a new constitution was developed. Nepal was declared a multi-ethnic, multi-lingual, Hindu, and constitutional monarchical kingdom. For the first time, several rights of minority groups were recognized: to follow their traditional religion, to preserve their native language and culture, and to ensure that their children were educated in their own mother tongues. "Where, before, issues of ethnicity and cultural disadvantage could only be alluded to indirectly, now they could be addressed openly, publicly, and officially."[9] Indigenous groups (*janajatis*) felt a deep sense of relief; indeed many expressed that "a great weight had been lifted from their shoulders."[10]

On 13 February 1996, the Communist Party of Nepal (Maoist) (CPN-M) launched simultaneous attacks against police outposts in Rolpa and Rukum districts in the mid-west, a government agricultural development bank in Gorkha district in the west, and another police outpost in Sindhuli in east Nepal. Other attacks occurred soon afterwards in Jajarkot and Salyan districts. The CPN-M also distributed pamphlets on the revolt in the urban centers of more than 60 of Nepal's 75 districts. The "People's War" had begun.

Perceiving the insurgency as a law and order issue, state security forces responded with aggressive police operations such as Operation Kilo Sierra 2; the ruthlessness of these indiscriminate operations brought terror to rural villages of the mid-west almost overnight.[11] However, by the end of 1999 Maoist insurgents were active in around three-quarters of Nepal's 75 districts, and a growing number of districts and Village Development Committees (VDCs) were being deeply affected by the conflict.[12] After 2001 there was a marked escalation of violence and a contraction of the economy. Five years after the beginning of the insurgency, Nepalis in urban and other areas outside of Maoist strongholds began to consider the conflict as a serious issue. Whelpton notes that until 2001 opinion polls revealed that the average Nepali considered issues such as corruption and unemployment as the country's most pressing challenges.[13] That year also marked a turning point in international attention, in no small part due to the assassination of 10 members of the royal family on 1 June 2001, which attracted strong media interest in a country that had until then been portrayed as an idyllic and peaceful land.[14] A state of emergency was declared on 26 November 2001, thus suspending a number of constitutional articles and clauses that guarantee civil liberties; the Terrorist and Destructive Activities (Prevention and Control) Ordinance (TADO) was also instated, which allowed security forces extraordinary powers to arrest and detain suspects.

The Hindu notion of social differentiation according to caste and sub-caste, as well as large differences in socioeconomic opportunities and access to resources, had resulted in domination by upper castes (Bahuns, Chhetris including Thakuris, and some Newars) and classes. The initial hopes for the opening up of political opportunities for previously sidelined groups failed to materialize. Rather, with many of the *Panchayat* regime's politicians (*panchas*) having moved into democratic politics through the major political parties, the "stranglehold" of the upper castes tightened throughout the 1990s.[15] Despite comprising only 30 percent of the population in 2001, this section of the population monopolized political power.[16] As the authors of *A Kingdom Under Siege* explain:

> In the two elected Panchayat legislatures (of the 1980s), the share of Bahuns and Chhetris was 50 per cent. This proportion increased to 55, 63, and 63 per cent respectively in the 1991, 1994, and 1999 parliaments. (Most strikingly, only one Dalit was elected MP in

> these three elections.) The imbalance has been even more striking in the bureaucracy. Between 1983 and 1985, 69 per cent of those who passed the civil service examination were Bahuns and Chhetris. This figure rose to 81 per cent in 1992/3; and by 2001 it stood at 98 per cent![17]

The "structure of inequality" of Nepali society had long resulted in "poverty for the majority," with women and other marginalized groups subjected to systemic discrimination in Nepali society.[18] These primary underlying causes of violence in Nepal were exacerbated by the "fragile balance of power" and sense of disappointment that marked the years following the 1990 movement.[19]

However, these factors alone do not explain the ability of the Maoists to mobilize such large numbers of men and women (up to 30 percent of Maoist cadres were women).[20] Despite a gross domestic product (GDP) growth rate of around 5 percent throughout the 1990s, there were insufficient employment opportunities for secondary school graduates, and high rates of unemployment further fuelled deep discontent.[21] Given high levels of poverty in Maoist strongholds, the prospect of equitable wealth distribution, employment, and cession of corruption—key issues of CPN(M) rhetoric—appealed to unemployed youths.[22]

The king launched a coup on 1 February 2005, which resulted in the dissolution of parliament, the arrest of several political and civil society leaders, and travel bans. In response, civil society, democratic political parties, and the Maoists launched the People's Movement II in April 2006—a campaign to end monarchy and restore democracy. This movement brought ideologically conflicting parties and civil society into alliance against the *ancien régime* of the Hindu monarchy.[23] Their efforts led to the CPA, signed on 21 November 2006 between the CPN(M) and the Seven-Party Alliance (SPA) government, largely negotiated by Nepali political and civic actors themselves. The broad pro-democracy, anti-monarchy alliance is largely believed to have led the country toward peace and away from the People's War, which cost around 16,000 lives. On 28 May 2008 the long-reigning Hindu monarchy was overthrown with a peaceful proclamation by the 601-member Constituent Assembly, the supreme political body directly elected by the people, which voted to establish a secular democratic federal republic.

International and national actors and interventions

Throughout the conflict and especially after 2005, Nepali civil society campaigned vigorously for the monarchy's end; human rights defenders

(HRDs) played a vibrant role in reminding all sides of their responsibilities to keep violence in check. During street protests and human rights fact-finding missions, Nepali HRDs wore standard jackets that enabled them to be easily identified and recognized as symbols of neutrality. They arranged makeshift ambulances for the injured and administered first aid.

National civic actors also played a critical role in negotiating with both sides to prevent atrocities during crucial moments, such as when the Maoists stormed a police base at Holeri, Rolpa District, and took 69 policemen hostage. With no effective state response, civil society intervened, and in the end the abductees were released without casualties. Civil society leaders accepted by all sides were also crucial in facilitating the CPA. For the most part, Kathmandu-based civil society remained ignorant of the full extent of the conflict's brutal effects during the conflict's early years.[24] Its role therefore became most important later when its efforts arguably were a determining factor in preventing potentially explosive situations.

International and diplomatic actors also played a crucial supportive role, albeit remaining largely restricted to Kathmandu and other urban centers. Following the royal take-over, prominent political and civil society leaders, including one of the authors of this chapter (Karki), were under arrest warrant and placed on the travel ban list. Neighbors often sheltered these individuals from the police, and subsequently the diplomatic community provided them with safe passage out of Nepal. International protection enabled exiled leaders to continue lobbying Western and Asian governments as well as intergovernmental organizations outside Nepal, and to draw international attention to the conflict and the grave human rights situation. Other individuals were given temporary shelter in foreign embassies and UN buildings in Kathmandu.

UN and EU interventions calling for respect for human rights and compliance with international norms complemented local and national civil society initiatives. Nepali civil society successfully lobbied to bring the OHCHR to Nepal. The OHCHR's monitoring and reporting on human rights violations, as well as its technical assistance to Nepali human rights institutions, helped reduce excesses by belligerents on both sides. Security Council Resolution 1740 on 23 January 2007 established UNMIN upon the joint invitation of the Maoists and the SPA. While UNMIN originally had offices in four urban centers outside of Kathmandu, its presence is now largely limited to the capital and to major Maoist cantonments. Its mandate has been to monitor arms, register armed personnel and Maoist combatants, and provide assistance in monitoring ceasefire arrangements and elections for the Constituent Assembly. In recent years the credibility of UNMIN as an impartial player has decreased, resulting in it being less positively perceived by Nepali civil society and politicians.

Social and cultural institutions in Nepal

Nepal is often described as a cultural mosaic resulting from waves of migration from India, Kashmir, Myanmar, Tibet, and the People's Republic of China. While Nepali-speaking Indo-Aryan groups (comprising Bahuns, Chhetris, and "Untouchables" or Dalits) arrived from the west and south, ethnic groups speaking languages of Tibeto-Myanmar origin arrived from the north and east. Some groups such as the Tharu and Santhals have resided in the country's southern plains for over two millennia. Official figures indicate the existence of at least 103 distinct caste, ethnic, religious, and linguistic groups. However, identity in modern Nepal is multidimensional, composite, and changing—complexities that census figures are unable to capture. Today, non-Indo-Aryans make up around 40 percent of a total population of well over 30 million. The major groups are: Magar, Tharu, Tamang, Newar, Limbu, and Gurung; there are also numerous other smaller groups such as the Santhals. As part of the battle for greater rights and self-determination, communities and groups with their own distinct languages, cultures, and identities—who are often defined in public discourse as non-Bahuns/Chhetri—are commonly referred to as "indigenous nationalities." We use the terms group, community, and nationality interchangeably.[25]

Since its establishment by Gorkha ruler Prithvi Narayan Shah in 1768, the Nepali state has been dominated by a small elite primarily consisting of the upper castes (Bahun, Chhetri, and Thakuri) and to a lesser extent privileged sections of other groups such as the Kathmandu-based Newars. Bahun and Chhetri are the Nepali terms for Hindu Brahmin and Kshatriya, which according to the 2001 census make up around 15.8 percent and 12.7 percent of the population, respectively. Thakuris, comprising only 1.5 percent of the population, are considered a distinct sub-caste. The dominance of these groups led to the establishment of Nepali as the common language and the spread of Parbatiya culture and Hinduism, effectively resulting in the suppression of the cultures, languages, and religions of other groups. As Harka Gurung and Rajendra Pradhan note, however, perceptions of who is oppressing or oppressed vary among marginalized groups. Exclusion has been structured according to region, as well as class, caste, ethnicity, and gender.[26]

Prominent voices within indigenous groups claim that their autonomy was destroyed during the construction of the Hindu nation-state. Nonetheless, most indigenous communities also profess pride for having preserved their own customary laws and, to a lesser extent, traditional practices of governance including modes of conflict resolution. Many in rural and remote districts, for example, do not attend government courts to seek justice but effectively settle disputes within their own villages. Numerous scholars examining the nature of the state and the physical, symbolic, and cultural violence often perpetrated in the Nepali nation-building project view the state as having not only undermined and in some cases destroyed local practices, but also systematically discriminated against and marginalized indigenous communities.[27]

Caste refers to the Hindu notion of ritual hierarchy, which divides society according to ideas of pollution and purity. On the one hand, the caste system seems exploitative and exclusionary, including for those outside the system—the Untouchables who now are commonly referred to as Dalits. On the other hand, caste was traditionally also an interdependent economic system to which different caste groups contributed. Difficult now to find in urban settlements, traces are more visible in socioeconomic relationships in the countryside.[28] While such economic interdependency may have in the past been instrumental in avoiding violent conflict in Nepal, the dominant and exclusionary nature of society has been a significant source of frustration for large sections of the Nepali population. Access to land and other socioeconomic resources have led also to powerful discourses of class.

Religion in Nepal is syncretic and defies strict categorization.[29] Buddhism in Nepal includes Theravada, Mahayana, and Vajrayana traditions, and although Nepal's rulers were primarily Hindu, they often encouraged Buddhist practices,[30] resulting in a combination of traditions that varies across communities.[31] While this distinctiveness is essential to understand the history and philosophy of Nepali society, such as the role of Hinduism in supporting the nationalist project,[32] our research indicated that religious dynamics were not a salient feature in local people's explanations, reflections, and reasoning.[33]

Finally, outmigration, especially from rural areas, has been a defining feature of Nepal's economy and society through the twentieth century. Traditionally migrating to India, vast numbers of laborers now also migrate to the Gulf and Malaysia. As a result, mothers and wives have increasingly been left alone in communities to maintain households; in 2006 approximately 44 percent of households had one or more members who had migrated from the community for work.[34] The armed conflict exacerbated matters: fear of being recruited or getting caught in the crossfire exacerbated vulnerabilities of food insecurity, poverty, and unemployment. This trend has had deep implications for how rural people have responded to the terror within their communities.

Within all societies, social relationships are a fundamental aspect of human organization. In rural communities in Nepal, the family continues to play a critical role for economic production and as a first recourse for support in times of hardship. Kinship bonds also work in various ways to provide a functional social relation binding individuals across caste, ethnic, and even religious boundaries. For example, in both urban and rural Nepal, kinship terms are fundamental for individuals in addressing each other. Unlike most societies, names are not publicly known and used for addressing individuals; rather it is a kinship term that denotes the relation between those interacting. Kin terms are therefore not always derived from genealogical, consanguinal, and affinal bases, and one may observe a high-caste Bahun calling a Dalit *dāju* (older brother) or *kākā* (uncle) and vice versa.[35] In agricultural communities, individuals with different socio-cultural backgrounds but with similar ecological and thus economic bases may be bound together through common economic obligations, rights, and interests in which simple kinship terms may function as a coordinating factor. Throughout Nepal, social interactions have a significant impact on individual actions and activities.

The concepts inherent in the responsibility to protect—of security, protection, and support—find their reflection in *suraksha*, *samrakshan* and *sahayog*. While the first two have more direct connotations of saving human life and therefore of protection from atrocities, *sahayog* has broader connotations of solidarity and supporting those in distress. During the insurgency, neither the state nor any other organization protected those entrapped by extreme adversity, and in such situations, kin were the first port of call. Extensive kinship networks instinctively offered assistance and refuge from the brutality of belligerents.[36]

This reality existed for biological kinship as well as for kinship beyond blood (*mit* or *miteri*).[37] *Mit lagaune* (having/establishing a relation) is a custom prevalent across the majority of caste and ethnic groups in Nepal, which brings different and otherwise unrelated groups together into socially binding relationships.[38] In his study of the Gurung community, anthropologist Donald Messerschmidt explains that *mit or miteri* "is contracted between individuals and sometimes, by extension … groups, for both instrumental and affective reasons … *Miteri* serves to cement social interaction. Nepal's caste-oriented society normally restricts kinship to the horizontal ties of consanguinity and affinity. The *miteri* allows the alternative of forming fictive kinship ties."[39] Given the importance of such relations, which are often argued to be deeper than relations with blood relatives,[40] contemporary Nepali scholars concur that "fictive kinship" is not an appropriate description of *miteri*, which is a binding relationship between any two people and, by extension, between their families. As with senior kin members, a *mit* kinsman or *mitini* kinswoman must be treated with the highest respect.[41] Often "infused with the reciprocal responsibilities of kinship,"[42] the establishment of *mit* relations strengthens existing bonds of commonality, affection, or cooperation and takes priority over material or instrumental considerations.[43] In addition to its emotional worth, however, these relationships are economically valuable and, consequently, strongly nurtured.[44]

Thus, *mit* is a cultural institution with wider significance. The process of becoming a *mit* or *mitini* varies across communities.

As Suresh Dhakal posits, while there are variations in the ways that *miteri* relations are set up and sustained between different ethnic and caste groups in Nepali society, there are strong suggestions that such relations are in some way central to the avoidance of discord and conflict, and to the maintenance of goodwill and social unity across different religious, caste and ethnic groups.[45] Many of Nepal's most prominent scholars affirm its value for conflict settlement or prevention within communities. Indeed, *miteri* relations are often established to resolve interpersonal disputes.

Several incidents of protection by *mit* during the armed conflict have been recorded. For example, a Chhetri from Baglung district, who, after having his property confiscated and his life threatened by the Maoists, was sheltered for over four months by his *mit* of modest means from the Magar ethnic group.[46]

Respect for kin, elders, and teachers (*guru*) is strong across Nepal and played a safeguarding role during Nepal's armed conflict. The bond between *guru-chelaa* (teachers and students) led frequently to the protection of teachers by students. As many teachers and professors were active in the peace process and in demonstrations, as students and youth were active either as police or young soldiers, as Maoists, or as Jana Andolan activists. Numerous individuals were even protected by members of the "enemy side" due to pre-established/existing relationships of respect.[47]

Indigenous communities and cultural protection mechanisms: two cases

In examining the protective role of cultural institutions, we focused on Morang's Santhal community and two different Tharu communities—one from mid-west Nepal and the other from the eastern region. Although not located in areas where the insurgency began, these communities were deeply affected by the conflict. Moreover, existing evidence and discussions with Nepali scholars revealed that the response to armed conflict through cultural means was particularly marked within these two indigenous communities.

"Resisting" the insurgents by the Santhals of Eastern Tarai

The Santhals are one of the oldest inhabitants of Jhapa and Morang districts of Eastern Tarai, the belt that runs across southern Nepal. According to the 2001 census, the total population of Santhals is 42,398 and more than 39,500 live in Jhapa and Morang. Those inhabiting a certain territorial base are organized under the Majhi Pargana, an institutionalized formal political organization based on indigenous political and cultural systems the main function of which is to maintain harmony and peace within the Santhal social system.[48] The institution has a number of formal officials, including the *majhi hadam*, the headman of the *ātu* (the basic political unit under which one or more settlement clusters are organized), who acts as the spokesperson of the village. The *majhi* is elected by the *ātu*'s elders; he is informed of all important events in the village; all social, religious, and political functions are held in accordance with his instruction and participation. The *paranik* (deputy of the *majhi*), *jog majhi* (leader of village cultural festivities), *nayake* (village priest), and *gudit* and *dharuwa* also have essential institutionalized roles. The *gudit* is responsible for disseminating all necessary information among the villagers; he also serves as a security officer, who works under the instructions of the *majhi hadam* and his deputies.[49]

The *majhi hadam* settles all disputes, debates, and conflicts in the village. Santhals say that they discourage conflict and violence. If an individual is found to have violated Santhal rules and norms, he or she is immediately held to account and often punished. Furthermore, if an individual is fighting with non-Santhal people, a *bainsi* (village assembly) is held to decide whether their Santhal kin is guilty.

We investigated the response to the armed conflict among Morang district's Santhals, who were terrorized by both the Maoists and the state. During our fieldwork, informants recounted how they resisted and prevented Maoist insurgents from entering Santhal territory for over a year. Community resistance began after a Santhal youth from a neighboring village, having protested Maoist activity in Situng Tola, was gagged and beaten by Maoist cadres. Immediate and spontaneous outrage greeted this atrocity. The Santhals of both Situng Tola and Bādhi Tola enacted the culturally embodied practice of having the *dharuwa* walk around the village with a small green mango branch. According to Santhal custom, whenever a *dharuwa* is seen walking, every individual understands that the community is facing a collective emergency. It is the mango branch that communicates the existence of a problem; community members understand that a *baisi* (assembly) must be convened. Following the aggression, the Santhals gathered a *baisi* in this way, under the leadership of all the *majhi* leaders from different Santhal settlements. Thousands of Santhals from dozens of the district's *ātus* gathered and decided to not allow the Maoists to hold any programs and activities in the Santhal *ātus*.

During the resistance, youths used their *tamak* and *tumda* drums to produce a rhythm that conveys a crisis.[50] They guarded their *ātus* by beating their drums throughout the village in the evenings. In this particular case, both elders and youth took responsibility: the former fulfilled their responsibility for leading the *baisi* and making the collective decision to resist, while the latter guarded the community's territory. Respondents noted that none of these Santhal customs had been used recently but that the armed conflict provoked a spontaneous reawakening of traditional practices. Moreover, youth participated and thus joined their elders in working for a common goal. As one youth explained, "It was decided by our *majhi hadams* and *baisi* to protect our *ātus* from the Maoists, and we were ready to die to do this."[51]

This case demonstrates how indigenous peoples' cultural institutions can still bind members to achieve political goals. The Santhal communities used their own traditional apparatus to resist the Maoist domination. Why did they not approach the state's administrative functionaries, such as the VDC, police, or district court to seek protection? There are several explanations that help illustrate the relevance for R2P of the agency of conflict-affected civilians within rural and indigenous communities. First, local government offices were prime targets in the insurgent offensive; in the first seven years of the conflict alone, 1,683 VDC buildings were damaged by Maoists and rendered unusable, in addition to attacks on district and municipality offices.[52] Second, indigenous communities still had functional cultural mechanisms that helped find solutions to a host of problems including political conflict. Third, there was the potential of these performative expressions to not only promote the culture itself, but also to unite people in political solidarity when used in processes of resistance.[53]

Supra-familial networks and social cohesion: case studies among two Tharu communities

Tharus, one of the oldest inhabitants of Nepal's Tarai, constitute 6.8 percent of the total population of Nepal.[54] Their population stretches along the Tarai belt; they also outnumber any other groups of people in the Sunsari, Dang, Bardiya, and Kailali districts. Before their annexation to the Gorkhali state, Tharus had their own political, social, and economic administrators.

Among the *Morangiya* Tharus (inhabitants of Morang district) of Eastern Tarai, the cultural institution of *garamati* is seen as a mechanism to maintain the Tharu value that family members should cooperate and support both each other and other members of society. A grouping made up of four to fifty families, at least one member has to come from outside the kin group; some *garamatis* have up to 30 percent of members from outside the kin group.[55] The use of *garamati* has a role in helping to ensure a strong community bond,[56] and households are primarily represented by women. A *garamati* that is not helping one of its members is publicly criticized, which partially explains their willingness to go to such lengths to protect members.

During interviews, Tharu respondents particularly cited the following case. Around 2003, when army searches were common in the area, a local Nepali Congress Party leader, Nam Narayan Mukhiya, provided shelter in a rented house, about a kilometer from his village, to a Maoist cadre who was from his village and a distant relative. Although they were from opposing political parties and ideologies, Nam Narayan gave shelter to the man. Later, soldiers suspecting that Nam Narayan was hiding a Maoist began to threaten him. A neighboring woman informed Nam's wife that the army was conducting a search in the village, prompting Nam and his wife not to sleep at home that evening. That night army officers searched his house but found nothing that could prove him guilty. As the villagers emphasize, the neighbor ran an enormous risk, as even doing this for a minor could have led to arrest, torture, or, in some cases, being killed. This neighbor was not a relative and was from a different caste group. However, she belonged to the same *garamati*.

In Morang district, the *garamati* provided two essential roles for victims that are relevant for R2P, especially the multiple aspects of protection. First, when particular individuals were targeted by Maoists, security forces, or both, members hid individuals in their homes; women were often responsible for bringing information about events and threats. Second, members received support (*sahayog*) during times of distress, such as after the death of a family member. During these times of shock, trauma, and grief, regular visits and practical assistance from the *garamati* helped people to slowly come to terms with their heartbreaking reality.

The uses and adaptations of cultural mechanisms during the conflict, as at other times, were not ubiquitously positive. Usually a *garamati* establishes a common understanding and opinions about social, economic, and political affairs at the local level. For this reason, political parties or leaders often try to influence the most influential family of a *garamati* to influence the rest. The use of this institution by politicians during elections clearly demonstrates how customs and cultural practices can be manipulated.

We also conducted field research among the Tharus of mid-west Nepal. Here, under the leadership of the *badghar* (village headman), the *khyala* (village assembly) deals with various social, ritual, developmental, and political issues. The *badghar*'s roles (through the *khyala*) range from community development works such as repairing irrigation canals, trails, community buildings, and religious shrines, to finding common solutions to local issues and disputes. The *badghar* also performs various community as well as family rituals and festivities; he also coordinates practical issues for the community's collective activities.

The Tharus of Lakshamanpur village in Bardiya district recounted that the *badghar* as a social institution played an instrumental role in handling the Maoists and armed forces during the insurgency. If a Tharu was arrested by state security forces or was abducted by rebels, the *badghar* took the lead in searching for the victim. Without a functioning state apparatus in most Tharu villages, even the victim's family members and wider kin relied on their community's cultural leader or institutional headman.[57] Beyond searching for the missing and negotiating with belligerent forces, *badghars* also helped organize the cultivation of crops for those families whose kin had disappeared. In such cases, the *badghar* would call for *khyala* to discuss and decide with the entire community the ways in which they should aid the victim's family.

These local figures went beyond their basic duties, often putting their own security at risk. Villagers in Lakshmanpur recounted how local *badghars* in Bardiya district discouraged community youths from engaging in violence. They also mentioned that a number of youths interested in joining the rebellion abandoned the idea after listening to the *badghar* and instead left for India to find work and returned when the insurgency was over.

Similar cultural institutions across Nepal were not wholly successful and were on occasion co-opted during the conflict to fulfill different objectives, such as by the Maoists to extort cash and "donations." In Lakshmanpur the *badghar* arranged for the collection of all grains in one place and then organized the hand-over in order to prevent Maoists from raiding every dwelling. Elsewhere Maoists contacted and forced village headmen to collect in-kind contributions from all members of the community, which they often had to do in secret.

Leaders were trapped in between the proverbial rock of the insurgents and the hard place of the equally brutal state security forces. *Badghars* often had to follow the instructions of insurgents to keep the villagers safe, but were arrested by security forces for cooperating with them. "Protection" does not, therefore, have a singular and positive value; as villagers in Motipur appreciated, such actions came with great risk. The experience of Motipur's inhabitants illustrates that Tharu social institutions played a functional role in regulating most aspects of Tharu society throughout the armed conflict. Leaders acted as negotiators with the warring parties, and thereby guarded villagers from direct contact and confrontation with violent forces—both Maoist and security forces.

The cultural institutions and practices discussed are strong but dynamic. Within the Santhal community, *baisi* and *dharuwa* had fallen into virtual desuetude and were revived. Among the Tharu, Dhakal and Dambar Chemjong note that *khyala* has taken on new roles—within education, health and sanitation, infrastructure, and economic development.[58] Conflict-induced challenges to both communities revitalized traditional customs and also transformed them.

Research on these two communities has focused more on Maoist violence and intrusions, which does not suggest that Maoist violence or atrocities exceeded those of the government's armed forces. Individuals badly needed protection from both sides.

The two case studies from the Santhal and Tharu communities reveal that kinship as well as cultural institutions and practices are important. However, they certainly did not function in a mechanical and simplistic fashion. Moreover, we cannot claim that kinship, *mit*, and other cultural institutions and practices played an unequivocally positive role in preventing and resisting violence. Each of the cases took place within a context of deep fear and a high level of both real and perceived danger, which has implications for our understanding of social and cultural dynamics of protection. The next section explores the implications for both the analysis and implementation of R2P.

The disintegration of social safety nets? living within a "culture of terror"

Thirteen days after the beginning of the Maoist insurgency, Dil Bahadur Ramtel, a 14-year old boy, was shot dead by police forces at his high school in the Gorkha district. His "crime" was opposing the arrest of the school's head teacher, Bir Bahadur Gurung.[59] To what extent can one speak of "protection" from atrocities in a conflict in which up to 16,000 people were killed and hundreds of thousands of others (including the elderly, women, and children) were made to live with extra-judicial killings and torture and multiple other forms of terror? All this despite the presence of the OHCHR and many international human rights NGOs? This question demands careful consideration. Further, how can one adequately account for the psychological damage to Dil Bahadur's family and classmates? What were the repercussions of the cultural dynamics of protection? Mukunda Kattel vividly captures the ugliness of those days:

> Both the opposing parties in the conflict have used the harshest possible methods to kill and terrorise their enemies. People have been killed while eating, dragged out of their houses into the courtyard and killed in the presence of the family members, thrown off cliffs, killed after rape, tied to trees, hacked and shot in various parts of bodies to let them die of utmost pain. Both the Maoists and the security forces have increasingly failed to observe any code of decency in their activities.[60]

Moreover, as Shobha Gautam explains, "Women are among the most vulnerable and primary victims of any conflict regardless of the time, place or context—be it within the family, community, nationally or internationally."[61] Nepal was no exception. Given that approximately 87 percent of Nepal's female population resides in rural areas, where the violence played out, it is imperative that the gender dimensions of the conflict be highlighted and women's suffering rendered visible.[62] One-third of Maoist forces were women and thus direct targets of the police and armed forces. Raping and then killing women suspected to be Maoists was a "systematic instrument of terror and repression."[63] "Lucky" survivors were often subjected to heinous acts, including having to watch their relatives being killed before being gang-raped in the same spot where their loved ones were lying dead.[64] Based on research carried out in five heavily conflict-affected areas, a prominent human rights organization found that both sides perpetrated sexual violence, but that security forces were involved in more such atrocities.[65] Nevertheless, many women both joined the insurgency and left it due to rape committed by both sides. In the absence of male kin, women were especially vulnerable; those in Maoist-dominated areas were forced to give donations or more commonly meals and overnight shelter to combatants, which invariably led to a visit from the security forces along with sexual and other forms of harassment.[66] Female household heads, therefore, bore extraordinary burdens.[67]

Over the course of the conflict, the seeming arbitrariness and unpredictability of arrests, torture, disappearances, and other atrocities by both sides led to increasing anxiety, which began to have profound impacts on social and cultural institutions and practices. As Arjun Karki and Binod Bhattarai explain, years of "continued violence … resulted in breakdown of social and communal bonds … [T]he kin networks and neighbourhood relationships that bound communities [were] disintegrating because of fear, distrust and loss of self-confidence."[68] More and more frequently, rural people who had faced harassment from security forces were ignored by their neighbors and relatives, who feared becoming targets themselves; in this context, social networks began to rethink their protection instincts, or did so differently. When taking clothes to a father who had been captured by the police was enough to cause the rape and killing of a thoughtful daughter, it is no wonder that people became wary of providing assistance, even to their closest kin.[69] If villagers aided a victim of the security forces, or even a victim's family, they would be assumed to be Maoists—and vice versa. "In other words, they did not want to be seen as helping the victim, fearing retaliation."[70] Though the exact nature of this transition has not been investigated and thus cannot be delineated—certainly not on a macro-level—the existence of such a shift is widely agreed upon.

This growing disinclination was true even for the assistance of children. By 2003 at least 4,000 children were orphaned by the conflict;[71] in addition, children were disabled by gunshots, bomb blasts, or landmines. Gopal Siwakoti notes that though there were people who sheltered conflict orphans, they were often not keen to do so.[72] This is in dramatic contradiction to the lived beliefs and practices of kinship in Nepal during peacetime, when orphans would have been taken care of by kin or *mit* relations. However, during the armed conflict, those who defied the risks and sheltered orphans were forced to conceal their identity.[73] Fearing that assisting individuals from either side would make them targets, one interviewee explained how "the spontaneity with which people used to help those in trouble seemed to be vanishing."[74] Communities living under constant fear of attacks by both Maoists and state security forces became shaped by what Karki and Bhattarai describe as a "military culture," in which "patience, conscience, trust, humility and respect are rendered meaningless, replaced instead by an ethos of arms, order and obedience."[75]

The military culture echoes in meaningful ways "cultures of terror," a concept initially developed by anthropologist Michael Taussig and further advanced by others.[76] As noted by Linda Green in the context of Guatemala, when terror becomes normalized, it "allows people to live in a chronic state of fear with a façade of normalcy at the same time that terror permeates and shreds the social fabric."[77] Pettigrew applies this concept to the rural Nepali village of Maurigaun, where she notes stories of distress, suffering, and anxiety.[78]

The erosion of social and kinship networks led to deep fear and feelings of uncertainty.[79] This, combined with the complete inability of the state to provide security meant that villagers living in conflict zones had few options other than to agree with the demands of insurgents, knowing that "disobedience could even cost lives."[80] Further, criminals also began to exploit the atmosphere of impunity and relied on the Maoists or police as covers for their crimes. Villagers in affected areas often found themselves to be suffering at the hands of the police, the army, the Maoists, and looters or dacoits.[81]

The enduring culture of fear has three impacts in the Nepali context. First, as this chapter has made clear, the military culture and culture of terror within rural communities had acute effects on traditional cultural mechanisms of protection and support—and in particular on the readiness to assist in customary ways. Under the weight of enduring conflict, traditional social safety nets began to fray, leaving innocent Nepalis to fall through the mesh.

Second, despite prevailing trends and the distressing implications of the culture of fear, there are nonetheless numerous examples of people taking extraordinary risks to come to the rescue and protect others from atrocities and undue suffering. Carolyn Nordstrom notes that "[w]hat may be the most powerful aspect of studying war is not merely the deconstructive violence that attends to it but the creativity the people on the front lines employ to reconstruct their shattered worlds."[82] The case studies of the Santhals and Tharus and the examples cited in the discussion of kinship and *mit* illustrate myriad ways that affected communities took agency and found distinctive, creative, and culturally appropriate ways to protect their kin, communities, strangers, and even enemies during violent conflict.

We highlighted some of the ways in which Nepali women suffered at the hands of both sides. However, as Gautam highlights, "women are involved in conflict in a capacity other than that of victims. They are also continuously working, knowingly or unknowingly, to end the conflict and protect the ones they love from the worst excesses of violence. They involve themselves in humanitarian work such as caring for the sick and wounded, and providing food and shelter. These actions seem part of everyday life, especially when you consider that many of them are carried out without any awareness of their contribution to peace."[83] The example of Aamaa Toli, a mother's group established in the hill village of Baglung and consisting of mothers from the Gurung community as well as others to resist the conscription of children into the armed conflict, confirms such an idea.[84] Further, the mainly female members of the Tharu *garamati* provided shelter to those being pursued by the Maoists and armed forces, often endangering their own security in order to protect both kin and non-kin. Similarly, along with Nam Nukhiya's neighbor, there are many examples of villagers—often women—informing those at risk of impending danger.

Pettigrew argues that though it was not possible for women such as these to prevent Maoist intrusions into their homes, "they acquired a measure of control over their immediate destiny." Based on ethnographic research, she also makes the analysis that "[b]y drawing on cultural models such as … the right of an older person to maintain authority over a younger one, villagers challenge Maoist hegemony."[85] In addition to heroic risks, more subtle strategies were used in daily life to cope with the violence and protect oneself and others from its effects. There are limits, of course, but as Pettigrew's examination makes clear, even within a context of fear "agency provides a possibility for creative resistance."[86]

Third, people are often hesitant to let their stories be known. They fear revealing their experiences of the conflict, and what they might have done behind closed doors. They are even more reluctant to speak about the ways in which they negotiated their lives and actions in the space between Maoist insurgents and state security forces; hence, tales that reveal "betrayal" of one or both sides have therefore so far been under-reported in Nepal. There is thus a crucial constraint on gathering information on how ordinary people experienced the conflict and dealt with the brutality, anxiety, and suffering. The trepidation of ordinary people to speak out on the crimes committed against them by the security and Maoist forces also creates hurdles for the possibilities of community-level peace building and transitional justice in the post-conflict situation. Particularly, the ways in which ordinary people expected or articulated calls for protection from the state and international authorities and the ways in which they crafted their own strategies for protection in the absence or inadequacy of protective responses from outsiders are particularly important for a deeper understanding of R2P.

While since 2006 Nepalis have become more confident about lobbying vociferously for investigations into disappearances and torture, such "confidence" is not widespread. The high-profile case of Sita Tamang, a former Maoist child soldier who testified at the UN Security Council in New York in June 2010, may have been an inspirational example but just a few weeks later five combatants appeared at her home and threatened her life should she dare to openly criticize them again. Even influential businessmen with some degree of protection refuse to speak openly against threats, making understandable the hesitation of ordinary citizens. A clearer understanding of the dynamics of fear, the impact of impunity, and the military culture in each society experiencing mass atrocities is critical for implementing R2P.

Conclusion: end of atrocities or new divisions? lessons for R2P

Did the official termination of the armed conflict signal the end of violence in Nepal? The notion of Nepal having avoided mass conflict and returned to a state of idyll is fallacious. Aside from widespread impunity, especially in rural areas, political violence has not been definitively averted in Nepal. This reality is not only an outcome of the conflict, but of the process of political transition—a process in which the move from the *Panchayat* system to multiparty democratic politics has been crucial.

The Seven-Party Coalition government of Nepal and the Maoists signed the Comprehensive Peace Agreement on 21 November 2006, officially declaring the end of the decade-long "People's War." The two key features of the CPA were the Maoists' commitment to peaceful democratic politics and the commitment of all parties to a progressive restructuring of the state to ensure the bridging of the old divisions along the lines of caste, class, ethnicity, and regional disparities. Further, the parties committed to respecting international human rights and humanitarian laws and principles. The CPA provided the necessary common anchor for the country to enter a transition phase to move from violence to peace—a process that raised the expectations of the Nepali masses about receiving a genuine peace dividend. However, the Comprehensive Peace Agreement's weak implementation and parties reneging on their commitments have severely jeopardized the peace process. A vital challenge for all stakeholders is to consolidate and preserve tenuous political achievements.

Post-CPA Nepal remains deeply fragmented. The country now has more than 100 armed groups, many of which are not political parties and often readily use violence as a weapon to realize their demands. The rise and intensification of identity politics offers the prospect of empowerment, identity, and partial autonomy to long repressed communities. However, demands for ethnic federalism also deeply challenge political stability, raising fundamental questions of how to handle national integration and unity. These issues must be urgently addressed according to the tenets of justice, inclusion, human rights, and human dignity. It must be borne in mind that current solutions may be open to manipulation by political elites and therefore could provide further ground for a relapse to violence.

The emerging and inchoate dynamics can be seen in some ways as more challenging than the Maoist conflict. The Maoists tapped into the frustrations of excluded and marginalized groups, including ethnic ones, and recruited widely among them.[87] The current dynamics of ethnic politics, however, are not within their control. The expression of identity in purely ethnic terms has now become so normalized that observers speak commonly of "ethnic revivalism." During 2009 the issue of ethnic federalism gained momentum, and in December 2009 the Maoist Party declared several regions as "autonomous states" divided according to ethnicity. Among politicians and the public, federalism is a matter of great contention. The effects of strong identity politics are empowering for historically marginalized groups and hint at possibilities for an inclusive state, but the potential divisiveness of a state structure that is largely based on ethnicity remains worrying. Preventive social and cultural mechanisms that may have previously been successful may not be relevant in the changed political context of the post-CPA period.

This chapter has explored several previously ignored aspects of Nepal's civic and cultural factors and traditions that played a role in protecting populations, resisting violence, and limiting atrocities. We focused on three that were particularly crucial in the rural communities and among indigenous peoples who bore the brunt of the armed conflict. The first factor we highlighted was kinship, including extra-kinship bonds of friendship or *miteri* that transcend caste, ethnicity, and class. The second factor was traditional cultural institutions such as *garamati* among the Tharu indigenous group, and *dharuwa*, *baisi*, and others within the Santhal community. The third factor was the dynamics of fear, which acted in multiple and complex ways, and paralyzed and eroded formerly strong kinship ties and cultural institutions. Sociocultural institutions in rural Nepal and elsewhere are not unchanging; however, cultural institutions and values prevalent across Nepal's diverse society and ethnic and caste groups have remained active despite pressure and often have provided a vital pillar of support in times of crisis.

Despite a multiplicity of national and civic actors involved during the conflict from 1996 to 2006, our principal argument was that Nepali civic actors and cultural institutions took on the main responsibility to protect endangered lives and prevent an escalation of violence. First civil society actors in the capital made a vital contribution in the second half of the conflict, working for political consensus and mobilizing rural populations across Nepal and international public opinion. Second, traditional cultural institutions and practices were used, reactivated, and adapted to protect vulnerable communities and individuals caught in the cross fire, to resist incursions by both Maoist and government forces, and to prevent an escalation of violence or outbreak of mass atrocities. As noted by participants in the project's consultations, cultural institutions undoubtedly were co-opted by one or other side for political or military gain. However, cultural institutions filled a crucial vacuum and served to protect lives both within and across caste and ethnic lines, at a time when state institutions had failed and when international or nongovernmental actions were absent, particularly in rural areas.

These findings are, we believe, crucial for the development and implementation of the evolving R2P norm. In many societies, as in Nepal, mass atrocities and violence affect above all innocent civilians in rural areas far from the reach of state authorities and institutions, and also often out of the view of outside governments as well as intergovernmental and nongovernmental organizations. Who is to provide protection to vulnerable populations and by what means? Our study suggests that civic and cultural institutions and authorities can. Thus, it is important for those promoting R2P to understand the ways in which such mechanisms work in order to support them and also to prevent them from being co-opted or used for destructive ends. Civic and cultural institutions and practices should not be strengthened without due attention to ensure that they adhere to principles of justice, inclusion, democracy, and equity (including gender).

Local agency is the dominant theme in this chapter, and we have noted some of the ways in which women and men creatively responded to the dynamics of fear, prevention, and protection. Understanding the agency and possible creativity of affected communities is essential if the emerging R2P norm is to have local resonance. Researchers or R2P norm entrepreneurs should be deeply engaged with his or her subjects during armed conflicts, though inevitably this involves risks for them—as it does for human rights workers and development practitioners.

It is also critical for the development of the R2P norm and practice to understand how it translates into different social practices and idioms in each cultural context. In Nepal the concepts of *suraksha*, *samrakshan*, and *sahayog* were most salient during the worst periods of the armed conflict. Without knowledge of such culturally specific expressions and practices, R2P will not advance. While we have begun in Nepal, further country-specific work is essential.

Our findings from Nepal also lead to recommendations for regional and international actors. First, the UN's most helpful role is at the stage of escalating violence and potential mass atrocities, as an impartial and credible human rights observer and arbiter. The world organization must be able to use its moral authority to uphold human rights and humanitarian law and to routinely condemn even-handedly all sides, as well as to provide a safe haven for endangered activists when required. This approach characterized the initial OHCHR operation but was later lost by UNMIN, which was unable to play such a positive role in the post-2006 peace building process.

Likewise, other international actors can play supportive roles. In Nepal, for example, some diplomatic missions provided safe havens to threatened activists at critical moments and even escorted them to exile at considerable personal risk. However, other regional and international actors were counterproductive in trying to balance their desire to protect humanitarian law and promote peace with their national security interests.

The Nepali proverb *bhāi phute gawār lute* (if brothers split, others will loot) has echoes in all cultures around the world: unity and solidarity breed security while disunity and division breed chaos and violence. Even in the short period of a decade, the Nepali situation hints at the volatility and dynamism of various factors—be they cultural factors, such as kinship or other institutions, or the perceived role of particular international agencies or actors. Deep dissatisfaction at the social, political, and economic inequalities of Nepali society led to the emergence of armed conflict in the mid-western hills of Nepal, to which the state responded often with indiscriminate counterattacks. Under such exceptional circumstances, norms and mechanisms of protection and mutual help can unravel and thereby create the conditions that turn an armed conflict into a situation of mass atrocities. For this reason, an essential common task in Nepal and internationally is to reduce inequalities and exclusion, and to understand and reinforce our diverse cultural values and practices. These can be the foundations for protection and the prevention of violence, a vital step to prevent mass atrocities and institute the norm of the responsibility to protect in the twenty-first century.

Notes

1 This chapter is based on prior fieldwork and research by Arjun Karki as well as additional work carried out specifically for this chapter. The authors benefited from the support and insights of Suresh Dhakal of Tribhuvan

University (TU) and from commissioned fieldwork for the two case studies conducted within the indigenous Tharu and Santhal communities, by Dambar Chemjong, also of TU. The chapter also benefited from the insights of Om Gurung, who heads TU's anthropology department, and from feedback on an earlier draft from scholars and students convened during two consultations in Kathmandu held in August 2009 and 2010.

2 *Implementing the Responsibility to Protect, Report from the Secretary-General* (UN document A/63/677), 12 January 2009.

3 Carolyn Nordstrom, "War on the Front Lines," in *Fieldwork Under Fire: Contemporary Studies of Violence and Culture*, ed. Carolyn Nordstrom and Antonius C.G.M. Robben (Berkeley: University of California Press, 1995), 143, 129–53.

4 Stathis N. Kalyvas, *The Logic of Violence in Civil War* (Cambridge: Cambridge University Press, 2006).

5 Colin Millard, "Democracy and Dissent in Nepal: An Overview with Some Perceptions from the Valley of Dhorpatan," in *Resistance and the State: Nepalese Experiences*, ed. David N. Gellner (New Delhi: Social Science Press, 2002), 281–304.

6 For example, a 1998 World Bank report comments, "Urban Kathmandu Valley and the rest of Nepal, in effect, are two separate and unequal countries … In one, around the capital, where around 5 per cent of the population live, the incidence of poverty is around 4 per cent and illiteracy is 24 per cent; in the rest of the country, poverty is ten times as high and the chance of being literate almost three times lower." Quoted by John Whelpton, *A History of Nepal* (Cambridge: Cambridge University Press, 2005), 225.

7 As noted by Chhetri and Gurung, in recent decades the focus of these disciplines with regard to Nepal has primarily been issues of development, natural resource management, and empowerment of marginalized communities. Ram B. Chhetri and Om P. Gurung, "Anthropology and Sociology of Nepal: Retrospect and Prospects," in *Anthropology and Sociology of Nepal: Cultures, Societies, Ecology and Development*, ed. Ram B. Chhetri and Om P. Gurung (Kathmandu: Sociological and Anthropological Society of Nepal, 1999), 7. There are also notable exceptions regarding the anthropology of religious communities.

8 Carolyn Nordstrom and Antonius C.G.M. Robben, "The Anthropology and Ethnography of Violence and Sociopolitical Conflict," in *Fieldwork Under Fire: Contemporary Studies of Violence and Culture*, ed. Nordstrom and Robben, 1–24.

9 Ganesh Man Gurung, "Ethnic Identity and Politics of Ethno-Museum in Nepal," in *Anthropology and Sociology of Nepal*, ed. Chhetri and Gurung, 82; William F. Fisher, "The Politics of Difference and the Reach of Modernity: Reflections on State and Society in Central Nepal," in *Resistance and the State: Nepalese Experiences*, ed. Gellner, 113–32.

10 John Whelpton, David N. Gellner, and Joanna Pfaff-Czarnecka, "New Nepal, New Ethnicities: Changes Since the Mid 1990s," in *Nationalism and Ethnicity in Nepal*, ed. David N. Gellner, Joanna Pfaff-Czarnecka and John Whelpton (Kathmandu: Vajra Publications, 2008), xvii, xvii–xlviii.

11 Arjun Karki and David Seddon, "The People's War in Historical Context," in *The People's War in Nepal: Left Perspectives*, ed. Arjun Karki and

David Seddon (New Delhi: Adroit Publishers, 2003), 3–48; Deepak Thapa, "The Maobadi of Nepal," in *State of Nepal*, ed. Kamal Mani Dixit and Shastri Ramachandaran (Kathmandu: Himal Books, 2002), 77–99.

12 Whelpton, *A History of Nepal*, 208. VDCs are the basic political unit of the Nepali government's administrative system.

13 Whelpton, *A History of Nepal*, 225.

14 David N. Gellner, "Introduction: Transformations of the Nepalese State," in *Resistance and the State: Nepalese Experiences*, ed. Gellner, 1–30.

15 Deepak Thapa with Bandana Sijapati, *A Kingdom Under Siege: Nepal's Maoist Insurgency, 1996–2003* (Kathmandu: The Printhouse, 2004).

16 Shobha Gautam, "Armed Conflict and its Impact on Gender," in *Nepal: The Maoist Insurgency and Beyond*, ed. Arjun Karki and Mukunda Kattel (Hong Kong: ARENA, 2005), 133–55.

17 Thapa, and Sijapati, *A Kingdom Under Siege*, 77. As a result, there was "anti-brahmanism" around 1991 and 1992. Media reports on the theme became commonplace during this period. See, for example, "Kingdom of the Bahuns," *Nepali Times*, no. 153, July 2003, 11–17.

18 David Seddon, *Nepal: A State of Poverty*, 2nd edn. (New Delhi: Vikas Publishing House, 1993), xiii.

19 Whelpton, *A History of Nepal*, 202.

20 Arjun Karki and Binod Bhattarai, *Whose War? Economic and Socio-Cultural Impacts of Nepal's Maoist-Government Conflict* (Kathmandu: NGO Federation of Nepal, 2004); Mandira Sharma and Dinesh Prasain, "Gender Dimensions of the People's War: Some Reflections on the Experiences of Rural Women," in *Himalayan People's War: Nepal's Maoist Rebellion*, ed. Michael Hutt (London: Hurst & Company, 2004), 152–65.

21 Karki and Bhattarai, *Whose War?*

22 Millard, "Democracy and Dissent in Nepal," 293, 281–304.

23 This coalition is often referred to as a triangular alliance—between the CPN(M), the Seven-Party Alliance, and civil society.

24 Manjushree Thapa, "The War in the West," *Himal Southasian*, January 2003, 36–42.

25 Rajendra Pradhan, "Ethnicity, Caste and Pluralist Society," in *State of Nepal*, ed. Kamal Mani Dixit and Shastri Ramachandaran (Kathmandu: Himal Books, 2002), 16; David N. Gellner, "Ethnicity and Nationalism in the World's Only Hindu State," in *Nationalism and Ethnicity in a Hindu Kingdom: The Politics of Culture in Contemporary Nepal*, ed. David N. Gellner, Joanna Pfaff-Czarnecka, and John Whelpton (San Diego, Calif.: Harcourt, 1997), 20–1.

26 Harka Gurung, *Trident and Thunderbolt: Cultural Dynamics in Nepalese Politics* (Kathmandu: Social Science Baha, 2003), 11; Pradhan, "Ethnicity, Caste and Pluralist Society," 1–21

27 Pradhan, "Ethnicity, Caste and Pluralist Society."

28 Gopal Singh Nepali, *The Newars: An Ethno-Sociological Study of a Himalayan Community* (Bombay: United Asia Publications, 1965).

29 Whelpton, *A History of Nepal.*

30 Sushil K. Naidu, *Buddhism in Nepal* (Delhi: Kalinga Publications, 2008).

31 Whelpton, *A History of Nepal.*

32 John Whelpton, "Political Identity in Nepal: State, Nation, and Community," in *Nationalism and Ethnicity in a Hindu Kingdom: The Politics of*

Culture in Contemporary Nepal, ed. Gellner, Pfaff-Czarnecka, and Whelpton, 39–78.

33 Nevertheless, it is acknowledged that religious notions such as *karma* (fate) and *dharma* (right or virtuous livelihood) are significant in that they are integral to the cosmology of Nepali communities and society at large, and that religion continued to play an important role in the lives of individuals throughout the conflict.

34 World Food Programme (WFP), *Nepal: Comprehensive Food Security and Vulnerability Analysis 2005* (Rome: WFP, 2006).

35 See Gyanu Chhetri, "A Sociological Analysis of Dalit Occupational Caste Groups in the Hills of Nepal," in *Anthropology and Sociology of Nepal*, ed. Chhetri and Gurung, 56–68.

36 These are cases that have emerged during recent and previous field investigations.

37 In order to protect individuals and communities, anonymity has been preserved.

38 Bihari K. Shrestha, *Karnali Folk Culture: Thakuris of Diyargaun* (Kathmandu: Royal Nepal Academy, 2028 Bikram Sambat (Nepali year)); Peter H. Prindle, *Tinglatar: Socio-Economic Relationships of a Brahmin Village in East Nepal* (Kathmandu: Ratna Pustak Bhandar, 1983); Suresh Dhakal, "Rodi and Jhora in Rural Entertainment Customs," in *Local Democratic Practice in Nepal* (Kathmandu: Nepal Sirjanatmak Adhyan Kendra, 2064 Bikram Sambat (Nepali year)); Donald A. Messerschmidt, "Miteri in Nepal: Fictive Kin Ties that Bind," *Kailash* 9, no. 1 (1982): 5–43; see Ferdinand E. Okada, "Ritual Brotherhood: A Cohesive Factor in Nepalese Society," *Southwestern Journal of Anthropology* 13 (1957): 212.

39 Messerschmidt, "Miteri in Nepal: Fictive Kin Ties that Bind," 5.

40 Dhakal, "Rodi and Jhora in Rural Entertainment Customs." There are also common proverbs that relate to a *mit* friend or a relation having much deeper meaning than a sister, who, after marriage, is perceived in Nepali custom to have stronger ties to her husband's family or *ghar* (home) than to her own.

41 Prindle, *Tinglatar*, 106.

42 Ibid., 109.

43 Commonality based on sharing an economic base or being classmates is described by Judith Pettigrew, "Guns, Kinship, and Fear: Maoists among the Tamu-mai (Gurungs)," in *Resistance and the State: Nepalese Experiences*, ed. Gellner, 305–25.

44 Bihari K. Shrestha, *From a Himalayan Enclave: A Study of Chance in the Western Mountains of Nepal* (Kathmandu: ICIMOD, 1993), 27.

45 Dhakal, "Rodi and Jhora in Rural Entertainment Customs."

46 This incident was shared by Suresh Dhakal at the first interdisciplinary consultation held in Kathmandu in August 2009, hosted by Rural Reconstruction Nepal, for this project. Two additional consultations were held in August 2010 with university students and professors at Nepal's Tribhuvan University.

47 Personal anecdotes were shared by Om Gurung during the two consultations in August 2010.

48 Lagan Rai, *An Ethnographic Outline of Santhals* (Kathmandu: National Foundation for the Development of Indigenous Nationalities, 2010).

49 This information was drawn from research conducted by Dambar Chemjong for this chapter.

50 Respondents highlighted that there are distinctly different ways of beating *tamak* and *tumda* drums according to the occasion: festivals, ritual ceremonies, community crises, etc.
51 Unnamed youth interviewed by Dambar Chemjong in Majhare VDC in July 2010.
52 Karki and Bhattarai, *Whose War?* 66.
53 See, for example, Terence Turner and Vanessa Fajan-Turner, "Political Innovation and Inter-Ethnic Alliance: Kayapo Resistance to the Developmentalist State," *Anthropology Today* 22, no. 5 (2006): 3–10, for their analysis of ritual among the Kayapo of Brazil.
54 Central Bureau of Statistics, *Statistical Year Book Nepal*, 2nd edn. (Kathmandu: Ratna Pustak Bhandar, 2002).
55 Suresh Dhakal, *Participation in Public Spaces in a Diverse Society: A Case Study of Community Organisation in a VDC from Eastern Tarai of Nepal* (Kathmandu: Tribhuvan University, 2010).
56 The *garamati* also has deep ritual importance during birth and death rites.
57 There are no specific records about the *badghar* having located or successfully rescued abductees during the insurgency; however, people consistently note these community leaders to have been significant sources of help during these times.
58 Suresh Dhakal and Dambar Chemjong, "Social-Cultural Institutions of Tharus of Western Tarai, Nepal," in *Democratic Indigenous Practices of Nepal*, ed. Anju Khadka, Rajan Khadka, and Bidya Nath Koirala (Kathmandu: Nepal Centre for Creative Research, Kapurdhara, 2008), 10–30.
59 The case of Dil Bahadur Ramtel is not unique. Children were also subject to harassment in schools, for example, if their name (often falsely) appeared in the list of *krantikari* (revolutionary) students that would on occasion fall into the hands of security forces. When they were not directly victimized, whether seeing their schoolteachers arrested, harassed, or abducted, or seeing the bodies of dead relatives, children witnessed horrific scenes. Siwakoti, in Karki and Kattel (2005) describes the trauma and suffering faced by children who witnessed the atrocities of war. Gopal Krishna Siwakoti, "Children in Conflict: A Lost Generation," in *Nepal: The Maoist Insurgency and Beyond*, ed. Karki and Kattel, 111–32.
60 Mukunda Kattel, "Introduction to the 'People's War' and its Implications," in *The People's War in Nepal: Left Perspectives*, ed. Karki, and Seddon, 60.
61 Gautam, "Armed Conflict and its Impact on Gender," 150; Thapa with Sijapati, *A Kingdom Under Siege*; Kattel, "Introduction to the 'People's War' and its Implications."
62 María Villellas Ariño, "Nepal: A Gender View of the Armed Conflict and the Peace Process," *Quadernas de Construcció de Pau*, no. 4 (2008): 7. Available at: www.ceipaz.org/images/contenido/Nepal_%20a%20gender%20view%20armed%20conflict_peace%20process.pdf. See also Chandra Bhadra, Ava D. Shrestha, and Rita Thapa, "On the edge: the impact of the insurgency on Nepali women," in *The Impact of Armed Conflicts on Women in South Asia*, ed. Ava D. Shrestha and Rita Thapa (Colombo: Manohar, 2007), 105–36.
63 Shobha Gautam, Amrita Banskota, and Rita Manchanda, "Where there are No Men: Women in the Maoist Insurgency in Nepal," in *Understanding the Maoist Movement of Nepal* (Kathmandu: Centre for Social Research

and Development, 2003), 123; Kattel, "Introduction to the 'People's War' and its Implications."

64 This incident took place in Pipal VDC, Rukum district, on 26 February 1996. It was reported by the Informal Sector Service Centre (INSEC), a human rights organization in Nepal. Quoted in Kattel, "Introduction to 'The People's War' and its Implications," 61.

65 Research was carried out in Achham, Banke, Bardiya, Doti, and Rolpa districts. IHRICON, *Sexual Violence in the People's War* (Kathmandu: IHRICON, 2006).

66 Gautam, Banskota and Manchanda, "Where there are No Men." See also Thapa, "The War in the West."

67 Sujita Shakya, "The Maoist Movement in Nepal: An Analysis from the Women's Perspective," in *The People's War in Nepal: Left Perspectives*, ed. Karki, and Seddon, 375–404.

68 Karki and Bhattarai, *Whose War?* 82. See also Thapa, "The War in the West."

69 Gautam, Banskota, and Manchanda, "Where there are No Men."

70 Ibid.

71 See Child Workers in Nepal Concerned Center (CWIN), *The State of the Rights of the Children in Nepal 2003* (Kathmandu: CWIN, 2003).

72 Gopal K. Siwakoti, "Children in Conflict: A Lost Generation," in *Nepal: The Maoist Insurgency and Beyond*, ed. Arjun Karki and Mukunda Kattel (Hong Kong: ARENA, 2005), 111–32.

73 Siwakoti, "Children in Conflict: A Lost Generation."

74 Karki and Bhattarai, *Whose War?*, 82.

75 Arjun Karki and Mukunda Kattel, "The Maoist Insurgency and Emerging Militarization in Nepal," in *Nepal: The Maoist Insurgency and Beyond*, ed. Arjun Karki and Mukunda Kattel (Hong Kong: ARENA, 2005), 66.

76 Judith Pettigrew, "Living between the Maoists and the Army in Rural Nepal," in *Himalayan People's War: Nepal's Maoist Rebellion*, ed. Michael Hutt (London: Hurst & Company, 2004), 261–83. Linda Green, "Living in a State of Fear," in *Fieldwork under Fire: Contemporary Studies of Violence and Survival*, ed. Carolyn Nordstrom and Antonius C.G.M. Robben (Berkeley: University of California Press, 1995), 105–27; Marcelo M. Suárez-Orozco, "The Treatment of Children in the 'Dirty War': Ideology, State Terrorism and the Abuse of Children in Argentina," in *Child Survival: Anthropological Perspectives on the Treatment and Maltreatment of Children* (Amsterdam: Reidel, 1987); Jeffery A. Sluka, ed., *Death Squad: The Anthropology of State Terror* (Philadelphia: University of Pennsylvania, 2000).

77 Green, "Living in a State of Fear," 108.

78 The name of the town has been changed.

79 Karki and Bhattarai, *Whose War?*

80 Ibid., 84.

81 Pradip Nepal, "The Maoist Movement and its Impact in Nepal," in *The People's War in Nepal: Left Perspectives*, ed. Karki, and Seddon, 405–37.

82 Nordstrom, "War on the Front Lines," 131.

83 Gautam, "Armed Conflict and its Impact on Gender," 150–1.

84 This information was received by Om Gurung during the consultation on 11 August 2010.

85 Pettigrew, "Living between the Maoists and the Army in Rural Nepal," 282.

86 Ibid., 283.

87 They articulated the demands of ethnic groups and vowed to give autonomy to regions where ethnic groups had a majority, as well as to regions that had distinct geographical specificities. As noted by Karki and Bhattarai, people neglected to question how such an approach would relate to the "single-state, single thought communist model." See Karki and Bhattarai, *Whose War?* 39.

7 Conclusion

The contribution of cultural perspectives to R2P

Rama Mani and Thomas G. Weiss

- **Recommendations from the research process**
- **Recommendations from the thematic chapters**
- **Observations and recommendations from the cases**
- **Final reflections**

> I loathe all armies and any kind of violence; yet I'm firmly convinced that at present these hateful weapons offer the only effective protection.
>
> Albert Einstein, 1933[1]

> Duties of a juridical nature presuppose others of a moral nature which support them in principle and constitute their basis.
>
> Inasmuch as spiritual development is the supreme end of human existence and the highest expression thereof, it is the duty of man to serve that end with all his strength and resources.
>
> Since culture is the highest social and historical expression of that spiritual development, it is the duty of man to preserve, practice and foster culture by every means within his power.
>
> And, since moral conduct constitutes the noblest flowering of culture, it is the duty of every man always to hold it in high respect.
>
> American Declaration of the Rights and Duties of Man, Organization of American States (OAS), 1948[2]

These quotations encapsulate the dual challenge confronted by the responsibility to protect (R2P) in general and by this volume in particular. First, R2P's unique appeal and its Achilles' heel lie in the convincing but contentious commitment to deploy all means—including military force—to halt conscience-shocking human suffering. This challenge resembles Albert Einstein's struggle as a pacifist to mobilize an international peace force before 1939 to arrest predictable Nazi atrocities when other means had manifestly failed to halt Hitler's onslaught. Second, like the inspirational but largely aspirational Preamble to the

OAS's 1948 American Declaration of the Rights and Duties of Man, this volume makes a case for the mutual interdependence and reinforcement between legal and moral duties, between political conduct and cultural and spiritual values, to reinforce R2P's appeal and authority.

This emerging norm is based on the cosmopolitan notion of universal human rights and the equal dignity and worth of all human beings, whatever their circumstances and wherever they reside. The responsibility to protect seeks a consistent basis for the protection of human beings from mass atrocities, but it comes of age in the fraught context of a United Nations divided by the contradicting concerns of its member states that sometimes confound high principles and good intentions. The aging edifice of state sovereignty has proven permeable and fluid in some quarters, yet obdurately resistant in others to the transformative effects of the globalizing post-1989 world as well as to what Eleanor Roosevelt in 1948 presciently predicted would be "a curious grapevine" of the spreading human rights regime.[3]

This set of essays straddles the space between the cautious, albeit growing, consensus around the normative values inherent in the responsibility to protect, on the one hand, and its yet unfulfilled implementation, on the other hand. Traditional claims about sovereignty by some states and the application of double standards by others motivate this book. The aim is to identify the cultural and societal conditions under which there would be more local as well as international support for robust R2P actions to prevent or slow-down mass atrocities as well as to halt them once unleashed and to help mend a society afterwards. The six preceding chapters explore and provide some answers to two thorny questions: What is R2P's resonance in the diverse cultural contexts where one might attempt to apply or gain support for it? And can a study of cultural dimensions provide insights to strengthen R2P's normative consensus and weaken challenges to its implementation?

As we mentioned in the introduction and as the essays underline, the responsibility to protect has such normative and operational potential because the political bar is not impossibly high. The focus is on acute events and not on chronic conditions or root causes. The triggers established by the International Commission on Intervention and State Sovereignty (ICISS) for coercive protection were massive loss of life and ethnic cleansing. The World Summit narrowed R2P's remit to four crimes: genocide, war crimes, ethnic cleansing, and crimes against humanity. Thus, the legal, political, *and* moral case is—or should be—*a priori* uncontested. Advocates are not hoping to stop the 75 smoldering conflicts that the International Crisis Group is monitoring this month that could turn deadly; they are not trying to establish peace on earth; and they are not attempting to rid the planet of all human rights abuses. Proponents are, after all, speaking of eliminating mass atrocities as public policy options.

In reflecting on solidarity with the vulnerable, which constitutes R2P's very foundation, Mohamed Sahnoun reminds us in his foreword that this is not a contemporary phenomenon. Indeed, solidarity is the rudiment of all cultures, whether in the global South or North. Consequently, R2P is not a moral and political project that has begun from scratch but rather has built on this solid foundation. Each of the chapters reminds us of R2P's fundamental cross-cultural essence, namely, "the equal moral status of each and every human being [independent] of their particular familial, ethnical, national and religious affiliations."[4] In effect, the chapters spell out a concrete cosmopolitanism that is found in the specifics of each culture and each community. At the same time, this book as a whole and its chapters individually do not treat culture as a panacea; they acknowledge the frequent manipulation of religion, philosophy, art, and cultural traditions to foment violence and justify suffering rather than prevent or eliminate it.

The responsibility to protect is a logical extension of the evolving international legal order that sets moral limits to state and non-state action. R2P is the sharp edge of human rights, the widespread recognition that certain conscience-shocking crimes cannot go unpunished, no matter what their purported source of inspiration or authority. Mass atrocities are out of synch with global consciousness and constitute an execrable exception to the normal workings of human society, traditional or contemporary. By extension, R2P constitutes unusual measures in the face of aberrations in human conduct, highly exceptional efforts to head-off, halt, or heal from mass atrocities.

This research project has examined R2P through the prism of culture and resulted in a book the chapters of which lead us to formulate two sets of observations and recommendations. The first should specially interest scholars and funders of policy-oriented research and emerges from the interdisciplinary process. The second set should particularly concern policymakers and emerges from the thematic analyses and case studies. The specific lessons and recommendations in each chapter are not repeated here. Rather, our value-added is to put forward commonalities and summarize what we both have learned while conceptualizing and directing this cross-cultural, multidimensional, and multilingual undertaking.

Recommendations from the research process

The gamble, so to speak, behind ventures like this project and publication is betting on the sometimes tenuous link between research and its impact on public policy. To what extent can political decisions in the international arena be shaped by the findings and recommendations from researchers? To what extent might academics doctor their research to further desirable policy outcomes, or policymakers cherry-pick from research findings to justify policy decisions? While many analysts and academics believe that the research-policy link is strong and direct—or at least can and should be[5]—it is difficult to measure or discern whether or not research findings have actually shifted or crystallized concrete changes in policy and practice.

In our case, we confronted particularly unfavorable odds by delving into areas normally deemed irrelevant by policymakers and social scientists who advise them. We plunged into the domain of *culture*, which is not only nebulous but fraught and fractious since the controversy surrounding the publication a decade and a half ago of the *Clash of Civilizations*[6] and the polarizing events of 11 September 2001. What did we learn?

First, analyses by local scholars who have personally witnessed or endured mass atrocities and violence—as *subjects* of violence and *agents* of resistance and response—are markedly different from the findings of external scholars. Objective empirical research that dispassionately collects data and reports them is clearly invaluable but also has limitations in the face or aftermath of mass atrocities. Local scholars are privy to vital but implicit knowledge, hidden data, and contested versions of facts that are difficult for outsiders to access, in particular outside of urban areas. Most of the seminal work that has influenced the development of R2P—in conflict prevention, crisis management, and peace building—has been produced by Western scholars. In parallel, local scholars have conducted field research and engaged in collective reflections about the events surrounding mass atrocity crimes in their societies, but the publication of such work remains largely inaccessible to international public policy audiences; it is unavailable even in the best-stocked libraries of world-class research universities. Locally produced academic literature is essentially missing from the West's competitive publishing market, and Southern scholars are hard-pressed to find outlets beyond the neighborhood for their work.

Thus, there is a clear value in supporting investigations by local scholars in conflict-torn societies and making their findings more widely available. Not only should the best of such research influence international public policy, but it should also be accessible to scholars, students, and policymakers in other conflict-affected countries to help them grapple with their own crises. For example, during the conference sponsored by the project at Tribhuvan University in Nepal in August

2010, young graduate students from remote parts of Nepal avidly sought African and Balkan perspectives about the Rwandan genocide and the ethnocide in Kosovo in order to contextualize their own country's struggle.

Second, local investigations within the context of mass atrocities are dangerous, even after a crisis ends. The paralyzing impact of fear and violence remains a reality, as the Nepal chapter shows. Yet it is exactly in the worst situations that such hands-on research is most acutely required. Despite a cottage industry of research since the early 1990s on humanitarian intervention, and since 2001 on R2P, there remains a startling gap in analyses of the rural and remote terrains where most atrocities are committed—far from the gaze of international observers. How do ordinary people affected by atrocities locate survival avenues and express their dissent and explore nonviolent alternatives? In what ways do local cultural frames of reference provide support to endangered people that state and international mechanisms often do not? What are their messages to national, regional, and international decision makers about how best to intervene and protect affected populations?

The answers to such questions require field-based research in proximity of affected populations to better inform the responsibility to protect. Such research comes, of course, with attendant risks that could deter even the most intrepid researcher. We felt obliged not to choose Afghanistan, Iraq, the Democratic Republic of the Congo (DRC), or Sudan as case studies in this project because of risks to local researchers, while historical distance made Rwanda and Kosovo more approachable, though by no means risk-free. Nevertheless, an acute need exists for many more historical and real-time assessments conducted at the local, rural, and community levels to probe the civic and cultural realms missing from most R2P discussions. Pooling their hands-on experiences, local researchers could engage in shared reflection across the borders of their crisis zones to devise innovative approaches to mitigate real risks in conducting research in remote atrocity-affected areas; donors should support such initiatives as a priority.

Third, we have learned much about the ever-present temptation for both academics and policymakers to unwittingly manipulate research; cherry pick among findings; cite sound bites from interviews out of context; and select evidence that best suits ideological preferences or political expedience. We have worked closely with local researchers and traveled to field sites ourselves in order to minimize such pitfalls. The autonomy and professionalism of our contributors has resulted, we believe, in balanced and subtle analyses that eschew the temptation to simply bolster the case for R2P or cultural analyses. However, we are aware that readers could well interpret the broad-ranging findings of this volume to fit their respective academic, advocacy, or policy purposes. We underscore the ethical responsibility of researchers in such politically sensitive endeavors to be honest; we also trust that readers will be scrupulous in using findings.

Fourth, the cultural dimensions of R2P have so far not been examined and are so vast as to be overwhelming, "a recipe for indigestion" as one colleague commented. As explained in the introduction, we selected topics that would expose the iceberg but show that this was merely the tip of vast unexplored terrain. Our contributors are aware of the daunting nature of their assignments, cognizant that they are breaking new ground in bringing cultural analysis to the political arena. Each spells out the pros and cons of culture and is modest about generalizations and recommendations. Based on the outcome of this collective experience, we would underscore the considerable value of expanded academic analyses aiming to incorporate cultural insights into policy formulation and decision making about R2P specifically and conflict prevention and peace building generally.

Despite the evident desirability of such research, we cannot gloss over the considerable logistical obstacles. Identifying the right geographically diverse authors with reliable institutional partners was a significant hurdle. Another was ensuring that they were able to document and translate complex local realities to be comprehensible to international audiences with short attention spans and limited cultural familiarity. Our contributors faced as well the usual litany of technological obstacles, electricity outages, interrupted internet access, family disasters, and natural calamities that sometimes render even routine communications and project organization maddeningly difficult. Further, a multidisciplinary and multilingual undertaking requires translating multiple discourses, languages, and disciplines into a book that is accessible to an Anglophone international audience of social scientists and policymakers.

Notwithstanding these hurdles, the utility and necessity of multiplying such initiatives is evident. We would urge other analysts to take additional steps on the research journey that we have barely begun, and for donors to follow the example of the Carnegie Corporation of New York and the Arsenault Family Foundation in support of research that employs local scholars and explores the poorly understood domain of culture within mass atrocities and violent conflicts.

Recommendations from the thematic chapters

The first three chapters examine the themes of religion and spirituality, philosophy and ethics, art and aesthetics. They seek to inject into ongoing R2P conversations insights from sources that for centuries lay at the heart of political discourse but have largely disappeared in the contemporary period. Given that religion and governance were coterminous for so many centuries, the extent to which religion has virtually vanished from the study of politics and international relations is puzzling. It was re-admitted partially and reluctantly after 9/11, with a focus largely on Islam. The cursory examination of the gamut of world religious and spiritual traditions reveals how determining a factor faith remains for the vast majority of the world's population, particularly in the global South.

In ancient times across Greece, China, India, Egypt, and Mesopotamia, philosophy and politics were allies. Philosophical inquiry defined the polis and shaped political discourse. No king saw fit to rule without wise philosophers to counsel him; indeed, the ideal king was often himself a philosopher, in addition to being a spiritual guide and artist or poet. Philosophers elaborated the sphere of ethics, recognizing that they constituted the necessary foundation for functioning polities. Yet today philosophy is considered essentially alien to governance and diplomacy. Consequently, decision makers flounder while usually being bereft of either philosophical training or ethical grounding.

So too, art has been relegated to museums and concert halls rather than being at the center of daily life. Formerly sovereigns not only were sometimes artists themselves but also were frequently active patrons; they recognized that culture and civilization could be preserved, enriched, and passed on by cultivating the arts. Creative expressions were everyday activities not restricted to the elite but practiced and enjoyed by ordinary people as they cultivated their fields or plied their trades. The arts often provided imaginative insights into and analogies for political dilemmas—the Trojan horse being only one symbolic illustration.

As we hope became evident from the rich material in the first three chapters, our intent was to enhance both our understanding of the responsibility to protect and the analysis of international relations more broadly. Efforts to understand and analyze rarely venture beyond the familiar and contiguous fields of political science, law, history, and economics.

Chapter 1 by Mutombo Nkulu-N'Sengha examines spirituality and religion, focusing on African and more broadly Southern spirituality. Religion provides a fount of ancient but extant values drawn from the world's spiritual heritage that constitute a *firma mentis* for the R2P norm, across cultural contexts and religious divides. Nkulu-N'Sengha's chapter reveals that within and beyond African spiritual traditions—indeed, across the world's religions—is the notion of shared divine origin and thus of boundless human kinship. Also omnipresent is "the golden rule," providing a simple but powerful platform for the prevention of mass atrocities and for exercising the responsibility to protect vulnerable "others," whether close neighbors or distant strangers. Most striking for the responsibility to protect is the ideal of "the noble sovereign" in African spirituality as well as across other religions in divergent cultures. The injunction on sovereigns almost universally is to exercise their rule responsibly and not overstep their limits. Equally conspicuous is the globally resonant spiritual call for subjects to resist and even overthrow tyrannical or unjust rulers. These two globally resonant injunctions in themselves provide clear counter arguments against recalcitrant governments that resist the implementation of the R2P norm as allegedly a foreign imposition. Indeed, religion is a quintessential transboundary phenomenon because no visas have ever been necessary for the spread of religious convictions across borders, which is why "global village" has special significance in Nkulu-N'Sengha's chapter title.

In this regard, the shift in language from the "right to intervene"[7] toward the "responsibility to protect" reflects two realities underlying the discussion of religion and spirituality. First, state sovereignty is increasingly viewed as contingent and not absolute—that is, the usual attributes of a sovereign encountered in the 1934 Montevideo Convention—people, authority, territory, and independence—now a modicum of respect for basic human rights at least to avoid mass atrocities. Second, the language moves the focus away from the rights of outsiders to intervene toward the rights of populations at risk to assistance and protection and the responsibility of outsiders to come to the rescue.

African spirituality also offers some consolation for tyrants who have ceased to be *muntu* (a human being) and become *kintu* (a thing); it seeks the purification and reintegration of such fallen leaders for the collective good of society. This realization suggests that R2P should better incorporate notions of accountability—not merely in the retributive or punitive sense of modern law but in the restorative or reparative notions of African transitional justice—to overcome resistance and induce changed behavior and compliance with international norms from overbearing sovereigns.

Chapter 2 by Yolanda Angulo Parra probes the relevance of philosophy and ethics for R2P. While the harshest of critics often lambaste philosophers for confusing rather than clarifying issues—the infamous "paralysis by analysis"—she seeks a rapprochement between philosophy and politics by underlining what is most relevant from the former for the politics of supporting the responsibility to protect. In particular, "critical philosophy" deliberately and purposefully responds to suffering, oppression, and injustice; and so Angulo Parra favors Michel Foucault's genealogical approach, which has been adapted by scholars from the global South. She adopts it because here the philosopher has a social commitment to identify, oppose, and articulate alternatives to any form of domination, violence, and suffering—in stark contrast to the prevalent view today of philosophy as abstract critical enquiry estranged from the realities of social suffering. Liberation philosophy and its sister liberation theology—brewed in the blood-stained Latin American soil of Spanish and Portuguese conquest and genocide, and subsequent neo-imperialism and local dictatorship—capture why philosophy is useful in addressing the contexts that breed mass atrocities. According to the tenets of liberation philosophy, a genuine philosopher must rid himself or herself of the fear of losing positions or standing or being expelled from a country and segregated from society in the pursuit of justice for or liberation of the oppressed. Hence, the philosophy of liberation is critical of oppression and clarifies liberation praxis. Angulo Parra views philosophical critiques of oppression and the identification of pathways toward liberation that avert the descent into mass atrocities as useful tools for developing R2P's preventive dimensions.

The rousing potency and continuing relevance of Albert Einstein's mobilization against Nazism and of Hannah Arendt's cry against totalitarianism[8] illustrate the potential value of philosophy to R2P today—before, during, and after mass atrocity crimes. As such, Angulo Parra's examination of ethics underlines a universal obligation to protect "the victims of disaster" who have no other recourse. Nonetheless, she cautions that "responsibility" carries less moral and ethical weight than "obligation," recalling a theme that was crucial to the original formulation by ICISS. The use of the former to frame the R2P debate about halting mass atrocities once and for all may be a weakness.

Both Nkulu-N'Sengha's analysis of religion and spirituality and Angulo Parra's of philosophy and ethics suggest that R2P is nothing short of a Kantian "categorical imperative," which is spiritually and ethically binding on all human beings. Yet R2P lacks that status at present in international law and political practice, which in turn suggests stepping up advocacy to convert R2P from an emerging norm into an enforceable categorical imperative, and ensure its universal and consistent application.

Finally, Angulo Parra's formulation of what she calls "veiled" atrocities—what the literature usually refers to as "structural violence"—appears both potentially harmful and helpful to translating R2P into practice. In the view of the editors, the scope of atrocities falling under the purview of R2P's reactive dimension must remain narrow for the immediate future, on the one hand, in order to maintain a sharp focus that can energize political will and action at least in the worst human tragedies. It remains problematic to mobilize sufficient international political will even to react to conscience-shocking events.

Early action, on the other hand, as our three case studies emphasize, is of the essence. Hence, Angulo Parra's discussion of veiled (or hidden) atrocities is useful because the causal link to evident (or visible) atrocities that attract R2P responses clarifies the case for prevention. She urges us not to overlook brewing catastrophes because they have not yet taken on the proportions of mass atrocity crimes; she urges us ultimately to eliminate the conditions that breed the kind of violence that often result in mass atrocities. While veiled atrocities do not meet the threshold criteria articulated by ICISS or by the World Summit for coercive measures by the international community of states, tackling them obviously remains crucial to alleviating human suffering and preventing mass violence.

Despite the regularity and quality of powerful exhibits that adorn the halls of UN offices, and of humanitarian concerts that UN agencies sponsor, art remains largely peripheral to public policy debates. It rarely even affects elite political discourse at UN headquarters or anywhere else. Rama Mani's chapter makes a cogent case for correcting this disparity.

She describes "artistic responses to crisis" as inclusive, collective, participative, transformative, and emancipatory—admittedly more of an ideal than a reality. She argues that during mass atrocities or violent crisis, it is not the objective and dispassionate Kantian contemplative tradition inherent in the Western aesthetic tradition that is relevant, but the passionate engagement between subject and object, between art and life, which is encapsulated in Southern and feminist aesthetics. She argues that art is not and should not be distant from daily life. Art is life; creativity is survival.

Pablo Picasso's *Guernica* epitomizes the artist's capacity to express the horrors of war as no verbal communication ever could. Mani's chapter argues that *Guernica* is not an exception but rather that Picasso has many worthy but less-known peers. In societies torn asunder by violence and mass atrocities, artists and ordinary citizens have used the full gamut of creative expressions to communicate a range of vital messages that are otherwise invisible or inaudible. Mani urges us to pay close attention to the revealing lessons embedded in artistic expressions as they are directly relevant for R2P: they send powerful signals before, during, and after crises that could and should inform international and national peacemakers; they serve distinct functions of conflict prevention, protection, and post-conflict reconciliation and peace building.

Such art in the face of mass atrocities is not a bourgeois dalliance but a vital expression of vulnerable populations when other avenues for expression are repressed. In ignoring them, national and international policymakers may overlook vital clues from the local population about desirable actions that could be undertaken, as well as public assessments of their previous or ongoing efforts. In not registering the deliberate extermination of artists for resisting violence or articulating society's aspirations, they may overlook the onset of cultural ethnocide that Kayishema so evocatively describes in his chapter on Rwanda. Art, through its manifold culturally and contextually specific expressions, provides the signposts that policymakers desperately require to inform their vexed decisions in the calm before as well as in the eye of a genocidal storm, and to reflect upon them afterwards.

Mani focuses on the spontaneous expressions of art that emerge in war-torn societies rather than art sponsored by states or international agencies. In outlining the particular characteristics and functions of art in the three stages of R2P, this chapter draws on a wide variety of artistic experiences that substantiate the universality of creativity. As Ellen Dessanayake puts it, art is a human need as ancient as our species and as vital as food or shelter, and humans suffer its deprivation.[9] Mani examines creative instances not as isolated or random, but as part of a fluid human tapestry as worthy of protection during war as cultural and historical monuments. She urges policymakers, donors, and scholars to notice, interpret, and support but not co-opt or make instrumental use of aesthetic expressions. The chapter convincingly makes the case that art's contribution in the face of mass atrocities is not merely to entertain survivors or rouse charitable responses—although it does both—but more to portend, warn, inform, and guide local, national, regional, and international decision makers as they attempt to protect vulnerable populations.

Mani makes a broader point, which we underscore: there is need in the praxis of politics and international relations to restore art, aesthetics, and creativity to a central place. The bureaucratic stagnation and lack of imagination that bog down problem solving in governments as well as intergovernmental and nongovernmental organizations can and should be overcome. Creativity, imagination, and innovation in problem solving would be potent tools to rejuvenate governance at all levels.

Observations and recommendations from the cases

We selected three culturally distinct societies from separate continents that had experienced mass atrocities accompanied by different types of international intervention. As noted in the introduction, Rwanda and Kosovo were obvious choices given their decisive role in shaping the Canadian government's original initiative to convene ICISS; and Nepal's experience with non-military, "soft" international assistance in the form of human rights missions and diplomatic support provided a counterfactual to explore the notion that R2P is not synonymous with 11th-hour military action. For logistic purposes, we avoided acute ongoing violent cases and also wished at least some distance from the end of a crisis to provide historical perspective and safe space for research. Our selection provided a wide palette of lessons to capture the evolution of the responsibility to protect. However, as we have continually stressed, these cases are the first and not the last word in a complex mapping exercise.

Jean-Marie Kayishema's analysis of Rwanda highlights two key points the relevance of which has certainly not faded in the decade and a half since that country's nightmare. First, genocide is preceded by cultural ethnocide, or the gradual and deliberate erosion and manipulation of cultural values and practices by political authorities. The dissolution of this cultural foundation, Kayishema argues, makes people incapable of protecting themselves and their communities from the descent into the abyss of mass atrocities; it allows them to be manipulated to commit execrable acts counter to their own time-tested values and traditions. His evocation of Rwanda's unifying myth of common ancestry in Gihanga, of the one all-forgiving God Imana, and the multiple cultural and spiritual values and taboos that educed virtue and proscribed amorality joins Nkulu-N'Sengha's chapter on African religions and spirituality and Angulo Parra's on philosophy and ethics. Of course, we know all too well that myths and legends, like ethical positions and religious beliefs, can be used to foster brotherhood or to foment fratricide. The same Gihanga myth of shared ancestry was employed to allege or justify discrimination and sow discord between ethnicities. Rwanda's genocide exemplifies the horror that lurks with the disappearance of the unifying glue of spirituality and ethics that bind a society.

Kayishema's examination of colonial policies of cultural ethnocide fills a blank in most analyses, which tend to focus on the country's political and economic destabilization but overlook the profound consequences of cultural collapse. It remains, of course, for scholars to examine other post-colonial societies in which culture was eroded and politics was antagonistic but did not result in mass killings. Today, often it is considered quaint to discuss colonialism, which officially ended several decades ago but continues to cast a long shadow. The case of

Rwanda suggests, however, that it is essential to encourage countries of the global South to revisit critically their colonial histories as well as their more distant pre-colonial and more recent post-colonial cultures in order to bolster themselves against violent fragmentation of their societies.

The attention that Kayishema attaches to the systematic cultural devalorization and demolition under Belgium's colonial domination may be read simplistically as an attempt to blame a long-gone and malevolent foreign power that destroyed an illusory African paradise. Kayishema is not attempting to return to the "good old days" that never were, but rather to understand the elements of traditional society that, whatever its shortcomings, had not resulted in mass murder until 1959 and its seemingly ever-worsening aftermath. Indeed, one might even interpret as a tribute to Rwandan culture the fact that it took three generations to erode that cultural edifice and establish the perverse conditions that made the 1994 tragedy possible. Moreover, Kayishema is equally systematic and ruthless in his depiction of local leadership in the culpability for cultural ethnocide—both the Tutsi collaborating elite during colonial times and the Hutu leaders who followed after independence. There is more than enough blame to go around, and Kayishema concludes by emphasizing the responsibility of Rwandans themselves rather than finger-pointing at outsiders.

Kayishema could be faulted for not providing an analysis of the actions and failures by the international community of states during the 1994 genocide. However, this reality has been so extensively analyzed as to be redundant here, whereas his focus on the policies and practices of pre-colonial, colonial, and post-independence regimes provides an original approach to an overlooked phenomenon. Despite the many analyses by international experts, including the Organization of African Unity's high-level panel and by local scholars, many Rwandans remain persuaded that the UN withdrew completely from Rwanda, and that General Roméo Dallaire and his men were renegades resisting edicts from UN headquarters. That a few hundred soldiers remained hardly seems relevant in light of the needs, but it frequently emerges in discussions of the UN's stance. The resulting tarnished credibility suggests the urgent need for better UN public communications before, during, and after mass atrocities. Kayishema also eschews a discussion of the polemic surrounding the massacres of Hutus in refugee camps in the DRC following the genocide, and Rwanda's subsequent controversial actions in that war thereafter. These central considerations went beyond the scope of this volume and Kayishema's mandate to elucidate the cultural antecedents of the 1994 genocide. They certainly point to the continuing impact of the earlier weakening and destruction of cultural foundations.

Second, Kayishema argues persuasively that only the citizens of a country can truly protect themselves from mass atrocities and prevent their recurrence. His emphasis on self-reliance as the response and preventive mechanism of choice echoes Angulo Parra's ethical notion of "co-responsibility." Implicit in both analyses is a troubling question: if local capacities are a sine qua non of effective protection, does the existence of the R2P norm risk denying agency to vulnerable populations? Kayishema offers a powerful input into ongoing debates about building national capacities, the second pillar of Secretary-General Ban Ki-moon's R2P implementation strategy.[10] Developing a more intense responsibility within a population to take their destiny into its own hands—and not wait for outsiders to come to the rescue—could and should call upon the strengths of appropriately adapted and revitalized cultural values and practices that are still resonant with and accepted by the majority of the population.

Nita Luci's assessment of Kosovo brought to light the ancient cultural values of *besa* or honor and hospitality toward guests that characterized and accompanied the war in Kosovo, which predated the 1999 North Atlantic Treaty Organization's (NATO) intervention.[11] Three themes emerge from her anthropological analysis of culture and the weaving of Kosovo's cosmopolitan belonging to Europe with its revitalization of values and traditions to build solidarity and resistance to Serbian incursion.

First, the international community of states has created a self-fulfilling prophecy of sorts in that nonviolent protest rarely has any global impact but violence is almost immediately acknowledged. In Kosovo, for instance, a collective international yawn greeted the initiative that brought together the quasi-totality of the civilian population to prevent mass atrocities through nonviolent resistance in the 1990s. Sacked civil servants from the health, education, and civil services made common cause with other citizens to construct a fully functioning parallel government that delivered clandestinely the public goods that a state customarily provides to its citizens, but that Serbia had ceased to provide Kosovar Albanians. Philosophers, artists, and literary figures joined hands with politicians and discharged civil servants and energized a movement. Youth and university students as well as pensioners contributed to it despite substantial risks of retaliation. The parallel system was a form of resistance but also an edifying illustration of the cultural, ethical, and aesthetic values and practices examined more generally in the volume's first three chapters. However, its success as a civic, nonviolent movement was insufficient to avert the descent into mass atrocities as a result of international neglect and lack of effective pressure on the Slobodan Milosevic regime.

Luci argues that ultimately frustration with Ibrahim Rugova's "Gandhi-like" approach led restless and disenchanted youth to form the Kosovo Liberation Army (KLA). The international response was immediate, as was Serbian intensification of repression and violence. Extreme violence can drive up the terms of a settlement for everyone concerned. Perhaps this case can be made even clearer when thinking about Sierra Leone's civil war, where conventional wisdom has it that the grisly chopping off of limbs was pure insanity. Yet one rebel leader noted, "It was only when you saw ever more amputees that [the West] started paying attention to our fate."[12] In Kosovo it was the appearance of the armed KLA that appeared in the headlines and stimulated policy briefings in the Western capitals. Critics may accuse Luci of glorifying the KLA and condoning the criminal violence and drug trafficking that many observers customarily associate with the group. However, she would counter that these illicit activities were not the original motivation of the KLA.

If R2P prevention is of the essence, Kosovo is hardly encouraging. One of the consequences of responding after violence erupts and armed belligerents confront political authorities is that eventually gun-wielding warlords and entrenched elites determine the terms of peace; the presence of corruption and crime further complicated complex negotiations. Meanwhile, the majority of the population, who long courageously resisted violence, was excluded from the conversation. By contrast, negotiating the terms of peace during a phase of nonviolent resistance would bring to the table representatives of civil society and might produce a more durable settlement. As the UN bolsters its Mediation Support Unit within the Department of Political Affairs, this eventuality should receive attention. There is a parallel of sorts in academic research, as Luci notes: the shelves of indepth research stimulated by NATO's military humanitarianism contrast starkly with scant interest in and little investigation of the nonviolent resistance of the 1990s.

Second, this chapter illustrates how culturally specific local values can co-mingle with and reinforce universal, cosmopolitan norms of human rights. In the 1990s Kosovar youth and intellectuals relied on such values to help people overcome their blood feuds and unite in solidarity to defend against Serbian oppression. This intriguing illustration suggests that the culturally specific values evoked in the chapters on religion and spirituality as well as on philosophy and universal ethics can be mutually reinforcing.

Luci's chapter also shows how international attention to culture can misfire. She observes that the accord eventually negotiated under the auspices of Nobel laureate Martti Ahtisaari inadvertently "ethnicized" culture and heightened tensions between Serbs and Albanians. A powerful lesson for R2P and the wider field of peace building is the double-edged sword of culture. It cannot be said too frequently that the application of culture requires reflection and engagement to guarantee acceptable and integrative rather than counterproductive and divisive outcomes.

Third, Luci signals that even a muscular armed intervention widely appreciated at first by the vast majority of Kosovar Albanians can turn sour. She cautions that outsiders can exhaust the good will of local populations by making them "guests in their own homes." The swelling negative reaction to international peace-builders in Kosovo has remained largely pacific albeit vociferous; in Afghanistan and Iraq, by contrast, local reactions to outsiders have taken far more violent forms. Luci's chapter makes clear that the much-vaunted "local ownership" paradigm still underpins peace building in rhetoric more than in reality.[13] There is much to learn about how to appropriately handle post-crisis peace building in ways that do not infantilize and divide the local population but rather empower them, instead of strengthening the hand of political and economic elites or former warlords. Kosovo is a humbling classroom where much can be learned about how best to utilize the underappreciated dimension of R2P—that is, regenerating a resilient society after a military intervention for human protection purposes.

Arjun Karki and Jyoti Upadhyay's examination of Nepal shifts us from the national to the sub-national unit of analysis. Nepal was selected as a case of "the dog not barking," which provides crucial material because at several junctures in the period covered by the chapter (1996–2006), local media headlines pointed to "the next Rwanda" erupting in the idyllic Himalayan kingdom. Like Kosovo, we see non-violent activity among civic actors and cultural institutions in Nepal, starting with the pro-democracy movement launched in 1990. Unlike Kosovo, where the highly organized national (Albanian) civic resistance was unable to avert the descent into ethnic cleansing, Nepalese civic actors and cultural institutions were an essential explanation for averting mass atrocities during the country's Maoist insurgency.

While international actors—the UN's human rights mission, European Union (EU) diplomats, and others—were helpful, it is of particular relevance to R2P's development to note that community leaders and ordinary citizens were ultimately the most decisive agents in providing protection. This experience dispels the stereotype of Nepalis as apolitical subjects of an idyllic if repressive mountain kingdom passively accepting their *karma*. It also intimates that even in the face of repression, committed citizens and strong cultural institutions can often be more effective agents for early warning than top-down official institutions; this realization should inform the implementation of the secretary-general's R2P strategy regarding capacity building within weak states. The indelible images of civic society emerging in the streets en masse, accompanied by the mobilizing songs of musicians, the political satire of comedians, the pointed performance art and plays of actors and artists, flanked by religious leaders and political activists of all denominations and colors demonstrate again how faith, philosophy, and art are intimately linked to politics, particularly under violent duress.

It was civil society that ultimately removed the king from power and the country from the brink of a catastrophe—and not the UN, the EU, or such major powers as India and the United States, notwithstanding their contributions. Given that the balance of power was different in the two cases—the Serbian regime sought ethnocide while the Nepalese one sought to quash an armed insurgency—widespread civic participation and commitment had quite different results in the two cases. A crucial and essential variable seems to have been the heightened and timely attention accorded to Nepal by international institutions, powerful countries, and the global media. Without this critical input, the crisis might not have been so effectively dampened by the civic movement Jan Andolan. The mutually supportive role of national and civic actors, on the one hand, and international actors, on the other hand, appears crucial for both R2P prevention and protection. The identification of the most effective mixture of insiders and outsiders in individual cases remains an essential topic for future research. As we argued in the introduction, spineless international attention may or may not contribute to moral hazard and worsen the situation of affected populations, but the absence of international scrutiny almost certainly will.

The Nepalese case study reinforces the utility of the point of departure for this collection of essays, namely the growing recognition that more knowledge of local culture is a prerequisite to better design international efforts. The realization is making headway. For instance, a recent special issue of the journal *International Peacekeeping* focused on "Peacekeeping and Culture" and argued that "The lack of cultural knowledge can be substantially disruptive and contribute to the failure of a mission."[14] An example of the importance of this reality was the UN's presence in Nepal through the UN Mission in Nepal, which was tailored to local expectations and avoided any armed peacekeepers. The head of the mission, Ian Martin, described it as a "designer mission" because "[t]he pride the Nepalese Army and establishment took in Nepal's long-standing participation in UN peacekeeping was reflected in reluctance to become a recipient of blue helmets."[15]

Karki and Upadhyay also show how cultural institutions contributed to protecting populations where the armed conflict took the worst toll—in rural areas far from the view of UN, EU, and national officials. Norms more than laws are what make villages function; what effectively stand between stability and mass atrocities. So the two rural case studies in Nepal indicate a more extensive, intricate, and country-wide fabric of culturally-rooted and value-based survival mechanisms on which most ordinary people relied during what at the time and in retrospect certainly were looming mass atrocities. This admittedly small sample is intriguing but suggests the need for far more research in Nepal and elsewhere. At the same time, the cases also suggest that while cultural values and practices can exert a humanizing and civilizing influence—protecting enemy "others" as kin across caste and ethnic boundaries even at moments of great peril—they are not foolproof. Indeed, the dynamics of fear resulting from the spreading Maoist war quickly eroded traditional values and practices of inter-kin and trans-ethnic and trans-caste solidarity and protection.

Nepal rather eerily finds echoes in Rwanda. Is the perilous process of cultural dissolution only beginning in un-colonized and hermetic but now-porous Nepal? Will the new societal fissures opened during the 1996–2006 war fracture still further if ancient cultural values and practices are not renewed and updated? Will greater autonomy and recognition to Nepal's mosaic of indigenous groups and ethnic minorities be a recipe for integration—for unity within diversity—as hitherto disenfranchised groups are empowered, or the contrary? The reader is left wondering whether a future case study will document that the dog has barked.

This brings us full circle. Cultural and spiritual values, beliefs and practices, ethical imperatives and philosophical reasoning, creative and aesthetic manifestations provide a bulwark for societies to prevent atrocities and injustice, protect those afflicted, and help rebuild war-torn societies. They may underpin nonviolent and value-based civic resistance and help prevent mass atrocities, as suggested by Kosovo and Nepal; however, their success is not assured, especially if timely international support is absent. If the narrow window of opportunity for preventive action closes, the tyranny and fear unleashed by mass atrocities devastates ancient survival mechanisms and leaves victims bereft. Indeed, cultural values and practices may be deliberately demolished to pave the way for mass atrocities, as in Rwanda, and they are impossible to resurrect during the chaotic devastation. Yet the overall message is that civic resilience and values of honor, solidarity, and responsibility persist through these tragedies, and this fact offers hope for R2P.

Final reflections

Neither collectively nor singly do the six substantive chapters pretend to provide a comprehensive understanding or explanation of R2P solely within the realm of culture. Indeed, each chapter treads on the cultural terrain with caution. Each author clarifies that culture is not static but dynamic; that the idioms are specific; that the significance of events and subjectivities change constantly with time, place, and circumstances; that all too often culture is misunderstood or partially understood and even deliberately manipulated to foment violence.

These pages should not give the impression that we attribute magical properties to culture. Like our contributors, we are painfully aware that culture has been misappropriated across time and place, that it has too often witnessed gashes from both sides of this double-edged sword. We do not advocate a wholesale return to some mythical idyll of "traditional" culture, to the proverbial good old days that never were. Despite its dynamism, cultures do not necessarily evolve in tandem to a society's changing needs; indeed, all too frequently they have evolved in ways that oppress the weakest members with devastating effects on women, minorities, the disabled, the poor, and the indigenous. Yet shorn of this historic safeguard and divested of legends and traditions that provided meaning, unmoored people are not only more prone to the winds of violence but also less willing to respond humanely toward friends and foes who are whipped about by such turbulence.

Despite this cautionary note, the chapters as a whole clarify why focusing on this neglected aspect of the R2P puzzle is essential and worthwhile. The conditions under which local cultures are propitious for the protection of vulnerable populations are clearer even if much more research remains to be done. The cultural dimension has profound significance for understanding the phases of mass atrocities and the dimensions of the responsibility to protect. Further, they serve to underline ICISS's original wisdom in formulating three mutually reinforcing stages of responsibility that may be successive or concurrent depending on the situation—to prevent, to react, to rebuild. The 2005 World Summit decision emphasized prevention and protection, and the secretary-general's 2009 and 2010 reports reflect member states' preference for prevention and capacity building rather than military protection after the outbreak of atrocities; peace building is assumed to be part of prevention. All six chapters reinforce the emphasis on prevention and early action, and the three case studies suggest why greater reliance on civic populations and cultural mechanisms would be helpful. Nevertheless, the chapters also point toward the necessity to reinstate peace building as a separate emphasis with particular reference to re-knitting the cultural and political fabric of war-torn societies as a distinct part of the international responsibility to protect vulnerable populations. Such an emphasis would bolster the role of the Peacebuilding Commission and Support Office; and it will ensure continuity and congruence among the UN's principles, policies, and mechanisms.

The contribution of individual human rights was to free ossified and oppressive societies, and they remain an indispensable tool to restrain repressive regimes. However, the tacit price for the emergence of the individual was the loss of community, just as the consequence of an emphasis on rights was the disappearance of responsibilities. Individual civil liberties and entitlements along with modernization brought in their wake not only progress but also a gradual erosion of culture and traditional bonds of community, solidarity, mutual help, and protection that had previously helped societies worldwide to cope with numerous physical and existential threats to their survival.

The obstacles confronting R2P can be formulated as follows: an assertion of sovereign rights with little concern for sovereign responsibilities; a glut of individual interests fomenting violent conflict to the detriment of community values and safeguarding of human life. Yet R2P also encounters unprecedented opportunities, including the transcendence of human rights and cultural values into the global expression of solidarity with suffering strangers, and exhortations for generous government responses that override narrow national interests. The spontaneous trans-boundary civic response to Darfur, the Asian tsunami, and the Haitian earthquake exemplify this shift and suggest momentum. The dilemma for R2P is to bridge the unequivocal wish for survival with dignity of the UN's main constituency—"we the peoples"—with the equivocation of their governments. The solution is for governments to truly become the guardians of their citizens' interests and recognize that sovereignty as responsibility transcends borders.

So too, it is time to harmonize the individual and community, recognizing that one is the necessary counterpart and guarantor of the other. It is time to restore culture and spirituality, ethics and morality as the fulcrum of global governance and international law—so clearly recognized in the passage from the OAS's American Declaration of Rights and Duties that began this chapter. In the final analysis, R2P will be legitimized not only by a sense of universal values but also by its effective application and infrequent use.

While UN member states waged a futile fight during the Cold War over the importance of a so-called first and second and eventually third generation of human rights—over the supremacy of civil and political rights versus economic and social ones and then of group rights—in the academy the duel involved the respective merits of cosmopolitan versus communitarian perspectives. As Kosovo in the 1990s illustrates, the cosmopolitan values of universal human rights can coexist with and reinforce communal and culturally specific practices. Moreover, if cosmopolitan values are not rooted in the cultural values of societies, their foundations are unstable. State protection mechanisms can and must be anchored in local institutions and practices. To state the obvious, sufficient space exists in the international arena to accommodate the value of community with the worth of every individual.

A disconcerting revelation during this project was that older scholars and civil society activists in the global South normally were supportive and even enthusiastic about the emerging R2P norm, whereas younger participants in the four countries where project consultations took place expressed skepticism and often sharp reservations. Their reticence was not toward the norm but rather reflected their skepticism about the UN's willingness and ability either to move beyond the strangle-hold of the national interests of its most powerful members or to condemn sovereign states for tyrannizing the most vulnerable.

There is much that UN officials and governments can learn from the ordinary citizens whose voices are heard in this volume. The effective prevention of mass atrocities and the protection of affected populations demand creativity, imagination, and innovation, in short supply in intergovernmental organizations. They also necessitate such exemplary courage as demonstrated by the civic activists and cultural leaders in Kosovo and Nepal and the *justes* in Rwanda, also scant in risk-averse and consensus-seeking international institutions.

If the UN wishes to move beyond rhetoric and implement R2P—to make the norm more than a slogan—a central challenge is winning the trust of a new generation that is less indulgent than its elders toward the flaws of multilateralism as practiced since 1945. The UN—its member states and its staff—must act more consistently, creatively, courageously, and humanely. Youth, the majority of the world's population and thus the majority of the UN's constituency, will only be satisfied by a radically transformed world organization that takes seriously its idealistic Charter objectives and breaks loose from the shackles of bureaucracy and the power politics that fortify the status quo. The path of the R2P norm is hardly linear,[16] but it certainly requires younger and older norm entrepreneurs to emphasize the wisdom and ethics of philosophy, the values of spiritual consciousness, and the ceaseless creativity of art to prevent future outrages to the collective conscience.

As we go to press, the dramatic international actions against Libya illustrate why this project was valuable. Today the central challenge of the responsibility to protect certainly is not too little normative consensus. The red herring of Western imperialism is a distraction. There is cultural evidence across the global South to sustain robust humanitarian action, and support by the Arab League and the African Union for outside intervention in Libya is noteworthy and perhaps a harbinger. "Though some critics fret that R2P could prove to be a humanitarian veneer by which powerful states could justify military intervention in the development world, more often the problem has been the opposite," Edward Luck tells us. "The capable have stood by as the slaughter of civilians unfolded before the world's—and sometimes even UN peacekeepers'—eyes. They have looked for excuses not to act, rather than for reasons to intervene."[17]

The action against Libya was not about bombing for democracy, sending messages to Iran, implementing regime change, keeping oil prices low, or pursuing narrow interests; they may result, but the dominant motivation for military force was to protect civilians. A likely collateral benefit is that by encouraging (to date) nonviolent and democratic revolutions in Tunisia and Egypt will have a greater chance to be replicated elsewhere. Now that the Arab world is no longer a democracy- and human rights-free zone, Qaddafi's "model" of repression cannot automatically be interpreted as an acceptable policy option by other autocratic regimes.

Culture provides, indeed, powerful insights for R2P's future. Perhaps Libya will reorient policy and decision makers toward realizing the centrality of the responsibility to protect to both normative and operational issues.

Notes

1 "Einstein Against Nazism," available at: www.ppu.org.uk/learn/infodocs/people/pp-einstein2.html.
2 Available at: www.hrcr.org/docs/OAS_Declaration/oasrights3.html.
3 Quoted by William Korey, *NGOs and the Universal Declaration of Human Rights: "A Curious Grapevine"* (New York: St. Martin's Press, 1998), 9.
4 See David Held, *Cosmopolitanism: Ideas and Realities* (Cambridge: Polity, 2010), x.
5 See *Theory vs. Practice: Connecting Scholars and Practitioners*, special issue edited by Thomas G. Weiss and Anoulak Kittikoun of *International Studies Review* 13, no. 1 (2011).

6 Samuel P. Huntington, *The Clash of Civilizations and the Remaking of World Order* (New York: Simon & Schuster, 1996).

7 Mario Bettati and Bernard Kouchner, eds., *Le Devoir d'ingérence: peut-on les laisser mourir?* (Paris: Denoël, 1987); and Mario Bettati, *Le Droit d'ingérence: mutation de l'ordre international* (Paris: Odile Jacob, 1987).

8 Hannah Arendt, *The Origins of Totalitarianism* (New York: Harcourt, Brace and Co., 1951).

9 See Ellen Dessanayake, *Homo Aestheticus: Where Art Comes from and Why* (Seattle: University of Washington Press, 1995).

10 *Implementing the Responsibility to Protect, Report from the Secretary-General*, UN document A/63/677, 12 January 2009. This is also part of his more recent *Early Warning, Assessment and the Responsibility to Protect, Report of the Secretary-General*, UN document A/64/864, 14 July 2010.

11 Luci assumes a political stance and prefers "Kosova" to "Kosovo." Here we rely on standard English usage.

12 Quoted by Philip Gourevitch, "Alms Dealers," *The New Yorker*, 11 October 2010: 105.

13 For a discussion, see Laura Hammond, "The Power of Holding Humanitarianism Hostage and the Myth of Protective Principles," Peter Redfield, "Sacrifice, Triage, and Global Humanitarianism," and Jennifer C. Rubenstein, "The Distributive Commitments of International NGOs," in *Humanitarianism in Question: Politics, Power, Ethics*, ed. Michael Barnett and Thomas G. Weiss (Ithaca, NY: Cornell University Press, 2008), 172–235.

14 Maren Tomforde, "Introduction: The Distinctive Role of Culture in Peacekeeping," *International Peacekeeping* 17, no. 4 (2010): 450.

15 Ian Martin, "All Peace Operations are Political: A Case for Designer Missions and the Next UN Reform," in *Review of Political 2010 Missions* (New York: Center on International Cooperation, 2010), 9.

16 See, for example, Edward C. Luck, "Building a Norm: The Responsibility to Protect Experience," in *Mass Atrocity Crimes: Preventing Future Outrages*, ed. Robert I. Rotberg (Washington, DC: Brookings Institution, 2010), 108–27; and Cristina Badescu and Thomas G. Weiss, "Misrepresenting R2P and Advancing Norms: An Alternative Spiral?" *International Studies Perspectives* 12, no. 1 (2011): 1–21.

17 Edward C. Luck, "The Responsibility to Protect: Growing Pains or Early Promise?" *Ethics & International Affairs* 24, no. 4 (2010): 361.

Index